Not Just a Walk in the Park

My Worldwide Disney Resorts Career

 *by* James B. Cora
with Jeff Kurtti

DISNEP
EDITIONS

Los Angeles · New York

Published by Disney Editions, an imprint of Buena Vista Books, Inc. No part of this book may be reproduced or transmitted in any form or by any means, electronic or mechanical, including photocopying, recording, or by any information storage and retrieval system, without written permission from the publisher.

For information address Disney Editions, 1200 Grand Central Avenue, Glendale, California 91201.

ISBN 978-1-368-04364-9

FAC-021131-21267

Printed in the United States of America

First Hardcover Edition, November 2021

10 9 8 7 6 5 4 3 2 1

Were a star quenched on high,
For ages would its light,
Still traveling downward from the sky,
Shine on our mortal sight.
So when a great man dies,
For years beyond our ken,
The light he leaves behind him lies
Upon the paths of men.

—Henry Wadsworth Longfellow

This book is dedicated to the memory of Michelle Leigh Cora

July 29, 1964–August 28, 1995

Contents

Introduction: Bob Weis
President, Walt Disney Imagineering

WALT DISNEY famously said, "You can dream, design, create, and build the most wonderful place in the world . . . but it requires people to make the dream a reality." And few people have had as much to do with bringing Disney parks and Walt's vision to reality as Jim Cora did during his lifetime. Throughout the day I write this, literally hundreds of thousands of Guests will visit Disney parks around the world that still carry the influences of Jim . . . from Tokyo, to Paris, to Florida, and to Anaheim, where he got his start at Disneyland.

In 1981, I was a young Imagineer, riding my new scooter, heading across the dusty construction site of what would become Disney's first park outside the United States, Tokyo Disneyland. I was going a little too fast and was just a bit too confident about controlling this new scooter, when I cut off a car that was making its way through what would be the park's Adventureland. I looked back and gave an apologetic wave, and then realized the guy in the back seat was the legendary Jim Cora. Yes, he was legendary even back then.

When I got a call from him the next day, I figured I was in for a ration of something. Instead, Jim just asked me if I was okay. "You looked a little stressed out, are you sure you're okay?" he inquired. He knew the pressures everyone was under to finish the park. I was, I assured him. But Jim wasn't finished. "Do you want me to get you a car, so you can get off that scooter? I can get you a car, you know." And he probably would have! Alas, I didn't take him up on it.

Just the fact that he didn't call to lecture and berate me for cutting off his driver—that his concern was immediately about how I was doing—well that stuck with me. It was quite a way to first, literally, cross paths with a great leader who would quickly become a mentor . . . and a friend.

So much of what makes Disney unique is the tribal knowledge handed down from Walt's first generation of leaders, and subsequently passed down over the years. And that makes Jim's book and his reflections on and recollections of his experiences something really valuable not only to Imagineers and Disney Cast Members, but fans and anyone else who is in a creative business that inspires and serves the public. After all, this is the guy who proved all the naysayers wrong when they told him that the exacting Disney standards of service and courtesy would never translate beyond the United States.

A year after Tokyo Disneyland opened in 1983, I flew back to Japan with Jim and a team to present a master plan for the first phases of growth for the park, which had seen overwhelming success. It was the first time any of us had ever landed in Tokyo in the midst of a major snowstorm. By the time our Pan Am 747 pulled up to the arrival gate, Narita Airport was closing, and there were no drivers, taxis, or even buses commuting into Tokyo proper. Yet even after an eleven-hour flight, with all our plans up in the air—and a major presentation with our partners scheduled the next morning—I never saw Jim worry or lose his cool.

His primary focus first and foremost was making sure everyone from Disney on the flight got rooms at the airport hotel, which by then was booked solid. Jim never wavered. He took care of us all, arranging family-style meals and setting up meeting rooms for us to work and collaborate for the *three days* we were snowed in there. How did he do it? Jim just seemed to know and care about everyone and, more importantly, everyone knew and respected him in return, so much so that they were willing to go out of their way to help him and, by extension, us.

I was lucky to have Jim's mentorship in those early days. I was very green, but thanks to him I got to be part of the management and creative collaboration push that would set Tokyo Disneyland on its way to being the beloved cultural landmark that it is today. Jim loved creative thinking and dreaming. It's what drove him and those around him. That, and his very dry sense of humor.

Sometimes running the operations day in, day out anywhere can make one resistant to change. But Jim was always excited about possibilities, and he saw the potential in people and ideas. He knew these big projects took every bit of passion and commitment we all had, and sustaining the team through those long challenging years was the only way to get there.

I am grateful for the support Jim provided to me personally throughout his life, as well as all the Imagineers and Cast Members who benefited from his knowledge, wisdom, and experience. And I am so happy he had the chance to write about his years at Disney and how they influenced and shaped him—and, by extension, us. Jim's life was dedicated to Disney and now we all have a chance "to take a walk in the park" with him, to learn from his journey and gain perspective from a legend who helped bring so many wonderful Disney places, around the world, to reality.

Prologue: On Board the *Benito Juarez*, 1912

IT'S DIFFICULT to say with any certainty, but interesting to consider, what the thoughts and feelings of my maternal grandmother, Freda Boustany Morad, were as she gazed out onto the seemingly endless ocean, bound for North America—and a whole new life in a new and unknown place.

The passenger ship *Benito Juarez* was a comfortable and stable ship. And although not swift and grand like today's luxury liners, her engine hummed relatively quietly far belowdecks, and her keel cut a seemingly effortless path across the still ocean surface at a respectable ten knots, on a voyage to . . . well, Freda didn't quite know.

She had heard so much from the Lebanese friends and relatives who had immigrated to the United States, almost storybook tales about a fantastic land of opportunity. They had been told of a pristine nation of great promise—and even that (just like the oft-repeated legend) the streets were literally lined with gold.

Freda, already a practical-minded person (even at barely twenty years old), wasn't sure about that one. She had come from Deir el Qamar ("Monastery of the Moon"), a village southeast of Beirut in south-central Lebanon, and after having spent some time in Egypt, knew the difference between dreams and reality. But she longed to be part of the adventure—and the fortunes to be made—in America. Fortunately, this decision to immigrate was not due to religious persecution or economic hardship, as it was for so many of those from the Middle East at that time.

Her husband, Buttross (Peter) Morad of the Nayami family, a dry goods dealer and merchant, had departed a few years before, selling goods as he journeyed far and wide by cart and wagon, and then establishing a store, much like the "general stores" you see in old Western movies.

Although this was to be a new life, in an unfamiliar country, like so many immigrants, Freda carried her unique culture, her deep faith, and her core values—the intangible treasures that she would pass on and nurture in her children and grandchildren—to this "New World."

Tucked into her luggage were a few practical artifacts from the "Old Country." One was a bulbous black vessel, similar to a vase, which contained the family yogurt starter (a unique blend of ingredients that transform milk into yogurt, and give this treat its unique flavor).

Neatly trimmed and carefully wrapped alongside it were what appeared to be nothing more than some unadorned branches: just sticks with a few buds and tendrils. These were grape shoots, and would be given new life, just as her family would, in whatever place they would call home.

Part One: Influences of Youth

FTER some brief travels in this new world, Freda, or "Sitte" as we called her (Arabic for "grandma"), settled down and planted the grape shoots she had carried with her on the voyage; those vines began to take root—as did our entire family—in a remarkable place called Southern California. (It wasn't for the grapes that my grandmother brought forth shoots to a new land—it was for the leaves. Middle Eastern people will roll grape leaves with meat and rice, sometimes just with rice, and it's a delicacy. For decades after, when people in our family moved away, or were married, or had children, they always got a clipping from Sitte's original grape vine.)

My aunt Marge recalls family stories that our Sitte initially settled in Mexico, where she joined Buttross and helped run his general mercantile while they waited for the immigration process to unfold and approval from authorities to be granted to enter the United States. By necessity, they learned to speak Spanish; my grandmother already spoke Arabic, French, and Italian.

Ultimately, in the last week of 1912, Sitte, Buttross, and now a young son arrived by steamship at the Port of San Diego ready to begin a new year—and a new life—in a new land.

California Dream

Its streets may not have been lined with gold as the tales had promised, but Southern California was paradise—and in those first decades of the twentieth century, it was in many ways as much a fantasy one reads about in storybooks as any actual place could be.

Like my grandparents, many others found their home and settled in the Los Angeles area in the 1920s. Some two million people were also bound for California during this period as well it turned out; and most of them chose the same region. By the end of the decade, that once-sleepy pueblo had *tripled* its population, and practically overnight, became the fifth-largest metropolis in the United States.

In the process, a whole new "Southern California" way of life developed, thanks to a temperate Mediterranean-like climate. The region had rich indigenous, Spanish,

Mexican roots. There were fertile fields, and groves of fresh produce, and fruit that seemed to grow and thrive everywhere.

The environmental variety of the region famously shaped the decisions and experiences of the immigrants who had been drawn to this magic land. There was a growing urban center, many small towns, far-flung rural ranchos. In one direction was sand and shore; in the other, evergreen mountains and winter escapes. Forest and desert lived side by side in a land that simply seemed to defy normalcy and convention.

There was a now-legendary energy—fed by this fantastical landscape and temperate weather, no doubt—of flourishing *creation*, invention, and reinvention; it was happening in everything from agriculture to architecture, to creative arts and design.

And, of course, there was the emergence of that popular fantasy paradise that was soon known around the world by a single name: "Hollywood."

Boyle Heights

Sitte and Buttross settled down in Boyle Heights, an area east of downtown Los Angeles, which had been called

Paredón Blanco ("White Bluff") in the 1820s, when it was a territory of Mexico's. Years later the name changed, after Irish-American Andrew Boyle returned from the Mexican–American War and bought twenty-two acres of the heights that overlook the Los Angeles River there. (His name has remained attached to the neighborhood ever since.)

By the early twentieth century, Boyle Heights was a real "melting pot," with Jews, Christians, Latinos, Russians, Yugoslavians, Portuguese, Japanese—and Lebanese—all living besides one another and creating a rich multicultural neighborhood in an already-remarkable place.

I do not have as many details on my father's family's arrival in Southern California. My paternal grandfather, Hunna Bashara Hayek (who became "John Cora" during immigration—and whom *no one* ever called "John"), helped found the Lebanese church for Maronite Catholics in the Boyle Heights area. It would have a profound impact on my life . . . because this is where my mother's and my father's families came together. It was always expected that we would marry someone within our sphere, Lebanese Catholic, and that was how my father, also John Cora, met my mother, Mary Morad, and professed almost immediately that he was going to marry her. She laughed, said he was presumptuous, and walked away.

Presumptuous as he might have been, my dad was right, and he and my mother were married on February 9, 1936.

Marriage, a Market, and a Melting Pot

My dad worked in his father's business then (and later took it over)—a small neighborhood store called Johnny's Market. It was at 5123 Long Beach Avenue, in Watts, a neighborhood in the south end of Los Angeles, near the towns of Lynwood and South Gate. Watts had begun as a ranching community, but when the railroads arrived (the train tracks ran right alongside the grocery) and the Watts Station opened, it quickly became a thriving, independent city. By the time my dad was there running the store, Watts was being consolidated into Los Angeles proper. A true neighborhood store, Johnny's sold meats, groceries, sundries, liquor—and just about anything that was in demand from the locals.

For the first year of their marriage, my parents lived with my paternal grandparents. After I was born in

December 1937, we moved into a room in back of the store for about a year. I'm guessing there was a conflict of some kind that prompted my parents to leave my dad's parents' home. Maybe it was my arrival. I've been known to cause a little trouble in my lifetime.

When I was two, my sister, Marilyn, was born. Being only two years apart, we were very close growing up—and we still are. She understood and spoke fluent Arabic as a child, and a lot of what we know of our family history came from her recollections, gathered from our grandmother, mother, aunts, and uncles. With typical strength, she cared for my mother and father until their passing, and persevered after the loss of her husband to a rare lung disease.

Marilyn was the first of our family to graduate from college, earning her teaching degree from Long Beach State University. One of her early teaching assignments was on a military base in Germany, where she hosted my parents on their first European tour. I've always been so proud of her—she is a pillar of our immediate and extended family. Her contributions to church and family are numerous. God bless my little sister.

During my preschool years, Sitte would babysit us at her home in Boyle Heights. Buttross had passed away from cancer a few years before I was born, but he had invested in rental properties, which was fortunate. He left Sitte well provided for. I remember their large, handsome house on a hill, and its big porch, that overlooked the then-small city of Los Angeles.

Those were great days. That "melting pot" neighborhood brought such a wonderful variety of faces, voices, and flavors to an impressionable young mind.

I understood Arabic then, and heard many stories about the "Old Country" while helping Sitte tend to her chickens, and spent time with my aunts and uncles. They were my added mothers and fathers—and remained that way for the rest of their lives.

Although my grandparents talked about the "Old Country" and shared memories and traditions, they really never looked back—they strived to be all-Americans. And for me, as a California-born kid, the rest of the world was just sort of far away, full of exotic, somewhat legendary storybook places that the adults in my life had come from and knew well, but didn't really comport with my young life.

During family holiday gatherings, we always had Lebanese specialties—along with the local favorites like tamales and chile rellenos. We all looked forward on Sunday mornings to the arrival of the cart selling menudo—a hot, spicy Mexican soup (sometimes called *pancita* or *mole de panza*), made from a cow's stomach and seasoned with red chili pepper, hominy, lime, onions, and oregano. It was said to be a sure cure for overindulging on Saturday night. (Or so we were told. Quite frankly, our family wasn't . . . indulgent.)

Values and Community

Our family community was built around the Maronite church, which was pretty typical for those days. Monsignor Joseph Daher organized the local Maronite Catholics into a parish named Our Lady of Mt. Lebanon in 1923. Mass was celebrated in a house that was bought by the congregation, at Warren and Brooklyn Avenues. Father Paul Meouchi became pastor in 1926 and had a church, hall, and rectory built on the property. He was elected the Maronite bishop of Tyre in 1934 before becoming Patriarch of Antioch, a cardinal, and head of the Maronite Church.

You lived and went to school around wherever your church was. If you were a Maronite Catholic—we were Maronite Catholics—the oldest male child in the family is automatically a Maronite, and has to be baptized by a Maronite priest, as I was.

Both of my grandfathers were generous with their families, and with those in need. They were industrious, even a bit adventurous, and possessed of a deep religious conviction and devotion to their Catholic faith. That has been a family tradition, and an example to me for as long as I can recall. Not just the traditions and ceremonies of the church, but a core set of strong values, a relationship to a community beyond my immediate family, a sense of a purpose in life and a meaning to what we do, and an unending reliance on and belief in a higher power.

I was the firstborn of my family, and the first grandchild, so for my mother, it was all about "doing it right." Keep it as clean as you can, pick up your trash. You weren't allowed to have a sloppy room. You ate when it was time to eat—breakfast, lunch, and dinner were at certain times. You didn't snack; you weren't allowed to just open the refrigerator without asking permission.

And yet, I always understood the ideas *behind* such disciplines. I never thought my folks were too straitlaced, or too strict. I always felt that they were just trying to set a solid path for me to the way things should be, to make life better. Plus, it wasn't always rules and rigid adherence. We were permitted the freedoms and pleasures of that childhood in a much more innocent era. We were allowed to stay out until it got dark, or until we heard Dad's whistle, or Mom calling, "Jimmy!" down the street. And we all just felt loved, because we *were* loved.

A Shopkeeper's Classroom

I learned lessons about the world outside my family and church by working alongside my dad from an early age. When I was a boy, my father would take me with him to his store on Saturdays. We first stopped at the Grand Central Market to buy fruit and vegetables. (Today that market is a sort of chic urban "food hall," but then it was truly a farmer's market—there were more than ninety vendors whose goods included produce, meats, fish, dairy, dry goods, baked goods, coffee, and flowers. All our store's fresh goods came from here.) From there we went to Smart & Final, then a grocery wholesaler and now a supermarket chain, for various other goods. I watched my dad negotiate prices and haggle over the quality of product to secure the best value. I learned about customer service, display, impulse buying (like keeping items in the back of the store so people will buy items they may not have come in for initially).

Working in the store, I learned the importance of honesty, effort, consistency, and presentation—communicating your identity and values through your diligence. I started doing that when I was nine years old. Sweep up the store at the beginning of the shift . . . and again at closing time. There were certain standards that you had to follow, and they were pretty rigid, but I always understood why they were to be followed. The store was always clean, organized efficiently for the customer. The shelves were always stocked and tidy-looking; the labels on cans and boxes were all forward-facing.

I learned about a larger circle of community, beyond my family, beyond the church. An early understanding of these connections and relationships was both interesting and useful in my development. My dad loved to talk to people; he talked to everybody. He loved to meet people; he was very gregarious. Everybody knew my dad, and my dad knew everybody who came to the store—it was a true mom-and-pop business. He knew the cops on the beat, the mailman, and all the vendors who delivered by their first names—and made sure they got a little something extra before they left.

After two Saturdays my dad asked how I wanted to be paid. I loved chocolate (still do), so I chose the chocolate we sold out of open glass drums. Dad said, "Reach in and take a handful and put the candy in a bag." The next week I got a raise, and learned a valuable lesson—my dad told me to let *him* reach in and grab a handful. He had huge hands, hence my raise.

There was lots of fun, and there are lots of fond memories—but there was also a solid education, an expectation of attention, best effort, and responsibility that was deeply formative, and that I've never forgotten.

School Days

I went to a Catholic school run by the Sisters of Notre Dame. From the first through the eighth grade, it was St. Helen's Grammar School in South Gate, where I was an altar boy. The Sisters of Notre Dame were a huge influence on me, and I think taught me more than any other educational program I was ever in.

I was a bit of a clown in school, and learned some organization and leadership skills. I think it was because I wanted attention, quite frankly. I knew I stood out from other students because I was Lebanese. I was dark-complected, and everybody in the school was white—*very* white, perhaps because it was in a *very* white neighborhood. I tried to get people to focus on what a funny guy I was, or what I could accomplish, rather than focus on me.

My mom sat me down and straightened me out one day, when I was crying because kids had picked on me because I was dark. She brought out some books about the Phoenicians, and then said, "You know, you have to be proud of who you are and what you look like—you are directly descended from the Phoenicians. The founders of civilization."

I felt much better about myself. I actually felt a *lot* better about myself, and I began to be proud. I was so proud to be Lebanese, and from that time on I wanted people to know I was Lebanese.

I liked school. I liked all the sports. I played baseball, basketball, and football from grammar school, all the way through high school—and enjoyed that a lot. I have two buddies I still see on a regular basis who I met in first grade. We sold a Catholic newsletter called *The Tidings* door-to-door, back when it was safe to go door-to-door.

I won a prize for selling the most subscriptions for my school, and got to meet the bishop in Los Angeles, a very huge honor. I have memories of paper drives and fundraisers of all kinds. Schools and churches often conduct these, but at the time they were even more common—because, when I was just a boy, our country went to war.

The War Comes

World War II changed everything. There was rationing, coupon books, special windshield stickers for gas, and more in those years. No more gum. Beans were replaced with lentils . . . and young men were disappearing from the neighborhood.

There were blackouts! I was yelled at by the air-raid warden for running my toy train with the engine light on. (My dad was pretty upset with him for that and yelled right back at him to get the hell off our front porch.) After dinner, we sat by the radio and listened to commentator Gabriel Heatter tell us the international news of the day. His war-era sign-on was either "There's good news tonight" or "There's bad news tonight." Then he would give us updates about America's victories or losses on both fronts, and on how our allies were faring—the good luck they were having, or their misfortunes. But mostly I remember that so often his voice came across as the sound of doom.

We always flew the flag, and displayed two gold stars on a blue field for the two uncles we had in the army. My mother taught my sister and me to sing the marine, army, navy, and air corps hymns, and dressed us in military-style uniforms on special days.

When I was six or seven, I scoured the neighborhood for rubber and scrap metal for the war effort, and tended our Victory garden. (Part of daily life on the home front, Victory gardens were vegetable, fruit, and herb gardens planted at private residences and public parks. By "growing our own," we reduced pressure on the public food supply.) We also had chickens and rabbits that I had to feed. In addition, I mowed the lawn, and picked fruit. There were always chores that had to be done. My mother would set goals and schedule assignments that we needed to accomplish.

My child's-eye view was that the rest of the world was simply dangerous and untrustworthy. Japan was an enemy, as were Italy and Germany. China was a friend, as was

Russia. We didn't hear much about others. But we were *sure* we would win the war. And through it all, my mother always encouraged us to be proud of being Americans, and to respect our Lebanese heritage.

During the war, we welcomed another sibling: my brother, John, who was born in 1943.

I remember my dad getting a notice just before the end of World War II that he was to sell his business and get his affairs in order—he was going to be drafted. He had been deferred up to that point because of his family obligations, but by this time, things looked bleak, and they were calling up more people, even those who had received deferments.

Although he was one of the most patriotic guys I knew, my dad was really upset about it. My uncles, who always helped take care of those in our extended family, were both in the army already. But then, blessedly, the war ended. My uncle happened to be home on furlough just as the war ended. He and my dad went out and just got plastered. I had never seen either one of them, ever, drunk in my entire life . . . not before, or since. They came home singing; my mom put food on the table for them. It was a sight to see. Because now dad didn't have to go into the service, or sell his business.

Postwar: Relocation and Reinvention

After the war, everybody moved out to the suburbs. Postwar California was a microcosm of the whole country: everything was changing. The culture of the car and a national interstate highway system were gaining speed. Sitte moved to Walnut Park; my grandfather Cora headed to Huntington Park. Our family had already moved to South Gate in 1939, so by this time most of us were within a ten-minute ride by bicycle from each other. And Sitte's grape vines came with us, and took root, and thrived, again. Our relatives were always visiting one another. You'd walk over, or you'd jump on your bike and go visit family. Those days were safe, and we didn't fear venturing out alone.

A few years or so after the war, my dad did sell the store. I think he actually leased it to somebody who made payments, but he was retired for about ten years. Finally my mom said, "You know, you've got to find a job where you can supervise people besides *me*." He went to a local supermarket, observed that their liquor department was in a shambles, and asked if they'd like someone to run it for them—and they hired him. He ended up working there another ten years.

A Childhood Interrupted

In 1948, my parents were visiting relatives in Louisiana. They drove with my aunt and uncle, and took my little brother along; he was then about five. I still have a terrifying memory of getting a phone call from the sheriff in San Angelo, Texas, who asked, "Who will come identify the bodies?" I was eleven years old.

There had been a very bad car accident. My dad was severely injured, and my mom had broken ribs and bruises. I called my uncle John; he drove straight through to Texas in his 1948 Buick to help them. Both my mom and dad were hospitalized—and we almost lost my brother, John. My aunt got everyone out of the car before it burst into flames, but ultimately her husband died.

My father was told he would probably never walk again. But Uncle John built a "physical therapy" rig, a system of weights and pulleys that my dad used night and day, constantly. It wasn't elegant, and it squeaked and rattled and thumped, but through dedication and constant usage of this contraption, my dad was finally able to walk.

My brother remained hospitalized in Texas, a large part of that time in a coma. The Sisters of Notre Dame watched over him until he was well enough to come home. My work in the store, rather than being something of a loving "apprenticeship," became vital to the ongoing welfare of the family—I worked every day after school and every weekend along with my uncle John until my father could go back to work. When my brother came home, my sister and I would have to look after him, massage his feet daily, and generally support my mother and the household far more than we had before the accident. I got a paper route to help out more when I was twelve or thirteen, and delivered the *Los Angeles Herald Examiner* door-to-door.

Our family dynamic was forever changed after that. In retrospect, there are life-altering events. But I also think there are life-affirming and life-strengthening events as well. I realize now that in a formative sense, I had to leave a lot of my childhood behind at this time. I also realize that it strengthened my faith, my appreciation of family, my sense of responsibility, and a commitment to optimism and good work that informed the rest of my life.

High School

I spent my first year of high school at St. Anthony's in Long Beach and the rest at Pius X in Downey. High school was good, and when I finally got into Pius the Tenth, I even met up with people I had gone to grammar school with. Most of the students at Pius came from either St. Emydius in Huntington Park, or St. Helen's in South Gate. It was a good school, a good life; I made friendships there that go on to this day.

My high school principal, Monsignor Sharpe, was a navy veteran—he saw a lot of action in World War II as a pilot, then became a priest. He taught me even more about discipline. We remained friends for many years. He performed my first marriage (along with a Lebanese priest, because in those days you had to have a Lebanese priest there).

I loved history. A lot. I always got A's in history. And I loved English—later in life I was an English major. I thought I was going to be a teacher—or at least wanted to be a teacher. And it turns out I *am* a teacher, but that's getting ahead of my own story.

I did *not* like math! I just wasn't good at it. My dad was good at math, and stayed up late at night with me trying to get me to understand it. I didn't.

Because of my sports prowess, I thought I was *really* a hotshot when I got to high school. So, during my sophomore year, I went out for the football team. At 130 pounds, and five foot ten, they just killed me . . . just beat me up really bad. My mom decided *for* me (thank God), that I shouldn't be playing football. I couldn't have agreed with her more, and I didn't play any sports in high school at all.

But I discovered a couple of other things I was interested in at school. One was girls; the other was cars.

California Car Culture

After World War II, there was a massive industrial shift from the manufacturing of war materiel to a variety of consumer goods. By the end of the 1950s, one in six working Americans was employed either directly or indirectly in the automotive industry! People moving to the new suburbs commuted extensively by car. Economist Richard Porter wrote that "the automobile made suburbia possible, and the suburbs made the automobile essential." The "car culture" of the United States ignited shortly after the war ended, and had an immediate influence upon popular music, entertainment—and especially tourism. Southern California was rife with roadside attractions and auto touring destinations, with more to come.

At this point, there were a *lot* of old cars still around,

models from the 1920s to the 1940s . . . and a lot of young people who were approaching driving age. My first car was a hand-me-down 1940 Chevrolet, our family car at the time. I got it before I was old enough to drive it, but as soon as it was officially mine, I promptly nosed, decked, louvered, and lowered that car. And it was all by hand! I didn't know much about it, so I just learned as I went.

My father wouldn't let me drive until I could take the engine apart and put it back together. That was the rule. So I started taking it apart. When I got the car, I was fourteen. And by the time I was sixteen, I could take it apart, and put it back together. (My dad didn't know that I put a ¾-inch cam back in—and it wasn't the stock cam—so it would be a little faster than what other guys on the road had.) I was a big part of a now-famous era in California culture.

Famed writer Tom Wolfe immortalized this era in a mid-1960s Sunday magazine piece for the *New York World Journal Tribune*: "They cruise around in their cars in Harvey's huge parking lot, boys and girls, showing each other the latest in fashions, in cars, hairdos (male and female) and clothes in the Los Angeles Teenage . . . and Second-Generation Teenage . . . modes, Teenage Paris! Harvey's Drive-in!"

I cruised Harvey's restaurant in Downey. I cruised the Clock Drive-In restaurant in Lynwood. I joined a car club when I was in high school, The Counts of Southern California. We learned a lot more about cars, and we'd go down to the Santa Ana drag strip and drag our cars. As a club, we owned a dragster, and got into that. But in those days, it was all about fixing up your own car. There weren't any computers involved in it, and nobody had the money to take a car to a shop. You barely had money for *gas* . . . and sometimes didn't even have the money for that! So I got to be a "car guy," just because of that.

I have to credit my dad; it was a brilliant idea not to run something until you knew how it worked. It's an idea I've carried with me, and was a huge help to me in my career.

Unfortunately, at this time I also started smoking, because it was the cool thing to do. It's the worst decision I've ever made.

Part Two: Leaving Home

OF COURSE, I will always acknowledge and appreciate the upright and positive elements of my upbringing. The values of community, standards, and ethics. The principled people and institutions that I feel established a moral and ethical foundation for my whole life.

But as Mae West famously said, "I'm no angel." (Now I have sent you running to your references to find out who Mae West is. . . .)

I'm not making news saying those late teens years, for almost *anyone*, are fraught with conflicts, internal and external. In my case, too, when you add in the freedoms coming to the fore in a postwar Southern California and the importance of the auto to teen culture, there was more than enough fuel created to further ignite adolescent discord. That a conflict would arise between a father and his oldest son, therefore, is hardly surprising.

But I'm getting ahead of myself. The Catholic high

school in my area was under construction when I was in my early teens, so I spent my freshman year—as I already noted—at St. Anthony's in Long Beach. I took the Pacific Electric Red Car from our South Gate home to the school—it was an hour each way. The commute made for long days, was expensive, and worried my parents (since their kid was gone from the house for a *long* time).

So I convinced my parents to let me go to South Gate High School my second year, arguing that it would save time, car fare, and tuition. Being *closer* to home actually made me somewhat cockier . . . and, shall we say, "adventurous"?

Many years later, in conversations with my dad, we talked about the growing tension between us during this time. Public school had taught me how to be a smart-ass, and as I've explained, I had been brought up quite differently. There was no "spare the rod" when I was growing up. If you screwed up—you got the rod. Of course, I resented it as any young boy would. Later in life, I realized my father was just trying to keep me on the straight and narrow, because lots of folks—especially in the area we were living—were *not* staying on the straight and narrow, and he wanted to make sure I didn't go down that path.

But of course, the more I asserted my independence

and stood up to him—no lies, and I never tried to hide my behavior—and the more stubborn I was, the greater and more frequent, and sometimes physical, the conflict between us grew. I never cried in front of him, but I did privately.

I remember vividly an incident during this time that led to a life-changing explosion: one day (I don't even really remember why, except the increasing feeling of autonomy and "adulthood"), I did not come home after school. I had hitchhiked so I could use my fare to buy a snack before boarding the bus, but I couldn't get a hitch until late in the day. In fact, I was away until *well* after dark. My mother thought I'd been kidnapped—and my dad was *fuming*. In my adolescent view, I wasn't sure if he was mad because I was late, or because I *wasn't* kidnapped. My mother—who rarely even raised her voice—yelled a lot.

"Where have you been?" she asked, once I was home.

"I can take care of myself—you shouldn't make such a big deal out of me being late!"

My dad could put up with a lot of my guff, but something about my so cavalierly dismissing my mother's distress seemed to push his patience to the brink. This was the first and last time my father ever hit me with a closed fist.

That same week, a buddy and I joined the Air Force Reserve.

Basic Training

With all the military action going on around the world when I was growing up, and the presence of the armed forces in our everyday lives for years, I was actually excited and enthusiastic about going into the service. I left high school for a short time, joined the Air Force Reserve, and was quickly put into basic training. After a wartime childhood and Catholic schooling, it really was a natural flow into the military—focusing on loyalty, dedication, discipline, hard work, and love of country.

Air force basic training was a breeze. I was stationed at the Long Beach Air Force Base (now Long Beach Airport) and assigned to the 452nd Bomb Wing. My first flight was on a B-29, World War II vintage. We were marched constantly in precision order—readied to enter into combat that never happened. Classroom teaching was intense and varied, mostly about various aircraft identification and military protocol, as well as the Code of Military Justice.

There was time and training on the firing range,

and more drilling (always), plus some administration courses—including typing and lesson-plan preparation, which served me well in my later career.

The teen rebellion that had brought me to the air force was subdued by my deeper training and discipline, though. I was selected Outstanding Airman for three consecutive months, and became eligible to be interviewed for an appointment to the Air Force Academy. (I didn't actually find out about that opportunity until about four months into my later army enlistment. The army would have allowed me to be transferred back if I had chosen to accept—but that would have meant four years at the academy, followed by three to four years of active duty.)

As often happened over the coming years, I set out on a path, but allowed myself to keep the *destinations* somewhat vague. I stayed the course, but often let the journey lead me, rather than the goal.

Graduation and Administration

Around the time of my graduation from high school, the army had come out with a special program, set up through passage of the Reserve Forces Act. The program offered candidates shorter active duty time, and allowed them to choose their own MOS (Military Occupational Specialties). Five of us graduates jumped at that chance.

I had already been trained in administration by the air force, so I chose army administration. The air force granted me an honorable discharge, only on the condition that I was transferring to the army. So I stayed with my buddies and finished basic, and six years active reserve duty. Basic training at Fort Ord (in the Monterey Bay region of California) was tough, especially after the comparatively easy air force training.

Our weekend passes (if we got them) were limited to a fifty-mile radius, so we spent a lot time in Monterey and Carmel. It was interesting to me, after having grown up in an era with such fervent respect and admiration of the military, that the locals around our base in those days were definitely *not* glad to see us, and were certainly not friendly. A sign in a local park said, NO DOGS ALLOWED. But someone had crossed out DOGS and written SOLDIERS. I remember asking a girl who worked at a local movie theater out for a date. She said, "Sure—as soon as you get out of that uniform." (For the first sixteen weeks of basic we were not allowed to wear civilian clothes.) Of course, we all wrote home for clothes to wear off base, and although our haircuts gave us away, it was a relief to feel a little more normal.

After basic, I moved around; at Fort MacArthur in San Pedro (a port section of Los Angeles), I worked out of the company headquarters, handling clerical and office administrative duties. I typed orders and filed reports and such.

Top Secret

I was also assigned to an ordnance group. They always seem to be in the middle of nowhere, in some not-so-beautiful parts of the country, where it's vast and arid and there are very few people. Tooele Army Depot, in Tooele County, Utah, was precisely like that. But a really interesting incident took place there that still sticks in my mind.

One night, *truly* in the middle of the night—two or three in the morning—clerk typists from every company in the battalion were ordered to show up at a particular building, and asked to type up an enormous number of orders for officers and enlisted personnel: we were relocating families, setting up housing, registering kids for school; all of this was on the spot and done quickly, since we were contending with a huge amount of paperwork. We were also under the constant watch of military police the whole time we were in this barracks processing orders and manning our typewriters.

Then the MPs took all the carbon paper, all the trash bins, and all the rollers out of the typewriters, put them in huge containers out in the base's street—and set them on fire. Clearly this was something deemed *top secret.* We all had to take an oath that we were never to talk about what we had done. I may go to jail for publishing this— but here it is: we were setting up the first group of people being sent to the White Sands, New Mexico, Atomic Testing Grounds for the Nike Hercules Missile Program.

Peripatetic Service

We got moved around through the Western states while I was in the service; I didn't do anything overseas. I served at the Texarkana Armory (in Texas) and in the Los Angeles Battalion, and then was reassigned to Fort Lewis in Washington State, about ten miles south of Tacoma. It was there that I had my first and serendipitous assignment as a trainer. Why they picked me for a trainer, I don't know to this day, as there were lots of us in that unit, but suddenly I was teaching classes, to new recruits, in a "learn-as-you-go" role that would prove so vital in my future career.

I didn't know anything about the subjects I was teaching, but I was given manuals and I had to develop lesson plans based on those manuals (and then teach from those lesson plans). Let me state this for the record: the army puts out great manuals. For a while, I taught CBR— chemical, biological, and radiological warfare. Again, it was something I knew nothing about. There were also the same classes for the nurses and other medical personnel, too, so they would know what they had to treat if anything CBR related happened. I loved presenting classes to the nurses—no fraternization, of course—but, come on, I was still a teenager!

This training—and instructing of others—continued throughout my reserve time, too—and was a vital part of my future career.

Leadership and Team Building

In addition to this training experience, I was able to pick my own teams from what I considered the most talented pool of people. I'm not sure I "learned" leadership conducting courses as much as I tapped a nascent skill I'd had since elementary school, when I had organized a collection and replaced a watch that one of the nuns had lost.

I think it's just a talent that you have . . . or that you don't have. Putting ego aside—just an observation across the decades of my life—I've concluded that it's almost impossible to *make* a leader. I think leaders are born, not made. You either have that gift, that ability, or you don't.

Homecoming

My military career ended, as T. S. Eliot wrote, "not with a bang but a whimper." I left active duty in 1957. Of course, I spent the next six years in active *reserve*, and went to all the reserve meetings. I think the last two years was *inactive* reserve, so we didn't have to go to meetings, but we had to keep our uniforms in shape.

Back home, my high school sweetheart had sent me a "Dear John" letter shortly after I joined the army. When I finally came back for good, I felt lost without her, and the things we had done together: movies, dances, family events. Even our local hangout, the Clock Drive-In, had closed. People—and their addresses and phone numbers—had changed, so I had some trouble reconnecting with many of them.

My mom saw this and cooked up a huge "welcome home" party for the five of us who had joined up in the army together. This was typical of her, and so thoughtful, and it was a huge morale boost that helped all of us.

My home environment was much more relaxed, as was my relationship with my father. He had sent me a letter while I was in the service, saying how proud he was of what I was doing to serve our country.

I had activities and interests, yet still felt listless, undisciplined—without purpose. I wanted to get on with something meaningful. I looked at Sitte's grape vine, which had grown enormous in almost two decades at our South Gate home, and couldn't help but see the symbolism. I needed to take root, to grow—to flourish somehow.

I had little interest in school, but entered a junior college with some of my buddies. I joined a local fraternity, called the Order of Thor. The members were mostly veterans at the time. I also played piano in a combo at a little beer bar in Long Beach. The name of the combo was the Thor Notes. (Get it?)

One of these frat brothers asked me to take a ride along with him to this place called "Disneyland," where he wanted to apply for a job. As I was waiting for him, the interviewer asked if I wanted a job, too. I declined, saying I thought I just wanted to take the summer off. Since I had never been to Disneyland before, he gave me an entry pass, and told me to come back in an hour to pick up my friend.

Part Three: A Magic Kingdom

ONE hour was all it took.

We were behind the pony farm, at the north side of the property—that's where Recruiting was in those days. I went out into the park, and I remember the first thing I saw was the Skyway, gliding through the air from Fantasyland to Tomorrowland and back again, high above my head. I didn't go on any of the attractions; I just walked through the lands. There was music everywhere, and the smell of fresh popcorn; the Guests were upbeat and smiling—and so were the employees; everyone seemed so happy.

I thought, *Gee, what a great place.* Later, I went back to meet my friend, and when I returned, the recruiter said, "What did you think?" I told him I loved the place, and sure, maybe I'd be interested in a short shift. I ended up with a six-hour shift, six days a week. I started at $1.60 an hour, which was more than I was making in the army, so I was happy with that.

Most of the people operating the rides were marines, who were working there part-time. (They were the foremen because they'd had some leadership experience.) No women, of course, were leads or foremen in those days— not yet, anyway. I enjoyed it a lot. And worked at the park until that summer ended.

I actually didn't see a Guest for about the first three weeks, except on my breaks. My first job was sitting backstage at the Mickey Mouse Club Theater, polishing 3-D glasses. (The theater showed a special compilation of 3-D shorts, a movie technology that was all the rage at the time, with new 3-D color footage of the popular TV stars of the *Mickey Mouse Club.*) In those days they didn't have a machine that cleaned the glasses. I was the machine that did that. I sat there for very long dull shifts—just me and boxes and boxes of Polaroid 3-D glasses. My first foreman was a guy named Ray Vanderwalker, the best foreman ever. I think he's one of the reasons I decided to stay there and keep working.

I tried to come back on weekends for other shifts, but I couldn't get them. You had to be "permanent part-time" for that. So I asked the manager of Fantasyland—Frank Hideman—how to *become* permanent part-time. He asked if I was available every weekend. When I said yes, he told me to just keep coming back and sit in front of his desk, and he'd find shifts for me.

And that's what I did. I sat in front of his desk, waiting for him to give me a shift to fill, if they had underestimated crowd size, or more often, to cover for employees out sick. He'd look around and he'd say, "Okay, Cora, you've got a shift over on Teacups." I trained on all the rides in Fantasyland, one ride at a time, all that first summer.

Learning the Lay of the Land

On the days when there were no shifts, and on my time off, I visited other lands and support departments, asking people what they did, and met with my co-workers, in an effort to see how this all came together. It seemed as if the more I learned, the more my curiosity grew, a trait that developed then, and continued throughout my career.

I kept working there while I was going to school. Now, honestly, at that point I thought school was a waste of my time, so I asked for more hours at Disneyland, and began cutting classes to sit in front of Frank's desk. I kept working there weekends for a long time, trying to go back to school at nights, and putting classes together. I never did go more than a year at a time before I dropped out, though. I loved Disneyland so much, and I was having more fun working in the park than I could have ever had doing anything else, any place else.

I learned how to operate all the rides in Fantasyland, and then the following Easter (spring of 1958), Frank asked me if I wanted to come back and work the Easter season. Then, as now, park attendance increased during the holidays, and staffing had to be adjusted accordingly. I said *absolutely.* He said, "I'll work you through Easter, then I'll work you on weekends until summer, then I'll put you on full-time for the summer season." So that summer, I was the only person who made permanent part-time in Fantasyland.

I couldn't believe that I could have so much fun working at Disneyland and still get paid for it. And I couldn't think of any other job that would offer me that kind of satisfaction *and* a paycheck. They didn't pay much in those days, but I sure was having a good experience. I couldn't wait to get to work. I lived twenty minutes away, so I'd breeze down there, even get there early. I'd always get there early! Then I'd walk around and talk to other people in the separate divisions to see what they were doing . . . try to hang out with the maintenance guys to understand how the rides worked; hang out with entertainment people. How do you produce a show, and where does the parade come from? Where do you keep it?

They made me a foreman my second summer, primarily because all the marines who had been in charge of the attractions were gone. That whole outfit got shipped out, and suddenly there were a lot of vacancies on the Fantasyland rides. I became foreman of the Snow White attraction. In those days, I had a crew of eleven people at that attraction. We were really overstaffed: we had people in the back, in charge of safety, maintenance, and preventing vandalism; and we had two unloaders and two loaders, and even a ticket taker. There was also a ticket booth right in front. At the time you had to buy an individual ticket for each attraction—there were no ticket books or passports back then.

A Carefree Culture

Disneyland's hourly cast in the 1950s was mainly made up of marines and schoolteachers on weekends; the permanent cadre consisted of city of Anaheim school system grads, as well as various people from the Disney Studio (artisans, technical personnel, and craftsmen—even spouses), and the local community; many of them even came out of retirement for a unique "late career" opportunity. Those overseeing the park's attractions came from those ranks.

Management and staff personnel were an assortment of studio chiefs and recent college graduates, as well as several who had worked in the defense plants that were shutting down (or scaling back) after years of producing materiel and weapons for the armed forces during World War II and the Korean War. It's why so much of our structure, and some of our terminology (such as "Operations") seem so military. It's because they were.

Morale was high on the job—throughout all of the park's units. We were young, and many of us gathered at the local watering holes after work to socialize. Hourly workers frequented a place called the Camel's Den (where ID was never checked), and if you were good at it, it was a great place to supplement your income by playing liar's poker. Another place, the Lounge, was attached to the Clock Drive-In on Harbor and Ball, across from the northeast corner of Disneyland. Supervisors went to Adamo's, and management staff went to the Lancers Restaurant on Harbor Boulevard. We did not stray into each other's territory. There was a clear hierarchy, but I was used to this from church and the military, and everyone seemed to get along. We were a much smaller group in the early days—I think there had been only six hundred or so original employees on the park's opening day. It was much more like a family then.

Fun and Family

And like any family, there was much play . . . and we had a lot of fun together. We took our jobs seriously—but ourselves a lot less so. We all felt it was important that we were part of a show, and entertaining the Guests was paramount. That didn't stop us, though, from entertaining ourselves, too.

We played a game called Hide the Bird, for instance, at the Jungle Cruise attraction. Operators would take a small stuffed bird and hide it within reach of the boat skipper, who could reach out and hide it again. Some cheated and jumped in and out of the boat and then back to continue the trip. This game was stopped when one day a skipper, didn't get back in time to jump back into the boat. It actually ended up coming back to the dock on its own, and rammed a boat stopped at the unload position. Luckily there were no injuries—except to the missing skipper's D-28 (that's an employee's Human Resources record).

While I was a steam train conductor on the Disneyland Railroad, I once took a box of lost sunglasses on my walk to check the track. This was done early in the morning, before the park opened. I placed sunglasses on the statues of Native Americans and their dogs along the tracks. Of course, everyone cracked up, including Cast Members and Guests. (It occurs to me that this might get me fired retroactively, since I never admitted to doing it.)

Growing with the Flow

I was taking it as it came as my tenure at Disneyland continued. I still didn't really know what I wanted to do. I thought I wanted to be a teacher at one point, but—as I noted before—I didn't pursue that as a profession, though I ended up being a teacher anyway (in a way), through a series of opportunities at work. Over my four years as a ride operator, and as a ride foreman, I ended up working almost all of the attractions in the park.

I began to understand Disneyland and get a feel for

the whole operation, but also better comprehend various strata of knowledge and culture. I felt a real growth spurt starting to happen in me, too. Like Sitte's grape shoots, I still needed to take root, to grow—to flourish somehow. And I began to see that Disneyland was a place I could do that at, and a place that I could see myself growing with the organization.

So I started to get a little impatient.

But then, in 1960, park management announced that they were looking for temporary summer supervisors, so I applied for that job. I was interviewed, and was hired as a temporary summer supervisor in Tomorrowland, in charge of the dance areas. During my first year in supervision, I was assigned to security on weekends, and then during the week I worked as a Tomorrowland assistant supervisor under a guy named Pete Crimings, who was manager at the time.

In those days, the weekend dance areas in Tomorrowland were the Yacht Bar and Space Bar (which later became Tomorrowland Terrace). On the Central Plaza was Carnation Gardens, which had a really terrific lineup of genuine big bands. And in Frontierland there was the tiny Oaks Tavern (which would turn its large patio fronting the Rivers of America into a dance floor. The Oaks Tavern became the Stage Door Cafe in 1978.)

In Tomorrowland especially, there were a lot of younger people looking for a date. Over there we were playing current pop hits at a pretty high volume, but the kids loved it . . . and it brought people in. We had lots of "date night" events and things going on weekend evenings. Yes, it was loud, it was boisterous, and that first summer it was frequently . . . unpredictable.

Here's a little "California culture" from those days: although it was a while before the hippie movement, there was still a growing clash in youth culture in those days, particularly in the case of Orange County (where Disneyland is located). Back then, it was the marines and the surfers who were slugging it out, every chance they got.

As many still do, the surfers in those days wore their hair long. The park, however, had a grooming standard in those days (and still does, though it's now far less strict). You couldn't have long hair and come in. Actually, a lot of the security guys that worked the main gate would help out the surfers; they carried scissors—and if a little trim would help them, they'd administer one. Or they'd show the surfers how to tuck their hair under their collar so it didn't show. We tried to get those kids in at the "edges" of the standards. We didn't have metal detectors or do body searches in those days, all the stuff that is commonplace now at entry gates (and at other parks).

As a result of what would now be considered lax protocols, though, lots of people snuck in a "little refreshment" that wasn't available in the park then. Many (both marines and civilians) drank too much, with the attendant changes in behavior and sociability taking place.

It was terrible.

I mean, any thought I had about wanting to be a cop ended after working security at the park. We were always breaking up fights, and taking people in to Security. Eventually we had to patrol with plainclothes military police ("Is that one of yours or is that one of ours?" we'd wonder when detaining those who were "misbehaving.") We'd grab the surfers; they had the marines. There was a wagon outside of Security where military police tossed those guys in and took them back to Camp Pendleton or El Toro . . . or wherever they came from.

The military police at Disney even provided some training. There was a martial arts expert who was in the 101st Airborne who taught us how to control belligerent people and crowds without doing bodily harm or physical damage. I'm not a very big guy, but there are certain places you can squeeze on a hand or an arm—and even the most bellicose will follow you anywhere. It was a brutal summer, but we got it all under control by the end of the season.

So the next summer, I got the same assignment: two days a week in the dance areas and the rest of the time supervising. Then, on top of all the other issues I've described, they decided to throw a live TV show at us, every Saturday night on KTTV-11 from one of the dance areas. Luckily I wasn't in charge of the TV show; I was just in charge of the dance areas. My little team did their job, while others were responsible for the TV shoot—but as I recall, it was a lot like CNN going out to cover riots. It was just a zoo.

Disneyland Days

Summers at the park were high-energy all day and evening, right up to closing time at midnight. When the season ended, we said goodbye to the summer help. Friends we had made were gone and we transitioned to our winter operation hours: open 10 a.m. to 6 p.m., closed Mondays and Tuesdays. Most of us loved the peak seasons buzz; winters were slow and boring. (During the rainy season, we would lose pay when the park would close during inclement weather.)

Disneyland was growing by this time—the big Matterhorn/Submarine/Monorail expansion was completed in 1959, and they were beginning construction on the Mine Train Through Nature's Wonderland attraction in Frontierland. It looked like things would only keep growing (and I didn't think being a bouncer in a teen club pointed to much career advancement). We looked forward to the expansion and the new attractions; we saw it as an opportunity to grow the park, and us with it.

Growing a Family

In 1961, I met Susan. She was a tour guide. Back then, we only had tour guides during reduced operating hours off-season. During summer and peak holiday times, they were rotated into handling attractions roles. I charmed and wooed her (at least in my own memory I did). I was working steam trains, and proposed during a romantic grand circle tour of the Magic Kingdom, with stops in the Frontierland, Fantasyland, and Tomorrowland stations, partly because of the "romance of the rails," and partly because portions of the route went through tunnels—and the Grand Canyon Diorama—where a fella could more boldly steal a kiss or two.

Susan accepted, and we were married. I was actually hesitant at first, because she wasn't Lebanese—she was really outside that sphere of "home." But luckily she was Catholic, so that was an advantage. My family was shocked, with the exception of my father, whose thought was, "You should marry whoever you damn well please."

Soon, our first daughter, Rene, was born.

Suspension and Supplementation

Once while I was a submarine operator at the Submarine Voyage attraction, I was assisting with the unloading of a docked boat. I was on the front hatch, and the rear hatch was manned by another operator. He signaled his side was empty, and so was mine, so I signaled the driver to proceed. As the boat began to move, an elderly couple slowly started up the stairs to exit via the rear hatch. The operator quickly lowered the ramp to allow them to exit, but unfortunately the boat was moving. Both the other operator and I yelled for the couple to back down the ramp, which they did (blessedly) and weren't hurt. But the ramp was mangled, and the attraction had to be shut down until repairs were made.

I was reprimanded and given a four-day suspension. That was tough, considering I was married with a tiny baby, and no savings, and my wife, Susan, not working. So, ingenuity and necessity had a little meeting, and I came to work each day anyway. I went to the Submarine Voyage break area with a set of poker dice, and earned more money doing that than I had working . . . at least until my supervisor discovered the break area was a little noisy, and *politely* (since I won't put down in writing the actual language he used) asked me to throw the dice in the submarine lagoon, and come back when my suspension was over.

Creating a Culture

I realize now that in those early days, we were writing the book on the first Disney park. We could pretty much do what we thought needed to be done to make the Guest happy. And the Guest was always right: that was our version of "the customer's always right" policy. As we grew, people hung back in making those "frontline" decisions, though; and things got more uniform and rigid. Things had to be done a certain way, decisions had to be elevated, and you couldn't violate that, or you'd get an oral reprimand, or worse, a written reprimand—or . . . worst of all, you'd get fired.

But I understood the reasoning. As things grew, our overall employee population had become less experienced by the simple nature of the numbers, and park management just couldn't let people make so many of those individual decisions anymore. Yet in another way, it's too bad that everything has to go through so many layers of bureaucracy, but I just think it's the nature of what happens when a business or project takes off. But even today, I think there's something to be said for empowering your local managers with the ability to make some sound and simple decisions.

As an example, during a rotation on attractions in Fantasyland, I was working on the Skyway. The Fantasyland side was perched in a Swiss chalet up above Fantasyland's northwest corner. The emergency power was controlled there through what was simply a Volkswagen gas-powered engine. I had taken out one of the suspended ride vehicles, which we called "buckets," for a routine inspection of the cable and towers, and while it was nearing one of the towers, it completely lost power and stopped.

I was the only guy that day who knew how to run the engine, as no one else had been trained. So I swung the bucket to get close enough to climb down the tower, just as the area manager, Bob Reilly, saw me and yelled, "Cora, what are you doing?" I explained that there was no one at the station who knew how to run the VW engine to power up the ride, and to evacuate the stranded Guests, as we needed to do. That's when I found a new religion: succession planning, and the vital importance of training (and cross-training). No one should ever be "the only guy" for anything.

During that same rotation I got a lesson on the importance of "catching Tinker Bell." At the beginning of the fireworks show each weekend and holiday night, a petite Hungarian circus performer named Tiny Kline (I didn't realize at the time she was in her seventies—and rode the bus to get to work every day!), dressed as Tinker Bell, would glide down a wire from high atop the Matterhorn to a landing platform out of the Guests' view in Fantasyland, spreading her pixie dust to begin the show. Skyway ride operators would be responsible for holding a blanket up at her landing site, in order to catch her. Everyone wanted that job because Tiny would tip you $50 for doing this each night. Naturally, that's something that just wouldn't and couldn't happen today—but back then, outside of the circus tent, such things hadn't been *done* before. ("Tinker Bell Catcher" isn't on any résumé I've ever seen, anyway. . . .)

The Lesson of a Submarine Mishap

While still an hourly, I was working an attraction rotation in Tomorrowland and assigned to the submarines. One morning, the safety engineer and my supervisor climbed aboard my sub, telling me that new guide wheels had been installed. They wanted me to take a test run for speed without any Guests on board. As we came through the waterfalls and into the lagoon, they asked me to "Open it up, wide open." I offered the opinion from daily experience that the guide wheels would come off the track. But they insisted, noting that it was the reason for the test, and that it shouldn't happen.

As the guides came off the track, we smashed into the load dock. I jokingly said, "We're sinking!" (which is, of course, impossible with those subs), and the supervisor yelled, "Pop the hatch," and jumped out onto the dock. Divers had to be called out to put the guides back on the track.

Then we proceeded through the load dock, past the switch, and I was asked to put the sub in reverse, and accelerate. I did as I was told, knowing full well what would happen. The back guide wheels immediately came off track, smashing the rear of the sub into the storage dock. I could have been awarded a four-day suspension, but because I was following a direct order from my supervisor, and the engineer backed me up, reporting that the guides were faulty, I escaped that punishment. I was, however, for a while known as "the guy who made a long submarine into a short one."

Like the Skyway incident, the lessons of this event stayed with me as I ascended in rank. When you're a boss, a big part of success is listening to your employees, trusting what their point of view is as they work on the frontline every single day. Don't swoop in from outside and start thinking you know everything that goes on. You don't.

In many ways, it was a lesson learned back when I was fourteen with that hand-me-down 1940 Chevrolet. I couldn't drive until I could take the engine apart and put it back together If you supervise, learn how the whole enterprise works, and what makes it work—and listen to those people who work with the components hands-on, every day.

Even in those more relaxed, seat-of-the-pants, make-it-up-as-you-go early days, a uniformity of behavior and a shared understanding of our remarkable workplace was required. The idea of solid training—and an even larger concept of developing employees over time—was a part of the Disneyland MO from the beginning.

Transition and Training

I was sent to see a guy with the unlikely name of Van Arsdale France. I didn't know a lot, except that with all the growth we had been having, he was setting up more thorough employee orientations and training programs. I'm not sure what I was expecting, but that name, Van Arsdale France, sounded almost to be of royal lineage.

Van had joined Disney in March of 1955, and had a background as an industrial labor relations expert. He'd been with General Dynamics, the U.S. Army in England (and later Germany), and Kaiser Aluminum Corporation. During his first few years at Disneyland, he'd performed several roles (because in those early days there was a lot of shifting and covering and filling in, all over), including area manager of Tomorrowland, organizational chairman of the Disneyland Recreation Club, and coordinator of the first Disneyland Cast Member magazine, *Backstage Disneyland.*

Van's office was in the administration building facing the parking lot. (The Grand Canyon Diorama actually ran through the center of the building.) Van was outgoing, and smoked during the time we talked. (We all smoked back then. God help us all.) He was also enthusiastic and gregarious, and talked at a clip about what he wanted to do.

He said, "Okay, Cora, you're my fifth guy. I've already picked four people to do this new orientation for Cast Members. I want people who have come out of the ranks. I want to use operational people." That was Food, Merchandise, and Attractions at the time. He later had us meet as a group to outline his plan.

First-Day Orientation

My job was a slide presentation, with those old carousel slide projectors, and the area Van assigned was Main Street. Of course, the balance of my work had been in Fantasyland. I mean, I knew about Main Street . . . but I didn't know all that *much* about it. I realized that may have been Van's intention, and my natural curiosity—and the time I had spent exploring on my own—may have paid off . . . and made an impression with others.

So, I started doing even deeper research. The other guys got the other lands, but we all would be working essentially together. In the evening, after closing time, the five of us would meet. We'd then look through music recordings, through slides and photos and art—all kinds of resources that were at our disposal—and then combine all of our segments into one "show." I think we used two or three trays of slides, and we taped the narration. Each one of us narrated our own segment.

We were a completely inexperienced bunch, though naturally, we thought it turned out pretty good, whatever it was we had set up. Van was the producer, or executive producer, and he must have thought it was good, too, because it all came together in a final presentation that became the new employees' first-day orientation guide. (Later, I added a *second*-day orientation, specific to each division. Everybody went crazy, and didn't want to do that. They said it increased their budget, paying for a day's labor for all these new people, and not getting any return for it. Well, you *do* get a return for it: now they're well trained, more invested in our goals and purpose, and thus more enthusiastic and efficient.)

This work was all on our own time, by the way. We still pulled our shifts inside the park. Training was not a full-time job for any of us—even Van. Everyone was still "doubling in brass," as they used to say. I think that was a kind of flexibility that I learned then, and that helped me grow, and established a kind of trust and enthusiasm for the work, and for the place. And I know it was something I really encouraged later in my career.

Van had begun a whole language and culture of working at Disneyland, one that really made even the newest employees understand the unique expectations we had, and also made them feel like part of a select group. The training handbooks Van authored featured themes such as *You're an Ambassador of Happiness* and *You're Here Because You Care*. They provided both a practical and a cultural foundation for the training of every new Disneyland staffer.

Part of the Show

Van also decided we were going to start calling employees "Cast Members." His orientation program was called "You Are in Show Business." That program was presented in Fantasyland at the Mickey Mouse Club Theater, and was made to be sort of a "special event." Before you entered the theater, you would see spotlights sweeping the sky outside, like a Hollywood premiere. Upon entering the lobby, you would spot a huge mirror with the phrase "You are in Show Business" prominently featured on it. You are a "Cast Member," and you are part of the "Show." Our customers are "Guests." If you were in front of our "audience," you were "Onstage." Behind the scenes, you were "Backstage."

It seems common now, where every fast-food restaurant and dollar store calls their customers "Guests." But back then there were only two companies that did this: Hilton Hotels and Disneyland. It was a transformative and utterly unique way to look at the experience that people would have at Disneyland, on both sides of the show's "footlights." It elevated the experience for everyone, and made every human transaction stand out for both employee and visitor. It was an exciting idea.

In retrospect, I think about the subtlety of that idea, especially when I transferred from Fantasyland to Frontierland, and I became a cowboy. When I put those boots on, and walked on those wooden sidewalks, I took a different kind of step. I really felt like I was part of that setting. Same when I worked on the Sailing Ship

Columbia; that was fantastic. I was a sailor. An army guy, but now I'm a sailor. You really felt like you were playing the part.

Fantasyland, I confess, was a problem because it was blue slacks, white shirt, blue tie. Nothing. Who cares? That was one of the things I worked on. We ended up with better "show" costumes later—lederhosen on the Skyway and Matterhorn and such—so that was kind of cool.

Van also did some fun and outlandish things. For some time we had a program called *Spring Tonics*, where the frontline folks had some fun poking away at management and supervision. These were great shows, produced by members of the cast, that provided both a way to vent some about workplace foibles and frustrations—and perhaps a little good-natured "education" for the higher-ups. Again, in retrospect, I realize how innovative and important the employee culture Van was building was—and how fortunate I felt to be in the thick of it, too.

Here's another key idea that came from Van: he hated the word "training." He said, what you're doing is not training people; you can train chickens to peck on little buttons on the ride, and it would continue to operate. But you have to *cultivate* people. "This isn't about *training*," he'd say. "It's about *developing* people." I often wonder if the common HR term "training and *development*" originated with Van.

Introductions and Opportunities

Van took me around to meet every division head. I realized that he had singled me out. He didn't take the whole team. He saw something in me that I didn't even see in myself, and wanted me to meet the top people. And so I met with the likes of Jack Lindquist, and with Ed Edinger, Disneyland's first marketing director and Lindquist's boss at the time. I also met with a guy named Tru Woodworth, who was in charge of maintenance at the time. I met with Jack Olson, merchandise director, and later vice president of merchandise for both Disneyland and Walt Disney World. And Jim Baker before him, in Merchandise. It was a great opportunity.

In addition to the other stuff I was doing on my own time, I was asked to write for Van's employee newsletter, *Backstage Disneyland.* Again, for some reason, I was writing about Main Street. (I never did ask Van why he kept having me focus on Main Street content.)

More Investment Training

Van and I also came up with a program called *The Business of Show Business.* In those days, finance was *not* my strong point. And it's not a whole lot stronger today, though it's certainly much stronger than it was in those days. We worked with the Finance division to put together this show, and we all attended it, along with anybody in charge of a unit. A unit could be a food location, an attraction, a shop. We got a sort of Disneyland fundamental overview of revenue streams, attainments, profit and loss, how to read and respond to financial statements. It was very helpful for many of us, and again was a program that provided an improved overview of a shared vision and efficiency.

We also developed a program that was eventually called *Good Show/Bad Show.* We worked with WED Enterprises (the design division of Disneyland, now Walt Disney Imagineering) and their creative leader, Marty Sklar. Operational people would lead tours into areas where we thought we needed WED help in design, supporting us on budget requisitions to get the job done. And in time, that's how we got a new Fantasyland. If WED agreed with us, we would pitch it to their management and Disneyland management, and we'd once again work together because of the belief in a collaborative structure and the support in a shared vision.

By this time, about 1962, I was a supervisor. I was still doing all this work with Van on my own time, but it was fun and exciting; I was constantly learning in a way no college course could ever have duplicated—at least for me. Plus, I really felt professionally fulfilled, respected, and trusted. Sometimes compensation doesn't come in a paycheck, and that's the way I feel about the investment Disney had made in me. There was a satisfaction I felt in that "non-paid" compensation, and in showing them a good return on that investment.

Prejudice and Pride

I think that maybe it also helped overcome an inherent discrimination that existed in the culture, because naturally my Lebanese heritage and origins made me look quite different from the "typical" Southern California boy of the era. After my initial experience with that prejudice—and my mother's transcending encouragement to meet it head-on—it really hadn't been an issue. And if it was, I kept believing in myself and dealt with it immediately and forcefully.

As Van put it to me one day, "You're not in a party more than ten minutes before somebody knows you're Lebanese, because you make it clear."

There was only one incident that stands out. I was asked about my nationality by a manager who nicknamed me "Camel Driver." He thought it was hilarious to have me lead the camel in the 1957 Christmas in Many Lands parade. Even though he was a manager—and I was only a ride operator—I met him in the local pub one night, and calmly explained why I didn't want him to call me that anymore.

He bought me a beer (even though I was underage), and that was that.

When you've been a victim of thoughtless discrimination, I think it makes you inherently aware of it in the world around you (or at the very least sensitive to it). For me it was always a sort of "sixth sense," and I never really looked at people by gender, race, ethnicity, sexual orientation, or religion. My criteria instead was whether a person was doing a good job, or had potential . . . or was acting in a collaborative manner with their colleagues. People are people. The rest is all decoration.

Retlaw

I was a full-time supervisor, and was doing a lot with Van in "Training" (which he had rechristened "University of Disneyland," and later "Disney University"), when I was asked to interview at Retlaw.

You're probably thinking, "That just looks like 'Walter' spelled backwards"—and that's what it was. Retlaw Enterprises was a privately held company, owned by Walt personally. Walt formed the company to control the rights to his name and likeness, as well as his compensation for his day-to-day "job" leading the Disney organization. (It may seem odd, but it makes business sense that Walt was paid a fee for the use of his name and likeness, because Walt Disney Productions was a publicly held company.)

Much as you would compensate any celebrity endorsement, Walt was given monetary compensation for that, as well as "points," a financial profit percentage in the films he personally produced. Retlaw also owned the steam trains and the Monorail. (Retlaw received net revenue of $75 million from the Monorail and railroad between 1955 and late 1981, according to U.S. Securities and Exchange Commission filings.) At one point, Retlaw also owned the

Viewliner Train of Tomorrow, as well as the horse-drawn streetcars on Main Street, U.S.A.

Retlaw paid rent for the attractions' rights-of-way, and employed the attraction staff separately from Disneyland Cast Members.

I took the interview. It all sounded good to me; I've always been a train freak. I met two old-timers there—a guy named John Welty, and one named Ken Kohler. Ken later was responsible for Retlaw maintenance, monorails, and steam trains. I ended up working with Retlaw for six years! What I liked most about it was that I was pretty independent from the rest of Disneyland's supervisory team—and I appreciated that they had a profit-share program, which Disneyland didn't have at the time. (Every time that turnstile turned, Retlaw people got paid for it by Walt Disney Productions.)

Hearth and Home

Through that profit sharing, I garnered enough money to put a down payment on my first house, so it really was a windfall for me. That first house was in Garden Grove. It was a cute little thing called a "Cinderella House." Builder and housing tract developer Jean Valjean Vandruff (no kidding) envisioned this charming-but-modern-home concept and ended up constructing several of them from 1954 and through the 1960s throughout the Western United States, in swiftly developing bedroom communities such as Anaheim, Claremont, and Pomona (in California) and other locales further afield, like Las Vegas, Albuquerque, and even Oklahoma City.

"These low-slung, ranch-style houses, marked by high-gabled, shake-shingle roofs and decorative gingerbread trim, sold a fantasy. These were storybook homes, designed through and through to appeal to the nuclear family at the dawn of the Atomic Age," writer Kriston Capps says.

I'm not sure I realized how this first home dovetailed into my personal culture at Disney, as well as into the larger culture that Walt Disney was so deeply influencing with what was now becoming widely known as a "theme park." (They hadn't been called such a thing before Walt's park.)

Of course, once we owned a home, our family tradition really established itself. We cut off clippings from the grape vine that Sitte had brought to America fifty years before, and carefully planted them, and then tended to their growth. We were ready, at work and at home, to get some roots established, and see the vines bear fruit.

A few years later, in 1964, our second daughter, Michelle, was born.

Breaking Some Rules

At Retlaw, meanwhile, we were forging a lean team with specific jobs. We were all trained to do time cards, payroll, accounting, and then ride operations for the steam trains and Monorail, of course. We had a manager, Jack Ater, who I learned a lot from. I was the supervisor, the full supervisor, working under him; and then we had an assistant supervisor, Paul Legg, and that was the extent of us—that was our whole team (plus the trains and Monorail maintenance people).

There was a little friction with park personnel, because Retlaw employees didn't fall under anybody's authority on-site. Plus, there was an attitude that we were the "chosen people," and I'm not sure we did anything to disabuse that notion. We always felt that we were a little cut above, and that was fine. We liked that, and took pride in that. Retlaw was a great experience for me. And I think for anybody that ever worked for it. We still had to obey the rules—and we wouldn't try to break any of them.

But I did run afoul of some unspoken and unwritten conventions while I was at Retlaw. I appointed the first female foreman at Disneyland. These were the days when you didn't promote women in ride operations.

You sometimes did, for instance, promote women to "leads" in food and in merchandise, but you did not make them foreman on attractions. It just "wasn't a job for women."

However, one afternoon, the regular foreman on the Monorails night shift called in sick. I looked around the platform for the best-qualified replacement, pulled out my schedule, and noted it was Dianna Stark. As far as I was concerned, Dianna was the best choice, so I made her foreman for the night. Dianna hesitated. She said, "You know you're going to get in trouble." I said, "I don't care, you're the best-qualified person. Can you handle it?"

She said, "Of course," and she did. (Naturally, I was biting my nails all night, hoping nothing went wrong where she'd get the blame—and then both of our jobs would be over.)

Unfortunately, a manager at the time turned me in for this "infraction." He ratted me out to the Retlaw supervisors at corporate, and I was called on the carpet. "Why would you make her a foreman?" I was berated.

"Because she's the best qualified."

"Well, we don't have women foremen, and you're not going to start a precedent."

"She's the best qualified, and I'm sorry, I'm not backing down from that," I persisted. "I'd make her a permanent foreman. So if that's a problem, then I should transfer out, and go do something else."

We resolved that I would check with a manager before I did such a thing again, which was fine with me, because he was never there in evenings or on weekends anyway.

Diana was simply a natural leader. She became a supervisor, and worked in Operations, and I think even in Merchandise. Later, she was involved with us at the first park in Tokyo. (She was the only person on that project whose "trailing spouse" was a man; all the other relocations were men.)

I always looked at people based on their performance. (And I also always tried to hire people smarter than I was. I didn't find any, but I was looking.) I hired people who were team players; I hired people who had performed, who had a proven track record, proved that they were open to training. It didn't matter to me whether they were Black, white, Asian, gay, old, young—I truly didn't care. It didn't make any difference to me. It was all about performance!

Maybe it's due to my amalgamated upbringing. My parents spoke Spanish . . . and they spoke Arabic, and English. My grandmother, in addition, spoke Italian and French. (I didn't know what the hell I was when I was growing up.) I was eating Mexican food alongside Lebanese dishes (along with hot dogs). There just weren't any prejudices, and I never heard any.

Continued Training

Of course my relationship with Van and the Disney University continued during my time at Retlaw. For a guy who'd thought about pursuing a teaching degree and then decided against it, I was doing an awful lot of teaching!

We developed the Qualified Trainer program. (Van used to laugh at the apparent redundancy. "Why would we have *un*qualified trainers?" he'd chuckle. We dovetailed the program into the end of the second day of orientation, creating a third training layer where new hires were turned over for more specific education within their attraction, shop, or restaurant. In a way, we had created orientation training that was as cinematic as the park experience: there was a long shot, a medium shot, a close-up. The "Disney Difference," as it came to be called, began here.)

For Qualified Trainer classes, we developed a checklist for each attraction. I say "we" because it was actually a team of Monorail and steam train people who actually worked on it, from the bottom up, and then became qualified trainers. I tried to get extra money for the qualified trainer role, but that never did fly. But it didn't make any difference. People wanted to be a qualified trainer. As I'd discovered, "compensation" doesn't always mean "money." It was like the next step to becoming a lead, or a foreman: we had their interest and enthusiasm—and a consistent training program.

The Retlaw experience was invaluable. I learned how to manage a slower business, basically. But it was also a dead end. After six years, I saw that, because of its fundamental nature as a holding company, nothing was growing at Retlaw.

Back to Fantasyland

In 1969, I went back to Disneyland. But first I said to Jack Ater, "I think I'm gonna see if Dick Nunis will take me back into operations after all these years."

So I went and talked to Dick Nunis. When Dick joined Disneyland in 1955, the park had six hundred Cast Members. By the time he retired forty-four years later from what was supposed to be a "summer job," Disneyland boasted thirteen thousand Cast Members and Walt Disney World had a workforce of fifty thousand.

Dick had learned about Disneyland through his USC classmate, Ron Miller, who was Walt's son-in-law. On a lark, he decided to apply for a summer job at the new park and was hired by Van. It was the two of them who initiated training Disneyland employees—and among members of their first class were Walt and his key park executives.

Dick soon worked his way up to attractions supervisor, developing the standard operating procedures for all of the park's attractions (many of which are still in use today). By the time I went to see him in my waning days at Retlaw, he was director of park operations.

Dick was, as usual, hard-nosed in his reaction to me at our meeting. "I'd like to have you over here," he said. "But I'm not going to give you a promotion. I'll bring you over laterally." Which is really more than I expected. I thought I'd have to start all over. But they brought me back as a full supervisor, working back in Fantasyland.

Once back there, I worked under William "Sully"

Sullivan, who, like Dick Nunis, had taken a summer job in the opening season of Disneyland and stayed for the rest of his career. He ascended from ticket-taker, to ride operator, to operations supervisor, learning all aspects of the operation along the way. (Sully had been my supervisor during my Submarine days, when I became renowned for turning a long sub into a short one.) He was sent to Squaw Valley (near Lake Tahoe) as a member of the operations team that assisted in the opening and operating of the Winter Olympics in 1960, where Walt Disney was in charge of pageantry. Sully then served as assistant manager for the Disney-designed attractions at the 1964–1965 New York World's Fair.

Welcome, Foolish Mortals . . .

My second stint in Fantasyland was actually fairly short, though. I was promoted to assistant manager of Frontierland/Adventureland in time for the opening of the Haunted Mansion attraction at the end of the summer in 1969.

Card Walker, who was executive vice president and chief operating officer of Walt Disney Productions at that time, and several other executives were really afraid that maybe we'd crossed a line, and that the opening up of a Haunted Mansion full of ghosts and frights wasn't the thing to do—that it wasn't a "Disney thing."

Card had called me, and had me stand at the attraction exit over three or four days to listen to people's comments, and call him at the end of each day to report what those comments were. I could only report that they had been favorable, the Guests liked it, and they came out of there laughing and smiling. They thought it was a great attraction. Everyone seemed to heave a sigh of relief.

Things to Come

Things at home ran "steady as she goes." But like so many young couples of this era, to a large degree, Susan and I had increasingly separate lives. This was a time when dads were typically absent a lot—and missed a lot of their family growing up. That was one of my greatest regrets, but truly not uncommon in those postwar times. I was the "breadwinner," Susan was the "wife and mother," just like on all the old TV shows. I don't think we noticed any increasing disconnection between us at that early stage of our marriage; or if we did notice, we just assumed that it was a part of the way lives were being lived then—which it was. So we just continued as we had begun, trying to balance my career with the very different needs of home and family. It was around this time that our third child, Jimmy, was born, in 1969.

At this point in my career, I was actually starting to question where it was all heading. I was respected and felt accomplished in my work, and was pretty confident about my career ascent. However, at this point in the history of Disney, there was actually plenty of uncertainty.

So much of what we did, what we planned, and what we aspired to was due to the vision and passion and commitment of one man, and he had left us, this earth, a few years before. We all thought about him and whether we were doing justice to his vision and tribute to his memory. This was becoming a "now or never" time for all of us to step up, and see if we had what it would take to honor the legacy of Walt Disney.

I hadn't forgotten: I owed my whole career to a chance encounter with him one early morning.

Part Four: Walt Disney

TODAY, it is hard for many to imagine that Walt Disney was real.

His name and image have become so iconic—and as we move further away from his lifetime, less personal, and more "legendary." It's easy to see him as a plaster saint, or as a sinister villain, because "Walt Disney" has also become fraught with meanings and interpretations—and scholarship and ignorance— far beyond the name and biography of an actual living, breathing, brilliant, fallible human being.

I was born about three weeks before the world premiere of *Snow White and the Seven Dwarfs*, so of course I never knew a world *without* Walt Disney in it. In childhood, and especially during World War II, the presence of Disney movies in the theaters, the characters in their cartoon shorts, the art and stories from Disney in books and magazines, and the seemingly omnipresent *music*—a lot of us from that era knew much of our "Disney" from the radio and records—was consistent and important, not only because they were fun and entertaining, but because there was a uniformity of philosophy and ideals that merged so well with the American spirit of the time, and with the culture of our country.

There was also something that resonated in the Disney productions that seemed to fit with the values I had learned from my family, and in my experience in church, and at school. It fit comfortably into my personal culture.

Behind the magic of all of these characters and creations, we knew, of course, was a fellow named Walt Disney. By the time I arrived at Disneyland years later, Walt's name and persona had flourished beyond the one I had grown up with, due to his weekly exposure on his television program, which begot additional publicity, and audiences, and fame as his reach through that young medium took hold. (Of course I later found out that he had presented the weekly TV program on ABC as a means to secure financing for the design and construction of Disneyland. That clever strategy was enlightening and remarkable, and only added to my enthusiasm over working at the park—and to my own philosophies about what we now know as the frequently clichéd and misunderstood term *synergy*.)

Walt Disney, Himself

So of course, as I began working steadily at Disneyland, I knew of Walt Disney's work, and who he was—and what he looked like. I'd seen him here and there in those earliest of my workdays in the park.

But one day, my personal relationship with Walt Disney changed.

I was hurrying through the park that morning, loaded down with notebooks and papers—I was still studying in school at the time, so I worked on my breaks, and whenever I could fit it in. Struggling both figuratively and literally with my workload, I was making my way around the roadway between Sleeping Beauty Castle and the Matterhorn, when I saw Walt headed directly toward me.

He was wearing a sport coat, and old slacks, and he had his hands in his pockets. The park wasn't open yet, so he seemed to be taking a stroll. I stayed close to the right rail, so as not to bother him or interrupt his thoughts. But suddenly I heard, "Hey, Jim, come on over here!"

And I thought, *My God, Walt Disney knows my name!* That there was a badge on my chest as big as my fist that said JIM on it hadn't dawned on me right then.

Walt asked where I was heading, and I told him I was on my way to the Matterhorn, where I was part of the opening crew. He looked at my armload of scholastic materials, and that famous eyebrow rise shot up in sheer curiosity.

"Are all those books and papers part of the job?" he asked with a sly grin.

"Well, part of this is that I'm a student, and studying for classes," I replied. "The other part is that I'm trying to come up with a more consistent training program than what we do now."

"Well, what do we do for training now?" he asked.

"We put the new person with the old person," I answered. "But sometimes the old person's not a great trainer, and we don't use any checklists—it's all whatever happens to be in their memory."

Walt seemed surprised. "Don't we have manuals, and standard operating procedures?"

"Some attractions do," I replied, "but some don't, so you have to pretty much wing it, and somebody just stays with a person until it's felt that they're 'trained.'"

In retrospect, I am still a little shocked at my own directness. I mean, this was *Walt Disney*, himself. Here's this pip-squeak employee telling the big boss stuff that maybe might get other people in trouble, or seem insubordinate, or even cocky. But I guess being honest, and with my own earnest enthusiasm motivating my candor—and maybe just being too naïve then to know any better—it all seemingly worked in my favor.

"Well, Jim," Walt said, "are you interested in training?"

"Yes, sir, I am," I said. "I like that. To see people learn, to make it all consistent, to train everyone to do it all the right way."

Walt sized me up for a minute and said, "I want you to go over to the administration building, and I want you to ask for a guy named Van Arsdale France. I think he may have something for you."

He then continued his stroll and walked past me toward Fantasyland, and in parting added, "Tell him Walt sent you!"

Yes, sir, I'll do that. You *bet* I'll do that! And so that was how I got my kickoff with Van France, a relationship that as I noted already has had a lasting impact.

That *kickoff* was because of *Walt Disney.*

Himself.

Memories, a Mentor . . . and a Martian?

These days, with Walt coming across more as a symbol, or an idea, or a logo—well, it's hard to describe how what he said and what he expressed and what he wanted stuck with you, became a rallying cry, a philosophy—even a religion.

There's an analogy that may be a bit trite now, that Walt was a great "orchestra conductor." He knew how to assemble a group of very talented people who could take their different skills and tools and personalities and points of view and still create magnificent music.

He selected people based on what they brought to the table. Sometimes he put people together *because* they were opposites, to see what kind of fire that friction might strike.

By putting me with Van France, Walt connected me with the only real mentor I think I ever had. I've had a lot of guidance, and influence, and leadership in my life and career, but Van is the only guy I'd ever consider a true mentor.

Walt liked eccentrics. Anyone who's looked at that group that coalesced into what is now the legendary "Nine Old Men" of Disney Animation knows that none of those guys was . . . well, typical. Yet in putting them together, Walt got an animation orchestra.

He did the same sort of thing at Disneyland. Van France was an eccentric guy, for sure. He reminded me a lot of Ray Walston, the famous character actor and star of *My Favorite Martian* on TV. Van wore glasses that were always so dirty I couldn't figure out how he saw through them. (Sometimes I took them off of his face and cleaned them myself.)

Like all of us back then, he smoked, but Van always seemed to have a cigarette with an impossibly long ash hanging from his mouth. He was gregarious and enthusiastic, but also very focused on a single idea: it was to perpetuate Walt's vision, and he saw the way to do that was to develop *people*.

Not Training, "Development"

Long before the term "human resources" was so ubiquitous, Van saw our people as our greatest asset, and our greatest opportunity. As I've noted, Van hated the term *training*. To him, it was about *developing* the staff: it was now about developing people, not just developing attractions or shows. This was an equal part of the Guest experience.

Van created programs such as "Laboratory and Communication Skills," so that people could learn how to talk in front of a group. He developed, for executive assistants, a program called "Put a Smile in Your Voice," which focused on phone etiquette and techniques. (We should have developed that class for everybody, come to think of it—a lot of our executives really didn't have a "smile in their voice" when they talked to us on the phone.)

There was education outside the workplace that the company paid for, too. For instance, Van suggested it, so I went to USC to take administrative leadership courses to help us *all* be better leaders. And I think it was a big help.

"Training" became a cursory thing; we left training for those people who actually had to run things—cash handling, food preparation, ride operations, merchandise, products, sales display, that kind of stuff. We still had those kinds of classes; that was training. But we wanted to develop people not *just* to be good ride operators, or good merchandise hosts. We wanted to try to train people to be good supervisors of *other* people, and then pass on what they had learned.

As we worked further on *developing* people, there

was also a real emphasis placed on improving their talent. Did they understand profit and loss? Did they understand "show"? Did they understand our relationships with other departments and divisions? We began building programs to broaden not only how they did their day-to-day work, but their future, and how they saw *themselves.* We put a lot of emphasis on developing our management technique, and how those managers developed those that were in line down below "in the ranks." Those ranks became a lot more important, too, because they were filled with the people who were in direct contact with the Guests on a day-to-day basis.

Van's "show" concept and "Cast Member" analogy turned out to be more and more accurate. People may have come to Disneyland for the attractions and shows and restaurants and shops—but for a majority of those Guests, a key memory or experience was something shared with one of our people, and personal interaction with our "onstage talent."

Backstage Development

We also looked at this whole idea from the other side. How did *we* treat our people? We instituted employee opinion polls on a regular basis, and if opinions came back pretty harsh on people's immediate supervisors, we'd take a hard look at them. Maybe they were miscast. Letting people go was the last resort; it was a better investment to move them to a job that they were better suited for. We did a lot of that: people, for example, say in merchandise who really should have been in maintenance—and we'd make accommodations for that transfer. If they were good people and believed in the *philosophy*, we'd find the right spot for them. If they were just there for a job, we'd gently suggest that they should move on.

Dick Nunis

Walt had hired Van France, and the first assistant Van hired was a guy named Dick Nunis. Dick had led the USC football team in interceptions in 1951 and was a member of the Trojans' Rose Bowl champion squad the next year, but in the second-to-last game of the regular season, before that Rose Bowl, he suffered a broken neck. His ambition to become a pro football player and a coach was sidelined; instead he focused on earning a bachelor's degree in education from the school in 1954, and Van hired him at Disneyland in 1955. A lot of how Disneyland approached training and development really comes from Dick and Van. They need and deserve to get the right credit for that.

Although his career ambitions had changed, I think Dick remained a sort of linebacker and coach. I learned from Dick—lots of people learned, but lots of them couldn't deal with his type of discipline. He was just a tough guy, and if that was your style he was a pretty good motivator. But Dick felt he shouldn't have to "hold your hand"; you should just *know* how to do the job. That's where Van France really was a good balance for me. Dick and Van were close. Van and I became close. And later in my career, Dick and I became close. Dick and I had the same standards—we just implemented them differently. I truly respect him for doing what he did, both at Disneyland and Walt Disney World. I don't necessarily agree with *how* he did it. But on the other hand, I'm not sure it could have been done any other way, in that particular era.

Dick really sat at Walt's knee, and used his particular personality and management style to do what we all wanted—to do it the way Walt wanted it, and to make Walt happy with the whole show.

Wear the Guest's Shoes

Walt wanted us out in the field, and said so. Dick would come into offices and see people, and he'd blow up. "Get the hell out in the field!" he'd holler. (Communicating out in the field was complicated back then. In those days, supervisors would wear orange ties—that's how you identified a supervisor "out in the field." Messages were delivered—remember, no cell phones or pagers in those days—through the Central Ticket Booth. If you wanted a supervisor, you called the Central Ticket Booth in Tomorrowland, or whatever area you were in. The ticket seller would flip on a light on the booth, so once in a while, as a supervisor, you'd check the light on top of it. If the light was on, you had a message.)

You know where I did my schedules in Fantasyland? On top of a trash can in front of the Welch's Grape Juice stand. I had a pad; I had a pencil (Welch's kept it for me under the counter). I'd go over there, and I'd pick up my pad, and on the trash can top, I'd make out schedules for the ride operators. Not in an office, not behind the scenes, but out there in the park. It's a lesson for everyone in a public-facing business. "Wear your Guests' shoes." Get out there and be where your customers are. See and hear and smell and feel the things that they do. You can't contribute to their experience if you have no idea what it is.

Another lesson from Dick came my way while I was an assistant manager, I think, in Frontierland/Adventureland. One morning, right as the park was opening, I was walking through when Dick came up to me, pointed to the French Market, and showed me that the chairs were still on top of the tables where they had mopped the night before. I made the mistake of saying, "I'm not in charge of [the] French Market." Boy, he let me have it. "You're in charge of everything you see when you walk through here! If it's not right, you go make sure it's taken care of!" That really stuck with me.

If you're a leader, you should care about all of it. If you walk through an area and can't find the food guy, or the merchandise guy, or the entertainment guy, or the manager and something *so obviously* needs doing—do it. I once read an interview with Ray Kroc, who built McDonald's into a empire. Even when he was CEO and worth a billion times what a hamburger cost, if he saw trash on the ground, or that the front of one of their stores needed hosing down, he just *did* it. That's the way we became at Disneyland.

Consistency that originated with show training

became Dick's purview to enforce. Employees had grooming standards, covering how hair and makeup and jewelry were to be appropriately worn and applied, because each Cast Member was out there essentially representing Walt Disney. Even though we all still (stupidly) smoked all the time in those days, we were conscientious about doing so out of the sight of the Guests. Even Walt was very self-conscious about this.

All of this came down to "sweating the details." It's a level of awareness that we instilled in everybody through training and through example—through good leadership. And that came from Walt, too. Walt was all about the details. During the construction of Storybook Land, for instance, someone mentioned that putting real stained glass into the tiny church and miniature buildings would be expensive to fabricate and maintain. If Walt would consider plexiglass instead, to replicate that "look," it would be quite a savings, and no one would notice the difference. Walt responded bluntly: "I would know"—and by extension, what he was saying was the Guests will know, too. People can tell, instinctively, when they enter a space where care has been taken, attention has been paid, and passion is part of the environment. Whether it's a garden, a retail store, a church, or a museum, attention to detail is a palpable part of an experience. Real handblown and stained glass was installed throughout the attraction.

There's an old adage, "God is in the details," meaning that something might seem simple, but contains greater complexity than it appears to.

At Disneyland, *Walt* was in the details.

Methods and Leadership

My mother's motto might have been "get it done, and get it done right, and get it done quickly." Another lesson from my parents was that I always felt I had to be firm, I had to be fair, and I had to be consistent. And if I wasn't, it'd catch up with me. I went to Catholic school, and that was formative and important, certainly. The nuns are tough on you—but they really instilled character in people, and helped motivate.

So, my parents, my religious background, and my educational background all prepared me to work for a guy like Walt Disney, who wanted everything perfect. Keep the park clean, keep it orderly. Don't take on fads when it comes to grooming, wardrobe, and behavior. "Get it done, and get it done right, and get it done quickly." All that just came together for me. It just felt natural. I had spent my whole life walking down the narrow path, and Walt had set up a narrow path, but one that was apparent and sensible, so it was a fine one to follow. In order to follow that path, it was wise to be firm, be fair, and be consistent. It was what I understood. It also made sense toward a shared goal. Leadership was defined, goals were established, expectations were clear.

Taking the Lead

I think a leader is someone who people will follow, somebody who gets in front of the issue and says, "Follow me." It's not someone who stands in the back and says, "I want you to get out there and get it done. I'll be right behind you." It's someone who works on the issues, no matter how small they are . . . whether it's making sure weeds get pulled in the planter, talking to custodial because they're upset about wages, dealing with a strike, or opening a new attraction.

I think leaders are basically born with leadership abilities. They can be enhanced. I know there are many arguments about whether you can *make* a leader or whether leaders are born. I think you can make a "better" leader, but I also do think they have to be born with a drive that spurs all good leaders.

I don't care whether it's at Disney or anyplace—it's how you're led. Who do you look up to? Who's taking you down that path? People look up to their leaders. Most people crave leadership and guidance, and they're going to follow in those footsteps. Do you believe in this dream? Do you believe in the philosophy? And if you believe in the philosophy, we'll develop you into somebody who can carry this philosophy on.

For me, above and beyond all, Disneyland had been about Walt's leadership. The ideas he instilled in Van, and Dick, and then me, and what I passed on over the rest of my career. Assume responsibility of everything you see. Disney was a culture we wanted to preserve, an experience and level of quality that Walt Disney wanted.

Walt's World

Of course with Disneyland Park, and the TV show, and huge movie hits such as *Mary Poppins* (and everything that came with that exposure and success), Walt only got more famous. I still marvel at how he did everything he did—a guy by this point in his sixties, which seemed ancient to me then (but not anymore). He was in the park a lot, frequently beaming proudly while leading dignitaries, movie stars, celebrities, heads of state, former presidents, and even royalty on a tour of this Magic Kingdom over which he was the benevolent monarch. More and more, he stayed in his cozy apartment over the Fire Station in the Town Square at the start of Main Street, U.S.A. We'd encounter him prowling or strolling through his creation at all hours of the day and night.

Sometimes when Guests were present, this could create a problem: he was so well-known that one request for an autograph could lead to a deluge of signature-seekers. He began to keep a fairly incognito look when around the park during Guest hours, and was rarely in his familiar suit or cardigan, often sporting a slouch hat or a straw fedora from Adventureland. And if someone did recognize him, he'd learned the trick of "pre-signing" his autograph on slips of his personal notepaper to quickly handle a fan and disperse an enthusiastic gathering without creating a scene—and without disappointing them.

Walt at times would also come to Disneyland with his daughters, Diane and Sharon, and later his grandkids. We'd see them around and "back door" them into attractions. The security call would go out when he arrived at Harbor Gate ("Code W"), so you'd know, as the animators up at the Disney Studio said, that "Man was in the forest" (watch *Bambi* again . . .). Those rare occasions when Walt's brother and business partner, Roy, came on to the property, it was a "Code R" that went out.

Tiki Times

When I worked for Retlaw, of course, I technically worked for Walt more directly, but I didn't see him that much more frequently then either, except for occasional special circumstances. One of those took place in the spring of 1963, when the Retlaw-owned attraction Walt Disney's Enchanted Tiki Room opened. I was assigned to the attraction to train personnel there. Walt would show up on a regular basis to see how the training was going. But he wasn't just an observer—he would jump in as the work was going on, and would say, "No, no, no, you didn't say it right," or "You've got to tap José's perch this way," and he'd want it done a certain way. "Wake up, José, wake up!"

Walt would really do that. He talked to Wally Boag (a really talented writer/comedian/performer who headlined at the Golden Horseshoe Revue in Frontierland) about narration and voices, and also spoke with the Imagineers (known as WED personnel then) there preparing the attraction, of course. I got to know a lot of the WED people then. We all worked on it very, very hard—and Walt was right there with us.

For the attraction's opening day that June, Walt conducted a press conference early one morning. He orchestrated everything that day, and wanted everything to run like clockwork. Despite all this, the conference wasn't capturing or generating the energy and attention Walt had hoped. Maybe it was because it was morning, but regardless, the enthusiasm seemed very low, and he was having a difficult time getting the reporters' attention to begin describing the creation and elements of the innovative show set to open. To change the mood, Walt pulled me aside and sent me on an errand "outside the berm." Shortly thereafter we were serving the sluggish reporters a little "Polynesian pick-me-up" of Walt's own concoction. Let's just say that pineapple juice wasn't its strongest ingredient (yet it seemingly did the trick). He'd managed to find a way to build sudden enthusiasm within the group, even at ten o'clock in the morning. Walt's unusual and quick thinking—and a long-developed understanding of this particular audience (and others)—always seemed to turn any event into a happening.

Endings and Beginnings

All I really remember about Thursday, December 15, 1966, was that I was on my way home from the park—just about like any other day. It was seemingly uneventful. The weather was mild; Christmas was in the air. We were getting ready for the Disneyland holiday celebrations, which in those days only lasted about two weeks. But when I came home, something was *really* wrong. Susan was in tears, and on the radio, they were playing "When You Wish Upon a Star." She looked at me so mournfully, and simply said, "Walt's gone."

I was stunned. Shocked. Speechless. I sunk into a chair and absorbed this horrible news. Rene ran to me and jumped into my arms, and I held her as she cried and cried. At four years old, she didn't really understand what was going on, except that something really bad had happened and Mommy and Daddy were both hurting, too.

To this day, whenever she hears "When You Wish Upon a Star," she cries.

The rest of that awful day is lost to my memory.

The next morning, Dick Nunis called an "all-hands" meeting. It was a rallying cry, a call to action, an admonition to the great culture and the clear philosophies Walt had left us in Disneyland. The park still opened for business, and the flag was not flown at half-mast, because Walt was still everywhere in the place. We carried on for him, for his memory, for the star he created that still shined . . . and that we could all still wish upon.

A Christmas Farewell

A few days after Walt's passing we had the annual Disneyland Candlelight Processional. It had begun during the 1957 Christmas season, when choirs followed the Christmas Around the World Parade from Sleeping Beauty Castle and headed down Main Street, U.S.A. before performing in a circle around Town Square. For the 1958 performance, bleachers were constructed in front of the Main Street Station, and the Candlelight Processional as we still know it today began.

Of course this one was the first without Walt in attendance. I remember it was a very cold night; temperatures dipped down into the high thirties after sunset. I was still a Retlaw employee, so I was at the train station, hosting the guest narrator for the Nativity Story, Dennis Morgan (an actor-singer who is probably best known for a series of Warner Bros. musicals he starred in during the 1940s).

There was still an unshakable somber feel to the "holiday cheer," and even as the choir prepared to begin its trek down Main Street, there was a bittersweet quality to the otherwise festive event. We were all looking up into the show lights just before they were to dim as the processional started, and a chilly mist began to fall through the crisp, cold winter air. As the assembled crowd watched in wonder, those crystalline water drops turned into tiny snowflakes. It didn't last very long, and nothing accumulated on the ground—but I don't think there was a dry eye in Town Square when that happened. Guest and Cast Member alike all shed a tear. Walt had said goodbye.

Part Five: A Culture in Transition

IN AN interview for the KNBC-TV program *Survey* in August of 1966, journalist Bob Wright asked Walt Disney if he thought his vision could endure, even if he were gone. Walt didn't miss a beat, and replied with this: "Well, I think by this time my staff, my young group of executives, and everything else, are convinced that Walt is right. That quality will out. And so I think they're going to stay with that policy, because it's proven that it's a good business policy! Give the people everything you can give them! Keep the place as clean as you can keep it! Keep it friendly, you know? Make it a real fun place to be! I think they're convinced and I think they'll hang on after, as you say . . . well . . . after Disney."

Walt had been optimistic, but I don't think any of us shared that feeling. To a degree, I don't think any of us believed Walt could actually die. I know that sounds ridiculous—everybody dies—but Roy E. Disney, Walt's nephew, said it well: "Walt had become kind of a mythical being even then to a lot of people, and especially to his own family. It was a sense of 'he'll be around forever.'"

There was not much communication from Burbank about how we should proceed after Walt's passing, so we all just put our heads down and continued to do what we had always done as best we could. Feedback was long in coming from upper management at the Studio down to us here in Disneyland.

Rumors and Suitors

But almost immediately there were rumors—of a shutdown, or a buyout, or a merger. Suitors circled and besieged the executive suite. Gulf + Western wanted to combine, and support, the Florida development. General Electric and Litton Industries expressed interest. Westinghouse Electric aggressively sought an acquisition.

Roy O. Disney, Walt's brother and business partner, was really instrumental in taking the lead on a vision for Walt Disney Productions. He ignored the suitors and decided to move the company forward, intact. He admitted that the organization would now have to be operated by committee, which he knew wasn't the best way. "But we will have to do it that way until the new leadership develops," he observed.

A week after Walt's passing, Roy O. assembled all the major executives and principals and department heads and spoke of the future. He said, "I want every one of you to do just exactly what you were going to do when Walt was alive."

At the Park

When Walt passed, we were all stunned and in shock, and a bit lost—especially the Retlaw people. We all worked directly for Walt's family company, and felt the loss pretty personally and severely. Bill Cottrell, president of Retlaw Enterprises, and Royal "Mickey" Clark continued to drive us, as did Chuck Romero.

And for those of us in Anaheim, it was really Card Walker who took the helm, and pulled people together, and set out the challenges and goals for us. Card had joined Disney by first working in the Studio mail room. (Walt believed that the mail room was the best place for a new employee to get to know the entire Studio operation.) From there he had moved to the camera department and then over to the production department as unit manager on short subjects. In 1941, Card enlisted in the navy, and after four years returned to the Studio to work in the story department, before spearheading a new thing called "market research," where he worked with a group called A.R.I. (Audience Research Institute) testing audience reaction to various film projects.

In 1956, Walt named Card vice president of advertising and sales. Four years later he was appointed to the company's board of directors. In 1965, he was made vice president of marketing, and—after Walt's passing—executive vice president of operations. (Card became executive vice president and chief operating officer in 1968.)

I liked Card. I thought he was a good leader—hard, strict, a veteran of World War II. Card had seen action, stood on aircraft carriers and guided airplanes in, and was targeted by kamikazes (at least three times from what he could recount, or wanted to reveal). Over the years he was very supportive of me and what I was doing, particularly when I took over responsibility for management training. I think Card understood the culture that Walt had created better than most people did. (I think that's one of the reasons that marketing was what Card did best. At

Disneyland it was all about attendance for him. I'm pretty sure he called the park on a daily basis to find out what the attendance was that day. Which was why we had a lot of admission giveaway programs. You see, Card never asked how much *money* we made, just how many *people* came through the turnstiles.)

Dick Nunis was also a huge help, giving direction to the operational people. Ultimately, we all just did the job the best we could.

Moving Forward Without Walt

Roy O. believed that we had "backlogged" enough projects with Walt in film, television, and at Disneyland Park to get us through about three years.

No matter the reassurances that began to trickle down from corporate, or the acceptance of a "new normal" that came as each day went by and the park seemed to be simply moving along smoothly, there was still an unease that would pervade through the entire organization for years.

"What would Walt do?" became the constant, annoying, and unanswerable refrain and question. What we eventually realized at Disneyland—especially Van and Dick and me (and all those who'd been involved for years in training and education)—is that "What would Walt do?" was a question we'd asked and answered every day . . . for years!

The Disney Way

The things we taught our incoming Cast Members (and all of those in our training programs) were based upon and inspired by Walt's words, his world views, his ideas, his values. Over the years, we had vetted and parsed and examined Walt's work and words to the degree that we had actually come to realize how *lacking* in complexity his big philosophies were. They were as basic as common sense and as practical as the golden rule. They were broad enough to be applied to any situation, and in the same fashion could also be added to and elaborated on.

Ethics

Ethics to me is a fundamental Disney idea. It's also a tricky business. As we know from politics, many ethical things aren't legal. Many legal things aren't ethical. Perhaps what I'm thinking of usually when I think about ethics is a kind of *decency.* Maybe the Golden Rule is the best example. In our culture back then, ethically, it was worse than a sin, or committing a real crime, if you were disloyal or underhanded, or "stabbed somebody in the back." If you backstabbed a colleague, talked badly about somebody, tried to get somebody demoted, or if you made up stories, anything . . . you were ostracized. You lost a lot of the regard and respect of people, and eventually those without decency tended to disappear. We were a lot like a family. People really treated their fellow workers as comrades.

Quality

Philip Stanhope, Fourth Earl of Chesterfield, said, "Whatever is worth doing at all, is worth doing well." Walt might have said the same thing. As he said in the interview cited earlier, "Quality will out." It's what Walt insisted on in everything he did. His animated films, TV programs—everything had to be *well-made* and "built to last." If a product licensee made shoddy products and Walt found out about it? That licensee either fixed it, or didn't get another contract. At the park, "good show" was about quality content, good storytelling, excellent craft with good materials. Walt knew that Guests might not notice such details, but they'd notice their absence. Quality was an expectation, and a big part of the Disney experience.

Value

Walt made the comment once (though I've forgotten in what context), "I don't care how much we charge, as long as when people leave they say, 'Boy, I really had a good time, and it was worth every penny.'" He continued, "I *do* care what we charge if they leave saying, 'Boy, that wasn't worth the money. Where was the value of what I just did?'"

Value meant to us that our Guests were satisfied that what they experienced at the park was worth not only their *money*, but their investment of time, and their effort.

To me it also meant this: did our storytelling carry value? Did they carry away a message, a feeling, a hope, or a dream that they didn't have when they came in the gate? Did they fulfill a hope or a dream based on what we had put before them?

We wanted that value to remain long after they left the berm. Our goal was to add value to their *lives*.

Uniqueness

In the early days of Disneyland, having a *unique* experience was practically a guarantee. There was simply nothing like it in the world. But even Walt knew that wouldn't last. Sure enough, variations on the Disneyland idea, imitators, and knockoffs popped up from coast-to-coast. Walt knew that he had a kind of protected uniqueness in the characters and stories that were so associated with his name already. He knew that he had an ability to promote his park through his television program that no competitor or imitator could match.

But he did not rest on his laurels. He created a service and experience culture that was highly unusual for its time, and one that I was happy to be a part of. We treated our customers as Guests. Every Cast Member was in place to enhance their experience. Whether through their personality, friendliness, attention, or facility with valuable information, our Cast Members and that level of service was probably more unique in the world than a flying elephant or a rocket to the moon.

So, as the question "What would Walt do?" was asked, over and over again, I began to realize that the distinctive place we occupied at Disneyland, as ambassadors of Walt's fundamental ideals directly to the public, uniquely quali-fied us with an expertise that as time went by was actually reassuring, and confidence-building.

It also brought us together as a culture. We were all in this together, we all had an investment in this dream, we all wanted to promote these admirable values in Walt's image, in his memory, and in his honor.

In many ways, I think our understanding of Disney-land Park and our connection there with Walt made us the best prepared part of the company to deal with his passing, and effectively continue his vision, carry out his plans, and elaborate on his dreams.

As the park project in Florida began anew, Roy O. admonished the business leadership, "We're going to fin-ish this . . . and we're going to do it just the way Walt wanted it. Don't you ever forget it."

And after a little time had passed, we felt ready.

Part Six: A Walt Disney World

I DON'T know that we actually recovered from Walt's death for several years. Maybe we never "recovered." But we persevered.

As I've said, I stuck it out at Retlaw, and it was about a year and a half after Walt's passing that I realized I had to move out, in order to move forward. Dick Nunis did take me back into Disneyland proper; as usual, he was no-nonsense—I certainly didn't get a promotion going back to the park, but the lateral return as a full supervisor to Fantasyland attractions was actually more than I expected. I actually thought I'd have to start all over.

After a brief time in Fantasyland, and another brief stint in Adventureland/Frontierland, and then helping with the opening of the delayed Haunted Mansion attraction in 1969, Dick approached me about joining "The Florida Project."

Looking Beyond the Berm

We'd heard rumors about a big "East Coast" project since the earliest days of the 1964–65 New York World's Fair. The four major Disney attractions at that project, and the success and publicity surrounding them, *really* started the talk that we ought to take the Disneyland idea out into the world, to a wider audience. There was serious planning during the New York World's Fair development phase about a project in St. Louis, too, in the riverfront area, which was undergoing a major redevelopment for the city's bicentennial celebration. I found out later that they had begun toying with the idea of another location as early as 1959, when some studies Walt had commissioned showed that only 5 percent of Disneyland's visitors came from east of the Mississippi River—where then 75 percent of the U.S. population resided.

Walt had said many times that whatever he did anywhere else wouldn't be Disneyland; he professed lots of doubts about just copying his original park. "I'm not sure we should be doing that," he'd said. "I'm not sure if it would work, and it takes away something from the uniqueness of Disneyland."

But the success Disney registered in New York broke the ice. We could get outside of this Anaheim bubble and do *other* things. In fact, it was these "other" things that motivated Walt's interest in Florida. He was unsure about taking that first step, but he wasn't a coward. His hesitancy to just "replicate Disneyland" made him think in other directions. Bigger dreams. Bolder ideas.

At the 1963 Urban Design Conference, held at Harvard University, pioneering American real estate developer James W. Rouse said, "I hold a view that may be somewhat shocking to an audience as sophisticated as this: that the greatest piece of urban design in the United States today is Disneyland. If you think about Disneyland and think of its performance in relationship to its purpose, its meaning to people—more than that, its meaning to the process of development—you will find it the outstanding piece of urban design in the United States."

What's an EPCOT?

It seems Walt took Rouse very much to heart. Even though he had begun to move away from the tales of Hans Christian Andersen and the Brothers Grimm toward the ideas of Lewis Mumford and Victor Gruen for his place-making inspiration, I think Walt was still motivated by a single larger idea: making *places* for *people.*

"The Florida Project," as Walt saw it, would present a distinct and highly personal vision for him. Original plans called for the theme park as a somewhat secondary, but necessary attraction to draw attention and public and corporate interest in what his *real* pursuit was: an "Experimental Prototype Community of Tomorrow" (EPCOT), a planned community intended to serve as a testing ground for "new city" innovations in a "living laboratory."

"We have done a lot of thinking on a model community," Walt said, "and I would like to be a part of building one—a 'city of tomorrow,' as you might say. I don't believe in going out to this extreme blue sky stuff that some of the architects do. I believe people still want to live like human beings. But there are a lot of things that could be done. I'm not against the automobile, but I just feel that you can design so that the automobile is there, but still put people back as pedestrians again. I'd love to work on a project like that."

Walt picked a site for this endeavor near Orlando, Florida, in November 1963. Over the next eighteen months, vaguely named dummy corporations—such as the

"Ayefour Corporation," "Latin-American Development and Management Corporation," and "Reedy Creek Ranch Corporation"—quietly acquired a cumulative forty-eight square *miles* of property in Orange and Osceola counties. "Here in Florida," Walt said, "we have something special we never enjoyed at Disneyland . . . the blessing of size. There's enough land here to hold all the ideas and plans we can possibly imagine."

Then on November 15, 1965, Walt and Florida governor Haydon Burns held a press conference in Orlando to announce the unveiling of a new "Disney World."

A little over a year later, Walt was gone, and a lot of people thought his Florida project would be gone, too. Was little Walt Disney Productions sitting on a white elephant of worthless swamp and scrub pine in Central Florida? Without a guiding vision and the prevalence of "committee think" in Burbank, whose would be the guiding hand for the future "Florida Project"?

Roy O. to the Rescue

The Florida Project had been Walt's priority, and his brother Roy O. now made it his.

"The process slowed down following the initial shock of Walt's passing," Jack Lindquist remembered. "Nothing happened because nobody would pick up the gauntlet and move forward. From December 15 [1966] for almost a year, there was doubt whether there would be a project. They went forward and secured the legislation, and some of the legal work was done. But nothing as far as the design and what the project would be."

Roy O. then did something else, seemingly trivial in the grand scheme of the juggernaut project we were facing, but deeply meaningful to those of us who had known and worked with Walt. "Everyone has heard of Ford cars," Roy said. "But have they all heard of Henry Ford, who started it all? *Walt* Disney World is in memory of the man who started it all, so people will know his name as long as Walt Disney World is here."

So in 1969, as drainage canals and roadways were constructed—and recreational waterways, and a theme park, and resort hotels, and golf courses were wrought from the Central Florida swamps—Dick Nunis and a large group of executives began the gargantuan task of staffing and readying this unfinished behemoth to receive visitors for a scheduled opening on October 1, 1971.

Bob Matheison

Bob Matheison had come into Disneyland when we were preparing staff to work on Walt Disney World. He had already been named director of operations after getting his start in the entertainment division. (In fact, Bob was the announcer for the Anaheim Angels for some years at Angels Stadium, just across town from Disneyland.) He was an entertainment guy no doubt, but I thought he was an even *better* director of operations. He asked me, because I had started that program called the Qualified Trainer, to take young supervisors and create uniform classes for all supervisors. So Van France and I put together a program called STP, the Supervisor Training Program. We began sessions consisting of eight to ten people per session. (I think the first program ran anywhere from seven to ten days.)

I was then asked to do an evaluation on each participant, what I thought they could do, and what they would be good at. These were mostly operations people, because Operations was going to run Walt Disney World. Some of those guys went on to become directors or vice presidents, and did a good job. But it was Bob Matheison who taught *me* how to be organized in training, instruction, recognizing one's talents, mentoring, and moving people along.

Roots and Shoots

At this point it seemed as if I was stepping into a stable new career path, advancing in the Disneyland hierarchy, and sinking some professional roots. It was time to do the same at home.

With the change of employment, and a growing family, we moved from the Cinderella House in Garden Grove to another Orange County locale, Mission Viejo (using the money I received from the Retlaw profit-share payout I received when I left). Our new home was a 1,600-square-foot Spanish-style house in a new development, with a terrific view. (True, we would regularly hear air traffic from El Toro Marine base; "sounds of freedom," we would say.) This house felt like a mansion to me, especially after living in a fairy-tale cottage. But in spite of that, it was pretty "bare bones"—no yard to speak of, and no fences or walls. I put those things in, as well as a sprinkler system, and landscaping.

I added one other thing as well: before we left Garden

Grove, we cut off more clippings from Sitte's grape vine. I replanted them, and they grew at our new home.

Discovering a New World

Dick Nunis approached me about heading down to Florida to lend a hand with the Florida Project. He said, "You'll be there for two or three months prior to opening."

I was there for nine months.

Like most major projects, everyone did whatever was needed. There were a lot of operational people pulled in to interview potential employees, because HR simply couldn't handle the demand and the volume of applicants. They were coming from all over the country. People were driving in from New York, and from all over the East. We had circus performers who weren't sure what Walt Disney World was going to be—they thought it might be a circus. We had tattooed ladies, contortionists, strong men, sideshow performers—it was quite a volume and assortment of people.

There were lots of people desperate for a job. People who wanted to break into show business. Some people also came from California; they'd worked at Disneyland, and they wanted to be there for the opening of Walt Disney World. (Those people were hired pretty quickly, because they had the background and the training and the experience.) Heck, they came from all over the country. They also came from Orlando, too, but not in great numbers.

The Disney Way of Leadership

My years with Van France had, naturally, identified and "typecast" me as a trainer. Van had written a book called *The Disney Way of Leadership*, and I taught from that. That was my lesson plan.

We were hiring people from hotels, other tourist destinations, and other amusement parks, so these people had to be brought together and brought into the "Disney Way." It wasn't the Marriott way, and it wasn't what you learned working at AstroWorld (an amusement park adjacent to the Astrodome in Houston), or Colonial Williamsburg, or Busch Gardens. It had to be the Disney Way!

We had training managers for every division teach the same class. We picked a manager from Fantasyland, merchandise, marketing, entertainment—all of them. Many of them had come from Disneyland, so that was an advantage: we needed to be consistent in all of our training. Thus, we used Van's *The Disney Way of Leadership* as text. The hardest part was getting everyone all together, so that I could train them and teach them that class. They were all working such long days and nights just trying to get that Florida Project open. To get participants into a class was tough. In turn, they understood the difficulties they would be facing as well, but they realized that training/developing was as important to the project as the floors and doors. They all came, and we had an almost 100 percent turnout before we opened.

And then almost suddenly, opening day was around the corner. I was moved to Fantasyland to work with Orlando Ferrante's group, which was called PICO (the Project Installation Coordinating Office). During the day, we would work with construction people, wearing hard hats and construction clothes, making sure the shows went to the right place. I was the operational representative for "it's a small world" and some of the rest of Fantasyland.

At night, we would go back to the still-being-finished Contemporary Resort hotel, use the shower (if the water was working), put shirts and ties on, and go back out and start training Cast Members. Those were long days, being active/on the move/teaching for sixteen, sometimes twenty hours a day. (Now, this is a famous tale that may be written about in other places—but before opening, we couldn't get all the landscape in. Dick Nunis called out all hands to get sod planted in front of the Contemporary Resort. The exterior lighting wasn't installed yet, and we were planting sod—at night, in the dark. Someone yelled out, "I don't know how to plant sod! How in the hell do you plant sod?" Dick yelled back, "Green side *up!*")

A Grand Opening?

But, as promised, we opened the park on October 1, 1971. Not surprisingly, Fantasyland was my job—I was responsible for all the operational stuff. We were ready for the deluge, the sweeping hordes of expectant Guests. But there weren't that many. Certainly not what we expected. We were all carrying two-way radios, and heard that there was no backup at the gate.

I was trying to get Fantasyland open, but I was also working out of Dick Nunis's trailer. Suddenly he said, "Cora, take my car, go down the road, and see how far back the lines are to get into the gates." So I took his car—and headed out. But soon after I tentatively radioed back to tell him there was nobody out there. "What do you mean there's nobody out there? Maybe you didn't go out far enough! The cops are probably holding up traffic!" So I kept driving, and as I went further out I saw a few cars here and there, but no big buildup, no traffic jams!

Down the highway I drove; there were police helicopters overhead, but there was nobody on the roads. That day we only had about twelve thousand people. We were expecting to be so busy that we'd have to close—turn people away! Instead, it was people who *stayed away* by the thousands, because they thought it was going to be so busy and chaotic. Luckily, this was a temporary condition, but it offered a great opportunity for a huge new employee base to get familiar with their new jobs without the burden of those *expected* crowds.

(I remember a woman running toward me at "it's a small world" with several children in tow, waving her "E Coupon" at me, and shouting, "What do I do with this?" I guided her to the attraction entrance, and suddenly realized I had forgotten to place an order to build ticket boxes for all of the Fantasyland attractions. So for the first few hours, we put the torn tickets in pockets and trash cans until the boxes could be fabricated. God bless our backstage support, especially the Mill.)

On opening day, we had about five thousand Cast Members placed at the Magic Kingdom. There were probably another 1,500 for the two hotels. And at the campgrounds there were another five hundred ready to help Guests. That's a *lot* of folks. But they all worked well together. Bringing people in from a variety of geographic locations made a big difference, and it was a great boon for Orlando, because their apartments filled up, as did their hotels/motels. It was great all around for the local economy.

Unfortunately, and this happens with all of our big projects, after personnel have experienced an opening— and the thrill of opening day—they start to leave. And so you've got to be prepared to start replacing those people with other folks.

A lot of people who had worked "above and beyond" for a long sustained period of time got really sick in the weeks after Walt Disney World's opening. It was a long, hard project, and we were building this thing in the middle of nowhere, really. There is a kind of PTSD I saw that sets in, that I would see again on all my later projects; there's just so much work and dedication that you see people get sick. I remember a fellow who I was working with, a good guy named Jim Murphy, manager of

Fantasyland. He dropped out right at the opening with a severe case of bronchitis, and didn't recover in time, and missed everything.

Behind the whole giant machine and rolling out of the project was Roy O. He was so committed to seeing through his brother's dream, so loyal and so passionate about his responsibility to Walt. He was there to dedicate the Magic Kingdom, and for all of the festivities and events tied to the opening. But it was clear that he was weary, he was tired. When Walt passed, Roy O. had cancelled his planned retirement. Just weeks after fulfilling his promise to Walt, Roy O. Disney died at age seventy-eight on December 20, 1971.

Home Again, but Not for Long

I returned to California, exhausted but ready to get back in the regular routines of home and familiar surroundings. There was certainly a feeling of personal and professional growth—you couldn't work on a project like Walt Disney World and *not* learn, and change . . . and grow. I was also satisfied that I'd been carrying the torch for Walt, and pleased with my colleagues. So many of them had stepped up to heights I know they themselves didn't know they could reach. Most of us survived, and thrived from the experience, and were proud of what we'd done.

I was way behind on the household routines, my children's school, family activities, home repairs, and everything involved in my personal life. Catching up was tough, and I feel as if I never fully did it right. It was catch-up for years. In fact, I think I'm still working on it.

The stability of career and hearth and home didn't last long. I don't think I'd been sleeping in my own bed for two months when I got a call from Dick Nunis again. The Walt Disney World hotels (the Contemporary Resort and the Polynesian Resort) were having a hard time. John Curry, from the Curry family of Yosemite hospitality fame, had been in charge. Dick said, "He's hired people from all these hotels; we've got people from the Hilton, Holiday Inn, Sheraton, Marriott—you name it! They don't all get along. They don't have the same systems, they all have different policies, and somebody's got to pull them together and do things the Disney Way."

I said, "Dick, I don't know anything about hotels."

"You know operations, you know entertainment, you know housekeeping, because that's custodial. And you know *Disney.* Put together a team and get back down there."

It took me a while to figure it out, but Dick put me in there as a "hit man." He could have picked somebody from Walt Disney World to be in there, but he didn't want to tarnish the Walt Disney World people, and he wanted the ongoing relationship between hotels and the park people to be good. Since I was coming in and then going back to California, it was okay if I was known as the "hit man." But Dick never told me that. It took me a while, but that's what I figured out.

Back to Bay Lake

The Florida hotels were riddled with problems, large and small. Floors weren't getting cleaned, staff didn't get along, Guests couldn't get checked in . . . or couldn't get checked out. It was a mess. People couldn't *find* the hotels! (We finally just painted lines on the pavement: an orange line for Polynesian, a blue line for the Contemporary. Just follow that all the way from the tollbooth. . . .)

I was assigned a couple of HR people (we used to call it "Employee Relations" in those days); they showed me organizational charts, summarized the roles and responsibilities, identified the specific staff people, and worked with me to digest the performance reviews of all the management in the hotel. They had already created their own recommendation hierarchy: people who were strong, people who were just okay, those who could be developed—and those who should probably go.

The Hotel Task Force

We put together a five-person team. Chuck Boyajian led the custodial group. The guy's an icon in Disney janitorial services, a World War II vet. He took over custodial, got the cleaning going right, and the floors to shine. I asked Karl Andrews to help with scheduling, security, and team building. Leroy Baza, who was an industrial engineer, worked on all systems, and flow, all the way from the gate to the hotel and back. Jim Haught, who was formerly my boss in Frontierland/Adventureland (once a manager there), took over the Polynesian. I took the Contemporary Resort, and we worked on it for several months—got it all organized.

The whole hotel task force team did what had to be done. I gave Dick recommendations, I reported to him every afternoon, four o'clock. I learned a whole lot from all those people, even those that John Curry had brought in from different hotels, about hotel operations. And it served me well later, when we started building hotels in Tokyo and France.

We also brought in our own people, trained operational people, and then trained them in the hotel business, and had the hotel people train them as well. There was still resistance, though, for us task force people that "flew in" versus those people that had relocated permanently. So we had to fight that for a while. We weren't just "seagulls" flying in, flapping our wings, dropping our little . . . bombs, and then flying out again.

For me, then, it was back to that 1940 Chevrolet. I had to take this thing apart in order to understand how it worked. The reputation that preceded me as a "hit man" was a huge burden. I had to constantly and consistently show that I was simply one of a team, with the goal of getting the problems solved and the issues ironed out. So I started to become part of the team. We'd go out for meals, or for drinks. We'd go look at the shows at the Top of the World, the penthouse restaurant and lounge at the Contemporary Resort—and the "only game on property" for adult beverages and entertainment for miles around. I just became part of the team, a guy just trying to learn the hotel business. But the word got out that I was Dick's staff assistant, and "heads were gonna roll," and so on. Luckily there were good people, confident people who really showed me the ropes, and took the time to explain hotel operations, plus helped to identify and define and equalize what hotels do . . . and what Disney does and what we were trying to achieve in Florida.

So once we got over that hump—and it took a while for that—we had to be credible. And once they realized we were credible, then things worked fine. One of the ways you make yourself *credible* is to get your hands dirty, right? I remembered that scolding from Dick, years before: "You're in charge of everything you see when you walk through here! If it's not right, you go make sure it's taken care of!"

Or if the line's getting too long, then you jump in and you help. Go back of house and find out what's holding up those reservationists and why they can't come out and help people. You find out quite possibly that you're short of staff, or waiting for somebody to come back from break, or someone didn't show up for work that day, and you solve the problem.

Once you become the problem-solver and the helper, then you're a lot more credible with your staff.

I learned more about the hotel business from two people in that early hotel division than I was ever able to teach them about Disney. The first was Harris Rosen. After leaving Disney he opened up a chain of smaller hotels, and today he's Florida's largest independent hotelier. He was a really good guy. I learned most of what I know about the hotel business from him. Harris really took the time to explain it to me. But he didn't fit in to the corporate strategy we advocate, and the way we do things at Disney, so he left and went off and did his own thing.

The other great influence in my "hotel training" was Tim Field. Tim's career had begun with his managing of the Colony Beach & Tennis Resort on Florida's west coast in Longboat Key. He oversaw the opening of the Contemporary Resort, prior to managing Arvida, Florida's Longboat Key Golf Club. Since then he's planned the development of the Inn on the Beach in St. Petersburg, Florida, and the Harbourside Golf Club in Longboat Key, and has personally developed waterfront residential single-family homes, waterfront condominiums, and commercial property in the same locale. Thank you, Harris Rosen and Tim Field.

Other people clearly didn't fit—or didn't want to. As we continued our efforts, Disney company president Card

Walker came to the property, seeking a thorough update on our progress from leadership. John Curry was supposed to be there. He didn't show up. There was deadly silence when Card finally said, "And where is John Curry?"

Dick said, "He's not here."

"Did he know about this meeting?"

"Yes, he knew about the meeting—he just didn't show up."

Card had a mixed drink in his hand, and threw it clear across the room. We all ducked, and it went over our heads, and hit the wall.

We never saw John Curry again.

People come and go at Disney, just like anyplace else. I've seen people leave Disney who were there during their college years. Perhaps it's been a part-time job for them, or a full-time assignment through the summer. They've made their money, Disney taught them a lot, and they went off to do their own business. There was a guy who could have maybe been president of The Walt Disney Company down the road, in my opinion—but he just didn't fit. Some became lawyers, some became doctors, some became developers or entrepreneurs of one sort or another—and were very successful at it. And they've always pointed back to their time at Disney and what they learned there on how things were done as one of the reasons they were so successful.

As for me, I don't think I could have done that. Because I liked show business, I liked the way Disney did show business so much. I was beautifully trapped. I was offered other jobs outside the company, and I just couldn't leave, even for more money—because I just loved what Disney did.

Homeward Bound . . . Again

I was tired, and ready to go home. I wasn't sure what getting back to "normal life" would feel like. In brief retrospect, I'd really enjoyed the work, and the people, and the feeling of breaking new ground—I took the grape shoot, and planted it in a foreign land, and made sure it had healthy soil and the best conditions to grow, and flourish.

I realized, that's what keeps you going. I can't say what keeps everybody else going, but what kept me going in all the projects I did was that we could bring Disney to people that might never get another chance to see and experience it. Many Americans may never go to California;

lots of Japanese people may never come to the United States. And so many people from France may never get over here. When will they ever get to see it? Now I always look forward to a new park's opening day. You spend *years* getting a project ready for that one week where you're able to watch new people come to that main gate—and then you turn it over to local people and get out of their way. That's what you do.

It's about bringing "Disney" to others.

Part Seven: Rising Sun

I HEADED back to California, and felt pretty confident that we had set things right with the Florida hotels. I knew that I had grown, and that I knew a heck of a lot more than when I'd left a second time for Florida. I felt confident that I had done a good job, and that I had been true to my own ideas about leadership, and the concepts we had been putting into training and development at Disney University for more than a decade. I also believe I'd done right by the Disney culture and values, too. I didn't know exactly where I was going to land when I headed back to Anaheim, but I wasn't too surprised where that wound up being.

It was a natural transition, I suppose, for me to come back and be the guy responsible for taking over the Disneyland Hotel.

Most people don't know that for a long time, the Disneyland Hotel was not an actual part of Disneyland, but operated under a license from Disney to the Wrather

Corporation. The placement of a hotel at the park had been a part of Walt's original plans, but his finances were strained to the limit as completion of the park neared. So in 1954 Walt invited his friend, the entrepreneur, petroleum businessman, and television producer Jack Wrather, to develop a hotel (with attendant amenities) in what was then an orange grove across from the park. (Wrather was probably best known for producing *The Lone Ranger, Sergeant Preston of the Yukon*, and the *Lassie* TV series in the 1950s, as well as for marrying actress Bonita Granville.)

Ground was broken on March 18, 1955, just four months before Disneyland's opening day. Designed by famed Los Angeles architects Pereira & Luckman, the original plans called for three hundred (later increased to 650) motel and hotel rooms, suites, and garden apartments. Due to several setbacks, including labor and material shortages, the still-unfinished Disneyland Hotel quietly opened—with just seven available guest rooms—on October 5, 1955. Finally, in August of 1956, the Disneyland Hotel had an "official" grand opening, when it had 204 guest rooms and suites, an Olympic-size swimming pool, seventeen shops, and restaurants and cocktail lounges. Over the years, the hotel expanded to include luxury guest room towers. (The first was the Sierra

Tower in 1962—which was expanded in 1966—and then the Marina Tower in 1970. A third tower, named after Wrather's wife, opened after my time there, in 1978.)

Back in the Hotel Business

When I came back to Anaheim in 1972, Wrather still owned and operated the Disneyland Hotel—but Walt Disney Productions was involved in serious negotiations to buy the whole thing from Wrather. In anticipation of this, Dick Nunis asked me to "do the same thing there [that] you did in Florida."

Of course, the hotel was all Wrather people, so I went through the same process I had with the hotels at Walt Disney World. The first thing I started to hear was, "You Disneyland people don't know anything about hotels." Except now I could speak their language. I understood hotels better. With these Wrather people, I used the terminology and the perspective that I had picked up in Florida, so I got their respect right off the bat. Almost immediately, their tone changed to this: "There's a guy who understands hotels after all."

We identified the strong people and invested in them, just like we had in Florida. Those identified as weak in their current role were reassigned or dropped. We then brought over new people from Disneyland, working hard to bring that Disney "show quality" to the namesake hotel. As I had before, I took the "Chevy engine" (the hotel structure) apart. I really got to know those folks. What I found was a corps of talented people: Thor Degelmann (later vice president, Human Resources, at what was then Euro Disney and now is Disneyland Paris), Donna Partin (manager of Guest Relations at Disneyland), Kathy Parker (supervisor, Disneyland Operations), Karl Andrews and Gary Wood (Disneyland Security), Jim Hilinski and Al Shelborn (Finance and Purchasing), and so many more.

While I was reorganizing the staff, Skip Palmer, who was the general manager of The Golf Resort (now Shades of Green) at Walt Disney World, suggested that I come meet with his manager, Hideo Amemiya. Once I got there I had to wait two days before Hideo could free himself up to meet—but I was so impressed watching all he did, that I hired him on the spot as front office manager at the Disneyland Hotel.

As negotiations for the sale of the hotel dragged on month after month, we worked with our own staff, putting new staff in place and laying off some people. We were doing all the training in the "Disney Way," and teaching them the Disney policies—while they were teaching us more about their experiences running a hotel in the Anaheim community. It was slow going, but I knew it would be worthwhile to create a cohesive Guest experience between Disneyland Park and the Disney Hotel. Such interaction further helped alleviate the feelings of stress and being bogged down as the business of transfer drudgery transpired (like counting of the silverware and doing other inventory, making sure we were getting what we paid for). Negotiations actually kept dragging on for two years. Then, suddenly, we got a notice: we had twenty-four hours to clear out! Why? Because of some problems with Wrather's role in local broadcasting and ownership of the early cable TV business TelePrompTer, there was some kind of legal action impending. All of Jack Wrather's assets were frozen. He couldn't buy or sell anything.

We notified my staff already on-site there. Dick wrote a nice letter to everybody thanking them. I also wrote a letter saying, "We're leaving." Between Dick and Disneyland's then-director of operations, Ron Dominguez, all the people who had come out of the park were given their jobs at Disneyland back.

Everyone who had been working toward that purchase and management change was justifiably upset about the whole thing. In retrospect, I think they probably could have cut a different kind of a deal; instead, we waited fourteen years and paid a lot more money for the property than we would have paid then.

Operational Appraisal

Well, now what?

When I first came back to Disneyland, many thought I was going to start firing people, based on the huge hotel reorganization performed in Florida and the work I was doing over at the Disneyland Hotel. It led me to a pretty unique culmination of everything I'd done up to that point.

It started with a call I got from Van France, who was a very good friend of Bob Allen's, who was president of Walt Disney World at the time. Bob asked Van if I could come out there and watch them do something they called "operational appraisal."

We had grown "fat" because of the opening of Walt Disney World. You always get *fat* when you open something new—you increase staff in a lot of cases ("throw some bodies at it") because you're not sure what to expect, or what support a new endeavor might require.

Operational appraisal was implemented to trim the fat. In addition, after Walt's passing, there were always corporate suitors and Wall Street raiders circling—so it was important to stay as "lean and mean" as possible.

Bob had each division head come before a committee and present a zero-base budget to them. Starting from the bottom, you justified a need for each individual in each particular job, plus the necessity for that job. Everything had to be justified.

Based on this exercise, people were reassigned to different jobs, or cross-trained, or laid off . . . and some divisions that were determined to need more support actually hired new people. They completely reorganized Walt Disney World in that manner. I only watched it for a while to understand the process, and then I came back to California and was asked to replicate it here. We had every Disneyland division head come in, zero-base budget their division, and present why they did things the way they did.

We had a committee composed of cross-divisional leaders—food, merchandise, attractions, and so on set up to evaluate and offer perspective on what was being presented. We discovered systems that did not interact with or support the rest of the park, and methods that had grown out of a specific or divisional need, but simply weren't necessary anymore. In this process, of course, operations and methods were streamlined and combined, and departments were transferred from one division to another.

The end result: we eliminated redundancies by combining roles so they had responsibility *across* divisions, not just to one division. Some people got laid off, some were reassigned to other jobs, and we didn't fill open requisitions. We built a much smaller staff. We eliminated a couple layers of management that were no longer necessary. Through this operational appraisal exercise, we ended up eliminating about $11 million in annual payroll.

Evaluations extended to individuals working at the park, as I had done at the hotels. Sometimes people were reassigned to more appropriate duties, or even more satisfying assignments. We evaluated performance reviews for individuals in key jobs, and came up with a training program to cross-train people across divisions. I thought about me and that 1940 Chevy again: it was imperative for people to understand how the whole business, the whole show, came together; and what made "that machine" function.

In the Food division, we created a department that

only did support for that division—quality control, recipes, menus, and so on. The operator ran the restaurant, this other department set up the criteria . . . and the product. We did the same thing for the Merchandise division.

We revised and then presented again that program we had developed called *The Business of Show Business*, which really addressed the practicalities of our enterprise, types of things you spent your money on, and where your revenues came from. It created a solid business base for all of us to understand and work from.

Area Concept

With a leaner team, we started cross-training people in other divisions. Van France and I called it the "Area Concept." The basis of the area concept is, if somebody is working an area, and that somebody is a Merchandise person, they're walking by an attraction, they're walking by food, they're looking at custodial—but they're only interested in the one thing—*merchandise* (or food, or whatever their specific discipline is). Well, that same person could be cross-trained to manage all of those things. The food person learned operations, attractions, merchandise, entertainment, custodial—and vice versa, every which way!

The result was that we didn't have four people walking through an area focused on their individual assignment or role. Instead, we had one person walking through, looking at the entirety of the show. (Van told me that's what Walt Disney wanted to do. He wanted a "mayor" of each land, and that person would have an overall responsibility for everything in it.)

Where the Show Begins

This streamlining and refocus on show really inspired Van, and the nomenclature at the business level changed: Employee became Cast Member. Employee Relations became Human Resources. (I think we may have been one of the first to do that.) There were three directors within Park Operations. We were now called production directors—we're producers of the show. We had stage managers, assistant stage managers, stage supervisors—everything tied back to and served as a reminder that our core business was to put on a great show. We combined support divisions—finance, maintenance, etc.—and merged the marketing and entertainment divisions.

People had started to forget that the heart of what we were doing was putting on a show. Famed theater owner

Marcus Loew used to say about his movie palaces that "the show starts on the sidewalk." And so we start at the main entrance. I take that back. We start at the toll plaza. This is where the show begins. Van said, "No, it begins before that." Where? "It begins when they're deciding to leave their house, and they're having a hard time getting those kids in the car. Then they have to come down that freeway. Then they have to fight all that traffic and people cutting them off. So by the time they get to the toll plaza, they don't care about our show. So we have to do a better job in the *parking lot* than anywhere!"

We named the parking lot sections by characters, instead of "A, B, C," and so on. It actually made a huge difference—so the show started there. Then you arrived at the gate; now you're in the main lobby of our show.

Van focused much of his energy in this period into creating new ideas and "plussing" existing ones with this idea of "putting on a show." One of the things I think is most relevant about the comparison is something that any theater student will tell you: it's not singing or dancing, or creating costumes or designing sets. Theater is about the totality of the experience being presented.

How does that show get there? Dozens, or sometimes hundreds of diverse personalities and disciplines and crafts work behind the scenes. They're all focusing on that show. Theater teaches collaboration and communication in a way that's highly relevant to what we do at Disney. Mutual understanding, respect for the craft and roles of others, and an understanding of everything that needs to happen to get that curtain up and perform for your audience are key.

It was also important, however, to *listen* to all the new ideas that emerged from this new way of managing our show.

Cups of Coffee and the "Corridor Culture"

Another component of performing arts that related directly to Disneyland, and to this area concept idea, was getting out of your "dressing room" and onto the damn stage! I seriously saw people in those days in adjoining office spaces who would send interoffice memos to each other (with copies to the people they thought should know), instead of getting up and walking over and talking to them!

It's that face-to-face, human interaction that solves problems and builds trust and creates relationships. I can't tell you how many cups of coffee I drank coming up through the organization, just because it was more efficient and effective to sit down with people and talk to them. In the Area Concept push, we got the leadership *out* of the Administration Building. I suggested that people go out into their areas and find office space, and I didn't mean luxurious suites with Eames chairs and potted palms. I meant a place to do some paperwork or make some calls that could be improvised, whether it was a storeroom, a back office, the side of a kitchen, whatever—but that supervisors were expected to be out in the field with their people.

And they were—and they were available, and they were accessible. One office turned out to be unused space next to the Golden Horseshoe; another was in an odd storage space in City Hall on Main Street. Mine was in an unused space left when the Carousel of Progress became America Sings. We were all out in the area, and that really worked!

Don't Pass the Trash

Unfortunately, as had happened before, there were those to whom this brave new world was uncomfortable—or even an affront to their ego. Many times I had run across arrogance over accomplishment, where people thought they could do a good job, but that it really wasn't necessary for the job they were in; that it didn't really require that much of an effort—at least on their end. Maybe it didn't require the homework necessary as you're assigned to something, an attraction or the emporium. Maybe you don't really need to understand cash handling. "I'm a supervisor and I don't need to get my hands dirty"—that kind of arrogance. That kind of "They're gonna pay me for doing the job; they're not paying me for doing somebody else's job" attitude.

My philosophy was know every job you're supervising. I learned how to embroider a name on a hat. It's a thing I had never done, and didn't know how to do. (I still don't. I was a terrible student.) But arrogance over accomplishment used to really bug me. People who I knew had the potential to grow within the organization and do better than what they were doing were the people I liked to transfer out. If I couldn't work with them—and couldn't get them to accept the job for what it was (and even more, what it *could* be)—I moved them someplace else. In some cases we let them go . . . period!

I had a philosophy: "Don't pass the trash." If you've got people who are *really* bad, don't give them to somebody else. Solve the problem yourself. If you can't develop them, if somebody else doesn't have a job for them, for their skills—or lack thereof—then they've got to leave. Disney wasn't for everybody.

Before the Sunrise

And yet we'd heard rumblings about a different kind of "everybody" who wanted to be a part of Disney. I would soon become acquainted with it very intimately—and it would change the rest of my life and career.

Since its earliest days, Disney had reached a global audience. Mickey Mouse cartoon shorts were released and playing in movie theaters all over the world, dubbed in several foreign languages. His popularity and the movies led to an array of worldwide merchandise and consumer goods, magazines, comic strips, and books. As Disney's movie output changed and grew, here and abroad, the meaning of "Disney" changed and grew, too. Each new nation being introduced to Mickey—and the company's brand—also seemed to adopt Disney as its own. Over time, many of these places came to regard Disney as a culture in and of itself, but with deep native ties and proprietorship. All over the world, Disney opened regional offices to supervise these businesses, promoting and protecting the name and identity of Disney and its characters and stories—plus its values of quality and decency, and trust in its quality. Once established, Disney's roots took hold worldwide, even before Disneyland came along.

With Disneyland, Walt had turned this notion around a bit, by creating a single *place* that was "Disney" and inviting the world to visit it. They did, from everywhere on the planet. The opening of Walt Disney World and its subsequent success only served to buttress and stimulate the idea of Disney on an international stage—and the idea that perhaps there were "worlds to conquer" that we hadn't thought of yet, or been thinking about at all. (Although, of course, Walt, as usual, was *way* ahead of us, and *had* thought of a Disneyland in Japan—but knew at the time that it wasn't for him. He was even quoted in 1961 saying, "Recently, a Japanese company came to me and asked me if I would start one there. When I said I wasn't interested, one of them asked me, 'Then will you loan us a set of your blueprints?'")

It's not surprising that in the tentative and careful "post-Walt" world that no one from our end was travelling the globe and knocking on doors "selling" an international Disney park idea. Disney, in the eyes of its corporate leadership, had enough commitments already—in Anaheim and to the project in Florida. Our plate was full, and our resources were limited and occupied. The Mitsukoshi Department Store chain, though, wasn't waiting for Disney to look outside the United States. Their people had proposed a site near Mount Fuji for building the first Disneyland not in the United States. (This was quickly rejected as an impractical location, for several reasons, though Disney established a long relationship with Mitsukoshi through a successful store in the Japan Pavilion at EPCOT. In fact, it is the only remaining branch of Mitsukoshi located in North America.)

But during this period there was another persistent international suitor who knocked on *our* door for *years*—and kept reaching out to us. It was another Japanese entity, Oriental Land Company (OLC). They persisted and stayed in contact with Disney for more than a decade about building a "Disneyland" in Japan.

Oriental Land Company

The Oriental Land Company had been established on July 11, 1960, as a subsidiary of the venerable Keisei

Electric Railway Company, Ltd., which was founded June 30, 1909, and established rail services in eastern Tokyo November 3, 1912. Its main line reached out to Narita in 1930 and Ueno in 1933. Their OLC subsidiary, meanwhile, was developing Maihama, an area of land in Urayasu that was created through land reclamation (as well as a few shopping centers in Chiba prefecture).

Their Oriental Land Establishment Plan prospectus of 1959 stated, "In this project, we would like to reclaim the sea off Urayasu to develop commercial and residential areas, as well as a large-scale recreational facility, so as to contribute to the nation's culture, health, and welfare."

From 1972 to 1973, OLC undertook a study of European and American leisure facilities in order to create a park tentatively called "Oriental Land." The results of the study led them to the conclusion that Disneyland was their ideal in order to best achieve that vision.

So, in February 1974, OLC made a formal request in writing to Disney executives to come to Japan on a fact-finding tour. Then in June, OLC president Kawasaki paid a visit to Walt Disney Productions to reiterate OLC's desire to bring Disneyland to Japan and again issued an invitation to the top Disney executives to visit Japan. That

July, the "Oriental Land Feasibility Study Report 1974," which outlined the project and the suitability of using the land in Urayasu, was submitted by OLC to Disney.

In response to these efforts and correspondence, Disney executives visited Japan, and on December 4, 1974, at Tokyo's Imperial Hotel, the proposal to bring Disneyland to the Urayasu site was presented to the Disney executives. After the presentation, the Disney contingent visited the Urayasu site, getting there by automobile and helicopter. Two days later, the two companies met again, and Disney agreed to begin negotiations for a Disneyland theme park project in partnership with the Oriental Land Company.

A basic agreement was signed a short time later, and OLC began work on a first phase in January 1975. That autumn, a summary of the first phase informational research and a Disney-produced site development plan based on that concept document was completed and presented in an "Oriental Disneyland Concept" package.

OLC and Disney then began to negotiate terms for entering the next phase of work, but a deal wasn't reached until June 1976, when an agreement to enter the concept-design phase was made. In March 1977, the project was officially named "Tokyo Disneyland," but another year of deliberations on the second phase followed, where extraordinarily complex and often-contentious business terms were ultimately hammered out.

Finally, on April 30, 1979, then OLC president Takahashi and then Disney president Card Walker of Disney signed a basic agreement concerning the design, construction, and operation of Tokyo Disneyland Park.

Walt Disney Productions had incorporated an entity called "Disneyland International" on November 20, 1961, to protect proprietary names being used by others worldwide, such as Frontierland, Mickey Mouse Theater, Fantasyland, etc. Later, this would become the name of the division that I oversaw, supervising all international park development.

In order for my team to begin supervising the training and relocation of hundreds of Americans, as well as getting them paid, Doris Smith (then secretary of the Disney Board) recommended we create a new entity. I cleverly called it "AROC." In the great Disney tradition of WED Enterprises and Retlaw, it was simply "Cora" spelled backwards. Later when Dick Nunis asked what this acronym stood for, I told him it was simply the "Anaheim Relocation Operational Committee." Walt Disney Productions even authorized shares, in order to be able to list it as a subsidiary.

A Promotion by Sandbag

By now, of course, I had heard about this Tokyo project. It had been rattling around the rumor mill for years. I hadn't thought a lot about it. But then I remembered Pete Clark, who was responsible for our corporate sponsorships (we called them "participants" in those days), inviting me to a dinner at a restaurant in downtown Los Angeles' Little Tokyo neighborhood with a group of Japanese people from this "Oriental Land Company." I went, not knowing why. Pete just said I'd like some operational people there.

I forget who was at the dinner, but I remember sitting next to a fellow. I had just assumed they didn't speak English. We bowed and acknowledged one another, then sat down next to each other. We didn't say much at first, and pretty soon our drinks came. That's when he extended his hand out and said, "Oh, by the way, just call me Mac. How are you?" The guy, Makoto Owada, spoke better English than I did. We got to be friends. He later became the manager of the Disney University. And we're friends to this day.

At about the same time, I was approached by Dick Nunis, who by this time was president of both Disneyland and Walt Disney World. I was chairing a park operations committee meeting when Dick whipped open the door of the conference room, and gave me one of these "Come over here, Jim" looks. I stepped out and he said, "I want you to go to Japan with us. We just signed a contract with a company called the Oriental Land Company, and we're going to be building a Magic Kingdom in Tokyo. I need someone to train the Japanese, both here and in Japan." I was still known as a trainer, somebody who knew how to teach and inform people.

"Dick, I don't know about this," I shot back.

"You'd have to live over there for a while," he responded, seemingly oblivious to my sentiments. "We'll bring the Japanese over here to train them; then you and I and the human resources team, and Van France, go over there, probably no more than two or three months. We'll select people from the Oriental Land Company, and we'll train them."

"That's a lot," I pointed out. "I can't commit to that right here and now. I've got to go home and talk to my wife and the family—it's a big move."

"Okay, you do that, and then get back to me," he said. "In the meantime, could you put together an organizational chart for [Disney CEO] Card Walker and [Disney chairman] Donn Tatum? How we're going to do training, how long it's going to take, personnel and resource requirements, and so on? We need to get that done by next week."

I said, "Yes, sir."

I went back in to finish my meeting. A short time later, however, Dick came bursting through the door. There were twelve directors in there, and Dick announced, "Well, you're all here! Let me announce that Jim Cora has been named managing director of operations for Tokyo Disneyland Resort, to be built, hopefully, in 1983. We're not sure about the date yet! But I want you to congratulate Jim!"

"Dick, I was going to go home and talk to my wife and the family, and get back to you!"

"I just talked to her," Dick said, "and she's okay with it. So you're on your way."

On Our Way

We put together a plan—me and a fellow named Tom Eastman, who was director of Disney University at the time. He helped me hammer out a timeline for how we were going to train. (I say *helped me*, though upon reflection, I think he did most of it, and I did the presentation.)

It was impressive, and had big foldouts, which we had to put on the wall in a conference room at the studio. I was so nervous about this—I'd never presented to the corporate leadership before. I can't even remember how we introduced it. But Tom and I sat down with Donn Tatum, Card Walker, and Dick Nunis, along with Ron Cayo, chief legal counsel, and Frank Stanek, who was vice president of strategic planning (and later led the Imagineering team for Tokyo Disneyland), plus a few others.

One thing to keep in mind, for context, is how people felt about our entering into this business in a foreign country. There was resistance internally. "This project will dilute or cheapen our product and brand." "It's a danger to consistency and quality if we don't own and operate." "Disney is not in the franchise business." "We shouldn't be 'leasing out' the Disney name." We heard it all.

Another important issue that cropped up was related to the age and experience of many of the people who would be building the project and working on-site. This was scarcely a generation beyond the end of World War II. There were people at Disney who had fought the Japanese forces. There were people who still carried a deep distrust and hostility toward the country and its people. Card

Walker was one of them. The World War II veteran had served on an aircraft carrier—and had seen deadly action. Card was *not* happy about doing a project in Japan—and was pretty vocal about it.

But Donn Tatum was more forceful than this contingent, and he pushed me toward the right answers about training people overseas. They approved the nine-month training program we touted first for nine trainees. At the time we had just gotten the Area Concept plan at Disneyland up and running. But I thought for the Japanese, who probably would not understand anything about how a theme park operates, we should go back to the divisional structure. It was just easier for them to implement. I couldn't cross-train them because they hadn't been trained at anything yet tied to theme parks.

(By the way, in Japan they still operate by divisional concept. They overstaff, by our standards. Why? Because they are legally obligated to hire a certain number of college graduates every year. It's based on their business, and the revenues they take in. You may come across conference rooms full of people doing paperwork that could be done by a computer, or go into a restaurant where five or six hostesses will welcome you; these people have the right to a job, so they must be kept busy.)

Finding Japanese Leadership

We had nine divisions, which is what Disneyland had in 1955, and we had to select nine key people. The Oriental Land Company put together the people we were going to interview, both from outside OLC and inside their company. I think we ultimately talked to 150 people on a four- or five-day trip.

In the meantime, Van France presented orientation sessions to the Disney/OLC executive management team. He gave orientations on how Disney operated to most of the salaried staff between Keisei Electric Railway, Mitsui Real Estate, and the Oriental Land Company. We finally selected nine people. I think there were only two from outside the Oriental Land Company. The rest were from OLC.

On my own, I started going to Little Tokyo more often. I went to the bookstores, and I talked to the Japanese people who resided there or were visiting. I would buy books at their suggestion that would help me learn about them. I began to understand Japanese food—I'd never eaten raw fish, of course, and sushi wasn't popular in those days. I'd never used chopsticks. I ate in restaurants, sat in sushi bars, drank sake out of wooden boxes. That was a learning experience; I spent a lot of time there. Then as we began to hire staff, I'd take everyone down there, and share what I'd learned, and we would spend time together getting as best a sense of the culture as we could.

Office Space

Dick Nunis said, "Go find yourself an office."

I suggested establishing project HQ in a trailer in the backstage areas somewhere.

Dick said, "We can't do any more trailers, the city won't allow it—just go find an office somewhere, a place where you think it would work."

So I chose the Walt's "apartment-to-be," a beautiful suite of rooms above the entrance to Pirates of the Caribbean. The space had been intended to be a shared apartment space for Walt and Roy O. and their families. But by the time construction on it was completed, Walt had passed away. The Insurance Company of North America, a park sponsor at the time, operated it as a VIP suite for a while. But they had pulled out, and it was vacant again. I had all the antique furniture and decorations moved to a warehouse and put in storage. We put office furniture in there, and turned the courtyard in this giant space over to our interpreters, who would work and prepare their lesson plans and other assignments for their people.

As we began hosting and teaching people with no background in how Disney operated, it really helped that we were in "Walt's apartment." Some thought we'd had it made specifically to be able to get a top-notch "show" facility, right onstage to awe and impress the Japanese.

But it was more than that; it was a reflection of the ideas we were putting forward, about heritage, and show, and the efficiency of running an operation like Disneyland. It was both utterly functional and deeply resonant. And it worked really well.

Quite some time after I'd furnished and staffed the office, Dick Nunis called me, and said, "Hey, I'm going to walk over to your office. Where in the hell are you?"

"I'm in Walt's apartment."

"Above the firehouse?"

"No, the one he never occupied, the old INA suite."

Dick barked, "What? What the hell are you doing in there? That's too nice for what you're doing!"

I reminded him that he'd told me to find an office, and had nixed the idea of a humble trailer backstage. He came over, ready to riot, but as he looked around at the way we'd utilized the space, he admitted that it was actually perfect for its function serving the Japan project.

"This is a great, great idea. Good for you," he said. "Good job."

Teaching a Course in the Disney Way

I went with the team to meet with Masatomo Takahashi, who then was president of the Oriental Land Company, and we gave him the names of those people we wanted to select for divisional leadership training. One of the people was a man named Toshio Kagami, who later became president, and then chairman and CEO of their company. Takahashi said, "You can have everybody except Kagami. He's my right arm, and he needs to stay here. If you're going to take all these other key people, then you can't take him." We insisted that if Kagami was going to be Takahashi's "number one," then he *should* be the guy who came to the United States to train.

We lost that one. Kagami never came stateside to train. Certainly that caused some problems down the road, because other people, including many staff members after that first training program, understood the project deeply, and had an awareness of what needed to be done in a way Kagami had missed learning. They understood Disney. Kagami, I don't think, really, fully understood it. I think he understood that the rest of us must know what we were doing, and so he went along with us, pretty much all the time. But ultimately it seemed every day later was spent negotiating with Kagami-san because he didn't quite understand *why* Disney operated that way. In fact, negotiating with OLC on almost every subject became a way of life.

For those nine trainees who came to this country, we had to find interpreters—because most of them quite frankly didn't speak English, and we certainly didn't speak Japanese. And even the ones who spoke English didn't want to rely on their English ability in their training. So the people I was meeting in those bookstores and in shops and restaurants in Little Tokyo became our interpreters. We hired them and brought them to Disneyland and provided an office space for them, then teamed them up with their respective trainees. If their personalities didn't match, they would on their own just make exchanges between a trainee and an interpreter.

Special offices for the Tokyo project training candidates were established in marketing, merchandise, food, operations, entertainment, maintenance, custodial, and security. Every evening after training, the director of administration, Ron Pogue, and I, along with the director of operations, Steve Llewelling, would meet with them and answer any questions. On a certain level, of course they knew what they were doing. Much of it didn't require very much training from us.

In fact, we learned a lot from them about how to operate in Japan. They'd come up with suggestions about how we were operating some things. I remember "it's a small world" specifically. One trainee came up with a suggestion for a better way to load and unload the boats than what we were doing, and cut down on labor to do it, by simply putting a smaller console control booth on the dock instead of up in the little tower. Over time, an unexpected team-building process emerged. Our training sessions and its participants were coming up together with lots of ideas that ended up changing how we operated Disneyland, and then were subsequently applied in Japan.

I'm thinking that us Disney guys came in pretty arrogant that first year, but it didn't take long before they started teaching *us* about *their* culture—not the touristy things like how to hold your chopsticks, but the more nuanced elements of the Japanese culture, such as how not to get angry. Getting angry is a sign of weakness to them . . . and there are plenty of occasions in a project like this where the frustration and the anger can begin to show. *We* had to change how *we* behaved. We were so impressed by this cultural wrinkle, and how important it was, that we hired a kind of "cultural acclimation company" to work with not just us, but the spouses and the families of those going overseas, to adapt to the culture. It was a program that started right here in the States, before those selected to partake, ever went to Japan.

Relocation

I made several trips alone and several others with our team to Japan before relocation. We were there at least once a month. A business trip there often entailed discussing things over with the Japanese representatives there, such as looking at the design. We wanted to make sure, in our estimation, that it was being built according to the design. Imagineering had it together, they knew what had to go where. So we worked hand in hand. We had put people at WDI who handled operational matters, and provided input. We also had Japanese at WDI who provided input.

It was all part of the process before I ever relocated.

At the same time, we had developed a social network here in the States. The Japanese and my team played baseball together. We had tennis teams—we played at the old Tennisland across the street from Disneyland.

At Disneyland itself we held annual Cast Member canoe races. These had begun in 1963 with a challenge between the Frontierland cast and Adventureland cast, and it would become a tradition that would spread to Walt Disney World (and later to Tokyo Disneyland, Disneyland Paris, and Hong Kong Disneyland). We formed a team with our trainees: they dubbed our DLI group *Cora! Cora! Cora!* They were as committed to success in play as they were in work, and the canoe team was a winning one. (Although probably not in the best taste today, *Tora! Tora! Tora!* had been a big 1970 World War II film . . . an American-Japanese co-production, allowing for a point of view from both nations. The title was a Japanese code word meaning complete surprise. It can also mean "tiger" and is an abbreviation of *totsugeki raigeki,* which means "lightning attack.")

We ate and drank together; we went out socially. They were invited to my home and others were inviting people to theirs. So we became a family, both Japanese and Americans.

The Japanese kept saying, "When we go, are you going to go?" And we weren't sure. But it became pretty apparent, at least a year and a half out, we were going to have to get over there.

I formed my core project team with known professionals who had done this before. We picked some trainers who had worked at Disneyland and Walt Disney World, and I started looking for the right people. I combed the staff at Walt Disney World, and we pulled a lot of the best experience from Disneyland. Thank goodness for Dick Nunis's backing, and especially the support of then vice president of Disneyland, Ron Dominguez. Every time I called for more help, I'd get the people I asked for. (Although maybe I was a little greedy; there was a point finally when Ron said, "You know, Jim, I'd like to continue running Disneyland, too.")

About a year and a half before opening, we relocated a major portion of our team to Japan. Not everybody went; we didn't need them all that early. But three months before opening we had a full team in place there.

Walt Disney Imagineering vice president Frank Stanek selected something like ninety employees to train at WDI in various crafts. We had about 190 people trained in different operational jobs by the time we opened. And I had selected three hundred people (including spouses and children) to go there to stay and train on-site, to reinforce what they had learned here in this country.

And by opening day, if anybody panicked and just couldn't handle the crowds, these people could step in and actually operate the park. It was overkill, as it turns out. The Japanese learned it, they got it, and they did a fantastic job on opening day.

I didn't have any doubts—or maybe that was naïve, or might have been a problem. But I just didn't doubt that we would be successful. Because it was Disney, and our Japanese visitors who came to this country loved us. Plus, our films did so well, and our publications did so well, and our products did so well. It never dawned on me that we couldn't be successful with Tokyo Disneyland.

On the Site

In their Oriental Land Establishment Plan prospectus from back in 1959, the Oriental Land Company stated, "In this project, we would like to reclaim the sea off Urayasu to develop commercial and residential areas, as well as a large-scale recreational facility, so as to contribute to the nation's culture, health, and welfare." This initial concept was the starting point of what became our project, and is now the Tokyo Disney Resort. The first difficulty the company faced was negotiations with the two fishermen's cooperatives in Urayasu-cho over the compensation for their loss of livelihood due to the offshore reclamation.

That reclamation, basically, entails stacking dirt on top of the area of shoreline you want to build up, and eventually it starts to sink, till it reaches a certain level. According to an engineer who supervised the reclamation work in Urayasu, soil dredged from the bottom of the sea was filled to a height of about sea level during the reclamation work. Then the filled surface was covered with hill sand transported by boats from the Boso Peninsula. The Japanese are very good at landfill and reclamation, and how to preserve its integrity from liquefaction during earthquakes. Tear down a mountain, put the mountain in the ocean, build on that. (I keep thinking that eventually you'll be able to drive from Hawaii to Japan. They'll just keep expanding that out there. It's going to be a wonderful trip.)

The reclamation of the Maihama section, where Tokyo Disney Resort now stands, was completed in 1970. (Of course, this presented special design and engineering differences from our existing parks. Because of the way the site was created, there was differential settling of the ground. Different areas of the site settled at different rates. We compensated as best we could predict. The load building and the show building of Pirates of the Caribbean are actually separate structures, and Cinderella Castle was built on a set of hydraulic "jacks," so that it can be adjusted for level based on shifts in site foundation.)

Reunion in Urayasu

A fellow named Tom Jones was the director in construction at Walt Disney World. Frank Stanek found him, and brought him onto the Tokyo team. Tom helped with the construction to make sure it went along with the way Disney had to do certain things for the specialized needs of attractions, and so on. He was paired up with a guy named Kajima-san. (We used to call him "Old Kajima." There was a "Young Kajima" and an Old Kajima.)

It turns out Old Kajima and Tom Jones had actually worked together on the same site in 1946, right after World War II. Tom was an army officer when the war ended, in the Army Corps of Engineers, and he was over to help with the reconstruction of Japan. Tokyo Disneyland is adjacent to a big industrial area that was heavily bombed during the war. Kajima was rebuilding on the Japanese side while Tom Jones was there, and when they met on the Tokyo Disneyland site after having not seen each other for twenty-five years they immediately recognized each other, and . . . well, it was a beautiful and moving reunion. They worked together all the way through the opening of the project.

For all of us, I think this was such a powerful symbol of the ongoing healing between Japan and the United States—major adversaries less than thirty years before.

Reflections on an Unexpected Culture

My formative years were during World War II. In the context of my time, the Japanese had been "the enemy." Not only that, but they were *vilified*, made monstrous and evil, in the name of wartime propaganda. Of course I still carried some of that attitude and feeling with me as I set out on this project. Thus, one of the most satisfying things about my experience in Japan was seeing how wrong those impressions were. I didn't see any of the stuff I used to see in those old World War II movies, or from my uncles and other veterans.

As a whole, I found the Japanese to be a gentle, patient, and deeply thoughtful people. My experiences, time and again, proved that the people of Japan are trustworthy, honest, and helpful. I can't tell you how many times I'd get lost on the streets in Tokyo. I wouldn't know where I was, and in those days hardly anybody spoke English—or admitted to it. Still, I found that if I was lost, someone would physically take me by the elbow, and walk me to the street corner, or to a cabstand . . . a safe place where I would not be lost anymore.

In Tokyo, a majority of the streets have no names. Large main streets do, but the streets of Tokyo don't follow the classical straight lines and ninety-degree street grids most U.S. cities feature. Add to that the city also having a very old and random street-numbering system in certain parts. Tokyo became a prominent political center in 1603. Many generations ago the first building in a neighborhood was numbered 1. The second, which today may be blocks away, was numbered 2. That means that sometimes building 7 can be next door to a building with the number 134.

I was also told that most of the street addresses were removed during the war to further confuse possible foreign invaders. We learned to spot iconic landmarks and use them as addresses. The OLC offices were near a huge billboard for Johnnie Walker Red, a popular brand of

Scotch whiskey. If you hopped in a cab and said, "Johnnie Walker," they'd get you to the right place.

I forgot where my hotel was all the time. I learned finally to carry a hotel matchbook (remember them?) in my pocket so I could give it to a cabdriver, and he'd get me back to where I was staying. (I admit, it took me about a year to figure out that the Imperial Hotel was the *Takako* to the Japanese. They had no idea what the Imperial was.)

I remember a similar "homing strategy" someone else tried, but with different results. Nancy Valeri was a sort of "spouse wrangler" for our team. One day she and a large group of her American charges were *very* lost in Tokyo. Their cabdriver spoke no English. She reached into her bag and found a set of Imperial Hotel chopsticks. She pointed to the inscription on the utensils and asked him to take the group there. He gamely drove along, but Nancy could tell he was going nowhere in circles. She finally had him pull over. Nancy then found a passerby who spoke English and asked him to translate the chopsticks. "Certainly," the helpful pedestrian said. "It says 'chopsticks.'"

On weekends, during my extended stay in Tokyo, I'd have nothing to do. Everything kind of shuts down, other than necessity shopping options such as grocery and hardware stores. So I'd putter around looking at hardware.

Maybe it's a "guy thing," but a lot of meeting of the minds happens in hardware stores. Maybe summits and treaty negotiations should be held in the hand tools aisle. I learned a lot looking at socket sets and drill bits with the natives.

A Proud Nation

I felt that in general, the Japanese more typically think with a "long view." They're thinking with a sort of cultural strategy. In the States, we tend to think ahead about one paycheck to the next, or how fast can we make a return on our investment. Sometimes it felt as if the Japanese focus ahead about a thousand years. They're thinking about how long whatever decision is made will last, and will their action make their *country* a better place.

When I was in Tokyo, they were still rebuilding from the war. That recovery took a while—this was 1979. There were cranes everywhere, rebuilding and building anew. I found the Japanese to be—well, *patriotic* isn't really the right word—deeply devoted to their country. Their country is supreme to them, and the emperor is still a god to many people in Japan. They also showed me an enormous national and cultural pride—they were proud to be Japanese.

I found a commonality between the philosophies and behaviors Japanese adhere to and those espoused and followed at Disney. That shared perspective only increased my confidence that Japan and Disney were simply a "fit," perhaps a better one than we'd even expected.

I had realized of course that within Disney we had a specific culture, a set of values, a philosophy, a way of behaving. And naturally, the Japanese have a culture. I began to see how much we were almost the same. Reverence to the past, yet moving to the future. Looking forward not to Saturday, or next year, but to generations and even centuries beyond. Living and working for value, not just profit, but the value of experiences, relationships, and creations. Keep things clean, be friendly, look to the new with enthusiasm and curiosity.

That's part of their culture . . . and it's certainly part of the Disney culture as well. This foundational agreement created some of the smoothest—as well as some of the most unusual and unexpected—interactions.

Don't "Japanese-ize" Disney

I think, at first, we probably wrung our hands a bit and wondered about what we'd need to do to bring a

Disneyland to Japan. What design challenges would we face? How would we need to redevelop what was done in California and Florida to accommodate the Japanese culture? What would they understand, not understand, misunderstand, in what we had been doing every day for decades for American audiences?

We needn't have worried about a tenth of the things we worried about. The Oriental Land Company wanted a *Disney* park. The Japanese insisted that we not "Japanese-ize,"—that was their word—the park. They wanted it Western style. They wanted it *just* like Disneyland.

Initially, for instance, we thought that the idea of a Midwestern American turn-of-the-century business street would be lost on the Japanese Guests. Imagineering developed an "International Street" idea, under a weather-protecting canopy. The Japanese hated it. They wanted Main Street, U.S.A. It sounds naïve today, but we were just beginning to realize that "Disney" was a culture all its own. It wasn't the historic Missouri Midwest that was the story to the Japanese, it was the *Disney* element of that story, and the evolution of it into something that represented "Disney." They got what's basically a version of Main Street, U.S.A., but under a majestic glass roof with weather-safe arcades. It's still called World Bazaar, for no *real* reason I can think of. There was a vague explanation about selling wares from all over the world in the locale. (This also may have been a first step in something we see today—the overall story we tell in many cases isn't the original one, but is the *Disney* part of that story. It's not an 1890s Midwestern town; it's a Disney town. The Shanghai park in particular tells *Disney* stories.)

Frontierland became Westernland, as it made more sense in the Japanese language than *Frontier.* OLC colleagues explained that frontier had a somewhat sinister connotation of a dark and mysterious place.

On the other hand, we hadn't planned for a Japanese restaurant, but rather one that sells the traditional quick-service items—hamburgers, hot dogs; very simple menus and an easy operation (though the hamburger is 50 percent soy; they didn't like the taste of 100 percent beef). Although we did have a Blue Bayou table service location, which served American cuisine. We offered some small snack and quick-service nods to comfortable local and traditional foods, but hadn't really *thought* about a traditional Japanese restaurant. That came about because, as our Japanese partners explained, older people did not even want to *try* Western food.

After opening, we regrouped and created a restaurant on the second floor of World Bazaar, and it was very successful. The older people and families liked that. It was more comfortable, particularly for visitors from outlying areas who didn't feel they were quite as sophisticated as somebody from Tokyo or Osaka might be.

Some things we had to insist needed to be "Japanese-ized." Safety signs, for instance, had to be displayed in more than one language. Not *all* the Japanese read English, and we knew we'd have a Guest population from China and Korea visiting, so we ended up with safety signs in those languages as well.

Throughout the project we argued and debated and discussed. Every day they asked about why we did things a certain way, and every night they told us what would and would not work in Japan. So, on a case-by-case basis, we either changed, or we changed their minds, or prepared for what we knew would change after the park's opening.

In many cases, our seeming arrogance rubbed against their desire not to appear unqualified or inept, but we maintained a good dialogue and a mutual respect born out of our shared desire to succeed.

Meet the World

We did make one really large concession to the Japanese: a one-of-a-kind attraction. Konosuke Matsushita, founder of the Matsushita Electric Industrial Company, had an interest in both Japanese history and in Walt Disney. He applied some pressure to create a Japanese version of a sort of Hall of Presidents concept. The result was a really ambitious attraction called Meet the World. The show was presented in a rotating theater, similar to the Carousel of Progress, and explored the history of Japan's engagement with the outside world. Meet the World featured animation, motion picture technology, and dozens of Audio-Animatronics figures—all with a score and original song by the Sherman brothers.

I kind of liked it. Nobody else did. The Japanese audiences sure didn't like it. It just didn't get attendance. Some Guests didn't like the idea that you could tell the history of Japan in twenty minutes. I felt bad about that, because they wanted it, they were heavily involved in the writing and design of it. Disney legend Claude Coats was a creative director on it. It was just never embraced by the Guests. Maybe because it worked too hard to "Japanese-ize" a

Disney experience. (It was also in Tomorrowland, which never made sense to me. Dick Kline told me that the facility had a hybrid art deco feel so that it connected more seamlessly to both World Bazaar and Tomorrowland—because no one was quite sure about what thematic foundation was in mind for it.)

Our Weakness Is Our Strength

The fact that they wanted and we needed so little new design for this project was actually a blessing in disguise. There was a real strain on available talent all across Disney, due to the enormous simultaneous demands being created by the design and building of EPCOT Center, which was scheduled to open in October 1982. I wasn't having any problem operationally, because most of my people got pulled out of Disneyland in California, and not Walt Disney World.

The good news was that we all got a great break from what we were doing, the Japanese included, because we *all* went over for the EPCOT Center premiere as scheduled and stayed there for about a week.

Our Japanese team got to see a real Disney opening. To me that was really important, so they could experience the kinds of things that happen on opening day at a Disney park. These are the kind of bugs you're going to have to work out, this is how people are going to react to a brand-new park—it's a lot of fun and a great team-building and learning experience.

Tokyo Disneyland's opening-day celebration turned out to be kind of a blend of our existing Magic Kingdom parks' unveilings. We used the same or similar designs in a lot of cases. Siting and attempts at creating proper operational square footage created some oddities and visual intrusion dilemmas, but they were ultimately solved. Berms and some camouflaging landscaping helped a bit—but it was a bit of a battle to get the money to address some of the issues.

The Haunted Mansion looked right down on Dumbo, for instance, because it was placed closer to Fantasyland than Westernland. I didn't like where it was on opening day, and I don't think we did a good job in transitions and separations from land to land. I directed that we start planting trees, adding planters, and making distinct land-scaping and hard-scaping breaks. We did that where World Bazaar ends into Tomorrowland—since that transition just didn't work for any of us. We worked on that, and I think did a good job—as the original design group did the best they could under the circumstances, and the engineering group, led by Don Edgren, executed a fantastic job.

I think in the end, one of the saving graces of working halfway around the world and away from the internal distractions of EPCOT Center, was that we were able to just work things out, find solutions, make decisions, and get the job done somewhat "under the radar." Disney corporate really didn't know what we were doing; all they knew was when it was supposed to be done. People came out for the ribbon cuttings and ceremonies, and publicity, and so on.

I think we just made it look easy—and they were inclined to just let us be.

Documenting Disney

Tokyo Disneyland had one of the most ambitious documentation projects in Disney park history. We'd (inconsistently) had what we called SOPs—standard operating procedures. Those got outdated very fast, and the Japanese wanted reference materials on every aspect of how Disney did things. In response we established the Tokyo Planning Center because the contract with OLC stipulated that we would provide operating manuals for every discipline. But we didn't have operating manuals for every discipline. So we started writing.

The lawyers thought this was great; it created credibility and consistency. We would point to documentation and verify how we'd instructed and agreed to every aspect of design and operational intent.

We hired writers from various parts of the parks, and they began churning out manuals on everything from marketing to maintenance, and food service to ride operations. It was a huge job overseeing a large organization of writers in Disneyland and at Imagineering, and then later at Walt Disney World.

A byproduct of the project was that we realized we were guardians of the Disney Way. Putting it all down in writing showed not only the methods and procedures followed, but the important ideas behind everything we did. It was deemed so important, in fact, that written manuals were eventually done for the whole organization.

I can't give Dick Nunis enough credit. He was the leader of that—he led the charge. Dick was a tough guy, but highly disciplined. If you think about it, back in the 1950s, there was no theme park rule book, and we were writing "the book" as we went. Every staff meeting with

Dick in those early days was full of new ideas—and we wrote a new book as we went in the aftermath.

In addition to the manuals, we did training videos. We formed two new departments: one for making training films, another for writing manuals. Bob Allen, Jr. was in charge of the A/V team, and he, along with Steve Kasper and Tom Carr, produced the training films and video documentation. Anne Okey led the manual/documentation team. We had no attractions to train people on in Japan, but we knew what attractions we'd have, so we did videos in Anaheim and Orlando. We knew we were going to have a Space Mountain in Tokyo, for instance, a Pirates of the Caribbean, a Dumbo. These video-training sessions ran anywhere from twenty to forty minutes and were combined with matching manuals. We had it supported visually, so they really got it.

We never had to point to a manual after the opening year. We never had to point to the contract after the opening year. We never had to say, "You're breaching." Never. It was a very honorable, respectful, and pleasant business relationship between two parties. I think as we (executives from our corporate side included) got to know the Japanese, the more we liked them, the more we trusted them. They never disappointed us. They're hardworking people who wanted it to happen, just as we did—and they believed in the Disney story, and the Disney philosophy, and the Disney Way.

Over the years, there were thousands of hours of meetings, and we negotiated everything: merchandise, operational policies, food product, you name it. *Thousands* of hours. We had to look at every object and action, and determine together the things that were—or were not— appropriate, at least not by our standards.

Collaboration, Cooperation, and Education

We typically had these three (or occasionally more) cultures in play in Japan: one was the American culture, which we worked hard to balance and temper. We didn't want to be arrogant to our hosts, or be seen as "Ugly Americans." We certainly had the Japanese culture in mind as well, which as I've said we found surprisingly easy, accommodating, and compatible with the thinking of that third culture—the Disney culture.

We spent a lot of time and effort balancing the desires and expectations of all three of these forces and in the end I think created a fluid hybrid that in many ways became a stronger culture all its own, a "Tokyo Disney Culture" greater than the sum of its parts.

There were certainly disagreements and struggles along the way. Many of them now seem quaint, or something where common sense prevailed . . . or even humorous.

Clean Ears: A Disney Tradition?

For example, we fought (as much as you can "fight" with the Japanese, who take pride in always maintaining politeness and serenity) on certain merchandise products that we didn't think were really suited to be "Disney" branded. Take an ear pick, as an example.

An ear pick is just what it sounds like: a type of curette, used to clean the ear canal of earwax. They are as common and conventional in Japan as toothpicks, or cotton swabs. However, in Japan, they are not necessarily used in a private way as they might be in the United States. Some Japanese even find ear-picking to be pleasurable; it's a service of many spas and salons.

We had yet to learn about this item when we were presented with a merchandise prototype, the Disney Ear Pick. It was actually rather handsome and well-made, of brass, with a black handle—and Mickey Mouse on the end.

You can guess our initial reaction.

But once we understood it (like so many things), it

was not as peculiar and "un-Disney" as it had first seemed from an American perspective. And this common Japanese gift item has since become a consistent and popular seller.

Disbanding a Boys' Club

One reason for the success of our Tokyo merchandise programs was the experience of an executive named Chris Lopez, our manager of merchandise, who worked for director of merchandise Bob Bowman. We owe much to Chris's diligence and close collaboration with the Japanese. One problem for our Japanese partners, though—Chris wasn't Christopher. Chris was Christine.

In the early days, the Japanese had said, "We don't want any women here in leadership positions." I said, "That's a problem, because half of my team are women."

I made the case that if they wanted "Disney," they were going to have to accept the successful organizations and strong leadership we drew on to drive our success. That included a lot of women. So we brought women over, and, of course, they did an *outstanding* job.

They didn't work as hard as the men—they worked *harder.* They knew they were entering an environment hostile to them, and they not only stepped up, they excelled.

And we've had many women working there in line operating positions, in marketing support divisions . . . you name it.

To their credit, the Japanese have relented from an untenable position and accepted them with open arms. They've looked to them for advice. They've become friends. They've even taken them out socially, which was *never* done in Japan before.

Everything Old Is New Again

Another interesting cross-cultural "issue" was our idea about how the park *looked* versus the aesthetics and expectations the Japanese envisioned. Disneyland was built by movie production designers, and part of the storytelling was making the park feel "real," as if the Guest was an actor in a movie, or walking into a historic site. So the Imagineers employed their movie experience in creating a look that was tidy but "lived-in"; or well designed, but as if it had been set in place a long time. They used painting and texturing techniques called "aging and graining" to give things the worn look of "time."

Around the Christmas vacation a year before its opening, late 1981, Imagineering had brought over their "agers and grainers" from the States. They distressed our brand-new Westernland to look a hundred years old. They did this as well to parts of New Orleans Square. We Americans all went home for Christmas vacation. When we came back, however, we noticed that all that work had been repainted, because the Japanese thought, "This really looks old and dirty. We're spending a lot of money on this place, and it had better look new." They had repainted it all to look fresh and clean. We had to bring all the agers and grainers back to repaint it. (Not just once, but twice. They just couldn't get used to the fact it *had* to look old.) Even to this day, I think Tokyo Disneyland looks a little "newer" than what we would prefer.

(Across from the Imperial Hotel back in Tokyo is Hibiya Park, the first Western style public park in the city. For nearly six years from the end of World War II, General Douglas MacArthur oversaw the occupation and restoration of Japan from an office on the sixth floor of the Dai-ichi Life Insurance Company building, located kitty-corner from this park. A gorgeous reproduction of the Liberty Bell, presented to the people of Japan by the general on behalf of the United States, occupies a hilltop in the park. When it arrived in Japan, the story goes, the installation crew noticed that the bell had a prominent crack in it. Being unfamiliar with the story of the Liberty Bell—they repaired the crack!)

Taking Out the Trash

The Japanese didn't want dumpsters in Japan. Our operations leadership was really puzzled. We had figured that we'd be generating thousands and thousands of pounds of trash every day, and it was going to take a *fleet* of trash dumpsters to keep order and cleanliness. Dumpsters, we reasoned, would be needed to abet the picking up and taking away of trash to landfills, or loaded on barges, or whatever—but there had to be an infrastructure to get rid of the trash. Yet there still wasn't one, up to an uncomfortably close time to the park's opening. We finally convinced our Japanese counterparts that we *had* to figure out a way to dispose of trash.

Well, they took our estimates and came up with a trash-disposal scheme. Here it is: they had all this undeveloped land, and they believed that they could establish a large hog farm where the pigs could eat all the trash (and then they could use the pigs as a source of income). We kept straight faces, studied that plan for about three minutes, and said, "Seems logical." (One of our industrial engineers, however, soon figured out it would likely take a hundred thousand pigs to eat all the consumable trash on-site.)

I also pointed out, "You know, the prevailing wind blows from the ocean—we *are* on Tokyo Bay—directly into the Tokyo Disneyland site. It's not going to smell very good."

They dropped that idea, and we started ordering dumpsters immediately.

Authentic Japanese Horticulture

When the Disney and Japanese cultures connected and harmonized, the results were spectacular. It was *better* than Japanese, it was *better* than Disney. The whole was greater than just the sum of its parts. Horticulture and garden design are a good example. Landscaping plays a deep role in Japanese history and culture, dating back to the Asuka period in the sixth and seventh centuries. Landscaping and garden design are deeply philosophical, in design and materials. The garden masters aspire to "authenticity" on two levels: a precedent-driven path where design comes from the *outside* and is imposed—on those who will use a garden, on the site, and on the choice of materials. The second (and higher) path follows a more metaphorical approach to the traditions, and the inspiration, for the design comes from *within*—from the desires and culture of those who will use the garden, from the site and its surroundings, and from locally available materials.

Without intending to, third-generation horticulturist Morgan "Bill" Evans, imposed this basic philosophy on his work at Disneyland. His forthright approach and innate understanding of how landscaping fit into the art of place making was a talent that must have not only pleased Walt Disney aesthetically, but was a godsend to Walt's ever-evolving design ideas about Disneyland. Evans quite simply knew how to use his medium for storytelling. He was as much an artist with living plants as others were with pen, ink, paint, or clay. After Disneyland, Evans continued to craft Disney's horticultural mythmaking for nearly half a century—including at both Tokyo parks.

Heading Toward Opening Day

We started to fall behind a little bit in landscaping, though . . . or at least we thought we were falling behind. I don't know whose idea it was, but in order to accelerate somewhat, we had a tree-planting ceremony. All of the construction personnel, and all the OLC and Mitsui Real Estate people, along with all of our partners and employees, were there. We had thousands of trees, and everyone adopted a tree. We conducted a huge tree-planting ceremony over a two-day period, plus created a map of where each particular person's tree was. To this day, people come back to visit their tree and say a prayer. My tree is quite large now.

A Blizzard in Tokyo Bay

Oh, and then we had a snowstorm. Seriously! It was a blizzard—in March of 1983, during our "soft opening" month! Traffic was at a standstill from Tokyo to the park site. The roads were blocked getting in from Tokyo. The subways were closed. The park itself was just terribly snowed in. I met with my staff—all of us from either California or from Florida, not exactly the "mukluks and snowshoes brigade." Could we safely operate the park? Two hours until opening, and here were a bunch of suntanned Americans trying to figure out how to handle blizzard conditions.

Then came a polite knock on the door, and a supervisor came in and said, through his interpreter, "There are twenty thousand people at the main gate waiting to open." Because that's the way it was those opening weeks. People would line up hours before during the night—even in a blizzard! The new teams went to the mill and started making shovels out of two-by-fours and flat pieces of plywood, and were beginning to shovel snow out of the pathways between lands, and between attractions, so people could get around. Piles of snow lay beside the walkways. Close to a hundred rented trucks were brought in and loaded up with all this snow, which was then dumped into the river adjoining the project site—and unfortunately into the Rivers of America inside the park itself.

The river froze. The *Mark Twain* was stuck in the ice. The Jungle Cruise's waterways froze, and didn't thaw until two or three days later. But our resourceful and industrious Japanese teams were already working on solving the problem before we could even think about how we were going to attack it.

Opening Day Arrives

Finally, after a monthlong "soft opening," the official Tokyo Disneyland Opening Day Ceremony event arrived.

The morning was mostly cloudy and overcast, and

chilly—it wouldn't get to be more than fifty degrees Fahrenheit all day. Because of our location on Tokyo Bay, it was also misty and wet. Our ribbon-cutting ceremony, which we had been planned to hold at the park's entrance, was moved "inside," underneath the glass-covered World Bazaar.

At Disney, we don't do openings without an appropriate sense of ceremony, and ritual . . . and most of all, *show.* This was no different. The host for the day's events was the popular Japanese actor and TV personality E. H. Eric. (He had served as the emcee for the Beatles 1966 concert in Tokyo.) As an assembled crowd of dignitaries, business leaders, and other VIPs watched, an opening concert of Disney music was performed by a 150-member symphony orchestra, and a two hundred-member chorale. Speeches were given by OLC head Masatomo Takahashi; Disney CEO Card Walker; Japan's minister of foreign affairs, Shintaro Abe; and the minister of education, Seto Yami.

Mickey, Minnie, Donald, Pluto, and Goofy escorted all of our 1983 Walt Disney World, Disneyland, and Tokyo Disneyland ambassadors, to the stage. There was also a parade of the children of our expatriates and employees of Walt Disney Productions, Japan—along with dozens of our costumed characters—who headed joyously through the seating area, waving and greeting the assembled VIP guests and filling the aisles.

An international children's chorus—consisting of girls from the Seisen International School in Tokyo, and boys from St. Mary's International School (along with that huge orchestra and chorale)—performed the Sherman brothers' beloved anthem "It's a Small World (After All)." It certainly felt appropriate, and truly moving, especially as a symbolic flock of white doves was released at the song's finale. As the sound of carillon bells tolled from Cinderella Castle, and the orchestra and voices concluded with "When You Wish Upon a Star," thousands of balloons were released—and headed skyward.

A multicolored ceremonial ribbon was held at intervals by the characters, and Mickey Mouse took center stage between Walker and Takahashi as the two men simultaneously cut the ribbon. Soon after the ceremony, thousands of Guests who had waited outside the park's turnstiles in the pouring rain were let into World Bazaar.

The dedication plaques, in both English and Japanese, can be found in the center of the Plaza (The Hub). The plaques read:

To All Who Come To This Happy Place

—WELCOME—

*Here you will discover enchanted
lands of Fantasy and Adventure, Yesterday and
Tomorrow. May Tokyo Disneyland be an eternal
source of Joy, Laughter, Inspiration, and Imagination
to the peoples of the world. And may this magical
kingdom be an enduring symbol of the spirit of
cooperation and friendship between the great nations
of Japan and the United States of America.*

*April 15, 1983
E. Cardon Walker
Chairman of the Board
Walt Disney Productions*

Rope Drop

Disney park veterans will know about "rope drop." It's pretty much like what it sounds—visitors accumulate at the gate or the end of Main Street (or World Bazaar), where there is a rope across to prevent entry. At opening time, there's usually a PA announcement or little show, and we . . . drop the rope. It's exciting, ceremonial, and builds anticipation, and it's become a part of the whole package for many people. Since Kagami never came stateside to train, I told him he needed to experience it. On opening day, he joined me at the rope. I told him that for safety's sake he better stand behind me—the crowd waiting to head in was going to come running down that street. Through the interpreter, Kagami countered, "No, they're not like you Americans. We'll just tell them to slow down, and to please walk and not run—and the Japanese will follow instructions."

So we gave the signal, and dropped the rope: a veritable stampede of visitors came tearing down that street. Floods of excited and happy and enthusiastic Guests created a wall of humanity. Cast Members were yelling at them, in both Japanese and English, to slow down, be careful . . . but they just kept on running toward us. I looked around for Kagami. He was crouched down on the sidewalk behind a trash can, scared to death.

I couldn't resist. "So, Kagami-san, join me out here tomorrow for rope drop?"

Nope, that was his last rope drop.

Merchandise Mania

We may have made a miscalculation on merchandise. Culturally, gift-giving is *very* Japanese. When they go on a trip, they always bring back something for somebody else—family members, or good friends, colleagues, and even co-workers sometimes. So with Tokyo, we just fell right into that existing tradition.

Early on, in a show of good faith, OLC had asked Disney to invest in the project. They said, "Why don't you invest in merchandise as we develop new product, and you can operate merchandise—now you're a piece of the project, and then we'll be assured that it's all going to work." Card Walker turned them down cold. He said, "We're not spending a dime on that project." OLC reimburses Disney for everything, but it's a straight-out license.

The night before we opened, I was doing a walk-through with managing director of administration Ron Pogue. The Emporium was just a mess. They could not get the shelves organized, they couldn't get the stock on the shelves, they couldn't get stock delivered from the warehouse—I mean, it was just total chaos. The poor Cast Members, who were already in costume because it was a dress rehearsal day, were sitting on the floor, just exhausted. I said to the lead, and to the supervisor, and to the general manager of the park that if this isn't cleaned up by tomorrow, ready for Guests, *you can't open*. So they got on it . . . they worked all night.

In the parks world, "101" means an attraction is down, or something is closed. Usually it's something like a mechanical, electrical, or computer failure, and then the proper people respond. On Pirates of the Caribbean, the area supervisors would respond. They'd evacuate it. Security would respond to help with the evacuation. Nurses might respond depending on what the breakdown was. It's an important code.

The day we opened; we got a radio call—the Emporium is 101. How can a retail site be 101? We hustled over there, and found the doors closed and locked. A security officer opened the doors to let us in, and here are those people still laying on the floor; half of them were now asleep. They'd been up all night, trying to stock the shelves.

"Oh, Jim-san. You said if we couldn't get this organized by today, we couldn't open. We couldn't get it organized, so we didn't open."

We quickly cleared up our miscommunication, they

hustled, and we got the Emporium open by noon. Everybody, including me, underestimated the power of the gift-buying society we were in.

Card Walker watched all of this and said to me, "You know, I turned down the offer from the Japanese to buy all of the merchandise rights for $25 million. I'm watching people buy things off the shelves so quickly, they can't even keep the shelves stocked! I want you to go back in and see if we can still buy in."

"Card, they're just going to laugh me out of the room."

"That's okay, better you than me."

So I went back in. Then I went outside, waited a credible amount of time, had a cigarette, and then came back to Card.

"Nope. They didn't go for it," I informed him.

Today, merchandise sales exceed the revenue from park admissions.

Keep It Clean

Overall, the Japanese performed brilliantly dealing with a kind of endeavor they had absolutely no experience with. There were certainly mistakes made, but there always are when you open up a new project. Nevertheless, our cultural separations were always interesting, informative, and fairly simple to work out.

For instance, the Japanese are a very clean society: they pick up trash, and they're not used to dropping it. Unfortunately, at the time, most amusement parks in Japan were dirty, and they didn't spend a lot of money on janitorial. Trash cans were always overflowing, there was always trash on the ground at those sites . . . and we knew that going in. So, we really focused hard on janitorial and training. We had the best of our custodial staff from Disneyland coming over to teach them, and they were trained well.

Unfortunately, they just couldn't keep up on opening day, and the Guests, used to the ways other amusement parks throughout the country handle trash, started being sloppy and dropping their trash on the ground at Tokyo Disneyland—which, as I said, is totally unlike them (but the acceptable behavioral pattern at other amusement parks).

We needed to have another big lecture. Afterward the park's janitorial staff worked all night . . . and the park *got* clean. The next morning, they had *twice* as many janitorial staff as we had the first day. (We were actually overstaffed the next day!) But this time they kept it clean, and it's been clean since. Today, if somebody drops a *popcorn kernel,* there's two guys there to pick it up. They clean their drinking fountains with toothbrushes. They're so into sanitation and making sure it's clean. They just continue to do a wonderful job!

Like so many Disney values, this originated with Walt. He had told us time and again that "cleanliness breeds cleanliness." If we keep it clean, the Guests will keep it clean. And as was often the case, Walt was right, and that philosophy worked in Japan as well.

Design Miscalculations

Speaking of drinking fountains, we had another little "cultural miscalculation." Initially, the Japanese didn't have drinking fountains in their plan, because at the time, nobody would drink tap water. They came up with a water purification plant backstage, so that we could have drinking fountains onstage with water that people could actually drink. The problem was, nobody *believed* it was purified water. So the drinking fountains pretty much stayed idle, and we sold a lot of water.

Another little misstep on our end was the design of the food-service counters: they were a little too high for the average Guest. (The height of an average Japanese adult peaked for those born in 1978 and 1979 at five foot six for men and five foot two for women.) The same thing happened with a now-ancient technology called the telephone booth. The public telephones were placed too high up on the walls. Users practically had to throw their coins and change to get them in the phone's slot. The phones were also plainly visible to the public. (We always try to theme and hide them.)

We spent a lot of that first operating year not only training park staff how to operate, or how to get up to theoretical capacity and so on, but also on how to reach and maintain those Disney standards, and to address various unexpected design issues and flaws. Haste makes waste. Time and budget allowed for mistakes.

More Unexpected Culture

The week we opened, I was summoned to the parking lot. I really didn't expect what I found there—dozens of vendors had arrived in the parking areas without any request or permission, and set up a sort of guerilla flea market. There were banquet tables and card tables all around, covered with merchandise, with aggressive sales and haggling taking place . . . and a lot of noise. Our Japanese partners seemed very hesitant to stop them—I think they assumed that perhaps they were affiliated with the Japanese Mafia and didn't want to mess with them—especially opening week—and didn't want any problems in the future. So they just let them stay out there. I said flatly and firmly, "You can't do that. First of all, the merchandise is unacceptable, and we don't want Guests thinking we are any part of this. These vendors are not authorized to be on the property, so you have liability issues for them *and* our Guests, and we need those parking spaces to put cars on."

But they remained unwilling to evict or enforce. So we gathered up our American staff—we probably had twenty security and expat people (our security people were already there training *their* security people). They formed a ring around the tables, and stood there, and wouldn't let any Guests come near the tables. They remained in place most of that day. That night, the interlopers packed up their tables and left—and they never came back again.

That was it. We set the standard. The Japanese were upset that we took charge, maybe a little frightened, or embarrassed—but on the other hand, they were grateful to us privately that we solved that problem for them.

Leisure Sheets

Leisure sheets were another one of our cultural struggles, flash points. The Japanese hate to get their clothes wet or dirty, and won't sit directly on the ground without something between them and the grass or pavement. A magazine or newspaper will do, but there is a common item known as a "leisure sheet" or "picnic mat."

There are also leisure sheet protocols. You don't wear shoes on one, or step on other people's sheets. They are also used to mark your spot . . . and you never move someone else's sheet once they've staked their claim.

Everyone there knows this and has at least one leisure sheet. They come with all different kinds of logos, designs, and characters. Snoopy would be on there, or Woody Woodpecker; all kinds of non-Disney characters. Not that I minded that so much, but the Guests would put them down on the ground along the parade route as soon as they came into Tokyo Disneyland, and use a sheet to secure their space. The Japanese are so courteous; if somebody had a sheet down at nine in the morning, that was their space for the parade—even though the parade might not be until two o'clock in the afternoon.

We had to divert our crowd-control people around

those sheets, so they could set up their stanchions and route the Guests and parade floats and Cast Members. It actually got to be a real problem. After a while, those sheets took up the whole parade route. People who arrived later would stand behind the sheets, but they couldn't stand where the sheets were, because that's how they respect somebody else's space. Operationally, and for safety reasons, I really fought to ban the sheets and the corresponding practice of not invading someone else's claimed space.

But there are some host customs you just can't shift, limit, or get rid of. Merchandise finally gave in, and came out with a leisure sheet with Mickey and other Disney characters on it. So there went my argument. I never did win it. To this day, they're still doing leisure sheets on the parade routes. And not just parade routes. If they see a nice shady spot under a tree somewhere, the sheet will be down, and it saves their spot for the whole day.

Two Cultures of Politeness

Interestingly, we don't use crowd-control stanchions or ropes much in Japan, because once you start a line, that line will be there until you close for that night. The

Japanese are orderly, and polite to each other. You don't have any "incidents" there. You don't have any fights; you don't have any arguments between people.

I think within the Disney culture, that's something Disney people do. We support goodwill and kindness. We have a lost and found for objects. We have a place for children who have "misplaced" their parents. That's part of our culture. Lots of places don't have such a thing. We have *friendly* Security. They're not guards, they're officers. I mean, it's a whole different type of thing. The blending of the cultures, time and again, proved to be easy.

Another surprising and reassuring Japanese custom we discovered was an innate sense of respect and honesty for others and their belongings. For instance, if you lose your wristwatch, camera, or any other personal item, you typically can come back to that same spot where you lost it, and it will be there. And more often than not, said missing item has been placed in plain view, on a bench, or hanging on a tree or fence finial next to it . . . or on a planter someplace where you can't miss it. And it will stay there. No local Guest would think of taking it, because it doesn't belong to them.

At the core of our success in Japan was this sense of a cultural synchronization between the parties. These

Not
Just a
Walk
in the
Park

James B. Cora
Disney Legend

Previous page: In 1979, I was named vice president and managing director of operations for Tokyo Disneyland Resort. I don't seem that important.

This page: James Bashara Cora premiered on December 3, 1937, just a few weeks before Walt Disney's baby, *Snow White and the Seven Dwarfs.*

My grandmother Jamile Moses and my grandfather Hunna Bashara Hayek—who became "John Cora," 1908.

A wedding photo of my "sitte," Freda, and Buttross (Peter) Morad of the Nayami family, 1906.

My dad, John Cora, and me, in front of his store, Johnny's Market, in 1938. We lived behind the store my first year.

My grandfather, me, and my dad in the store, 1947. Working there as a kid, I learned a lot about honesty, effort, consistency, and diligence.

My mom holding my brother, John, on my shoulders and my sister, Marilyn.

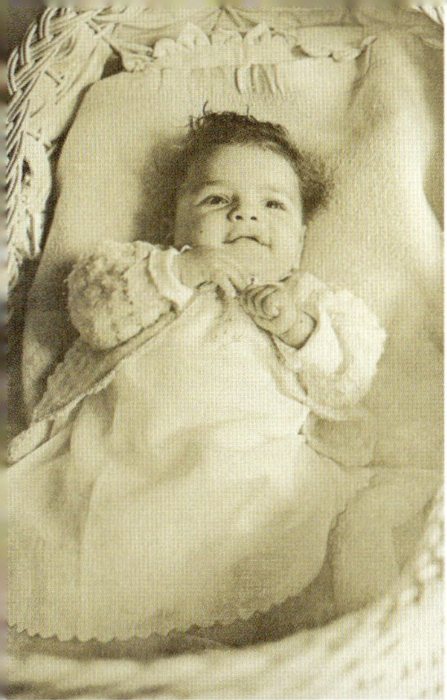

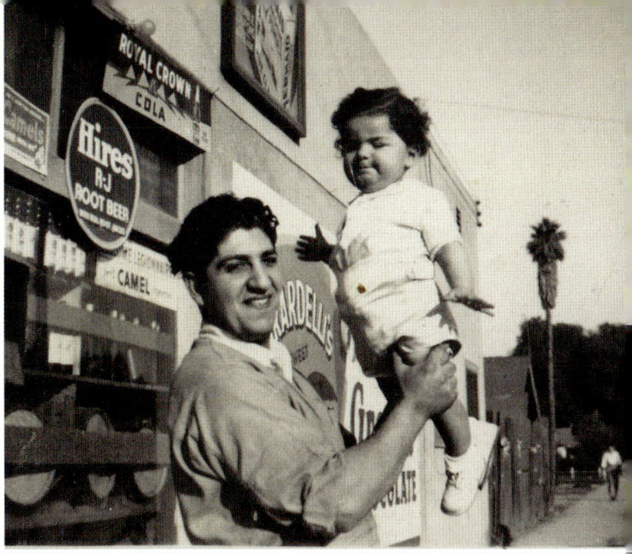
ROYAL CROWN
COLA
Hires
R-J
ROOT BEER
CAMEL

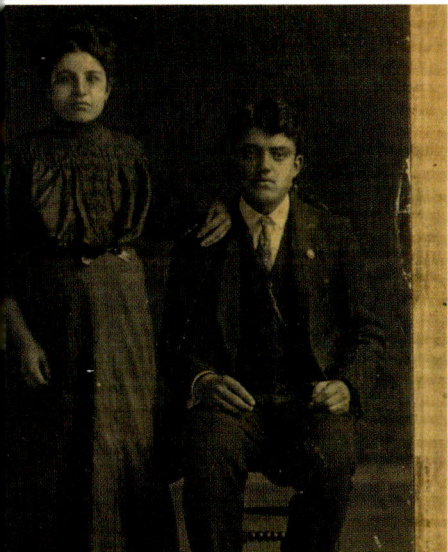

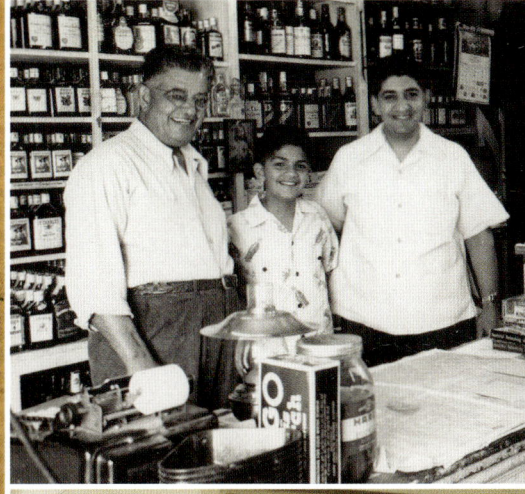

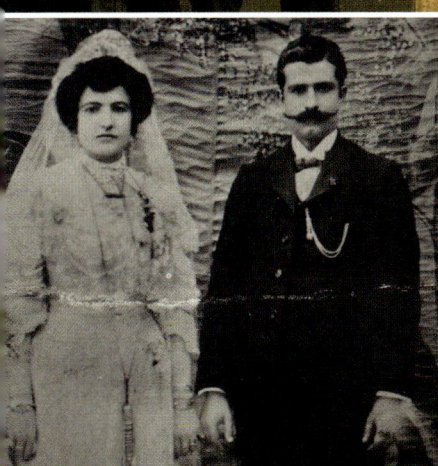

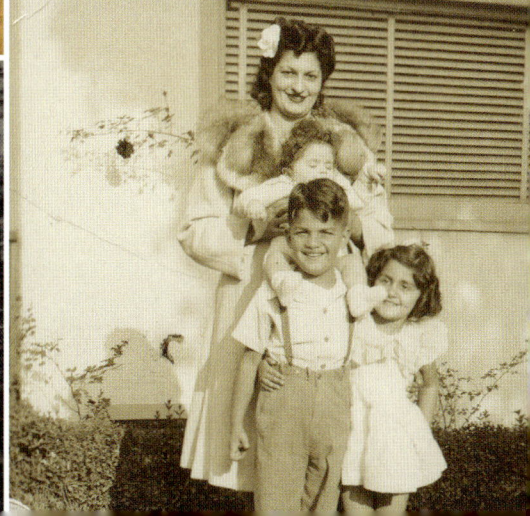

My mother and me.

Me, Marilyn, and John.

I left my active military
duty in 1957, but I carried
a lot of valuable lessons
with me, including those on
administration, training,
and team building.

Me and my aunties (Margie,
Annie, and Eva) and my
mom. I loved them all.

My mom, and my sitte,
Freda, with my aunties and
my uncle John. We were a
patriotic family; Marilyn
and I even wore uniforms
celebrating our uncle's visit.

I met Wayne Ferris while
at Pius X High School,
and we went through basic
training together. We've
been lifelong friends.

To My dear
Grandmother
Love + kindness always
Jim

U.S. ARMY

Daughters Michelle, right, and Rene. At work and at home, we were a growing family and, in the early 1960s, always adding to the "Cast."

In 1969, Dick Nunis brought me from Retlaw back to Fantasyland as a full supervisor.

Any guy who has worked at Disneyland knows that his little girl (here it's my Rene) feels like a princess when Dad shows off Walt's Magic Kingdom to her, and vice versa.

In my temporary summer role as a security supervisor in Tomorrowland's dance areas in 1960.

I was working the Skyway when I found a new religion: succession planning, and the vital importance of training (and cross-training).

Already charming, just like his old man, our third child, James Cora Jr. (Jimmy), was born in 1969.

To me, leadership involved learning, and being able to do every job. One I never could master was embroidering names on hats.

With Marty Sklar on a Matterhorn bobsled in 1977. He and I worked in tandem on many projects, but rarely so closely, over many years.

Tokyo Disneyland opening day. Managing Directors: *Top row:* Ron Pogue, Fred Duffy, Lee Lanselle, Steve Lewelling, Jack Myers, Dave Burkhart, Jerry Wright, Bob Bowman, and Bill Gair. *Bottom row:* Bob Coontz, Hideo Amemiya, Larry Billman, Gary Burson, me, Tom Gardner, Wayne Jackson, and Dick Kline. *Not shown:* Darrell Metzger and Bob Baldwin.

The first visit to the Tokyo site. Hideo Amemiya, me, F. Mori, Dick Nunis, Jim Pasilla, Frank Stanek, and Y. Kobinata are standing; kneeling are H. Takada and Van France.

The nine original Oriental Land Company Tokyo Disneyland trainees: *Top row:* M. Ikeda, T. Watanabe, Y. Natsui, Y. Tamaru, Mac Owada. *Bottom row:* T. Sakamoto, Yasuo Okuyama, Noburu Kamisawa, S. Natsuki.

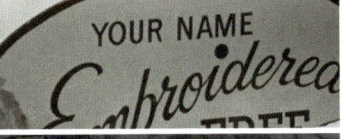

YOUR NAME
Embroidered
FREE

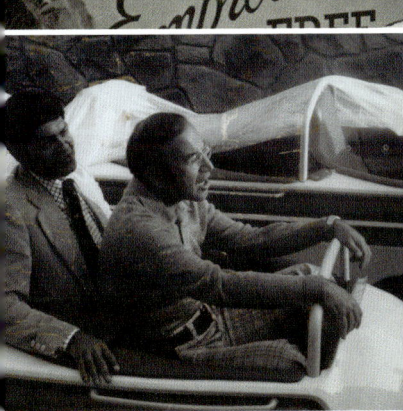

The training center team for Tokyo Disneyland.

Cast Members assembled to spell out "Tokyo Disneyland" at the main gate, 1983.

Frank Stanek (far left) with (left to right): S. Natsuki, M. Ikeda, Y. Okuyama, T. Watanabe, N. Kamisawa, Dick Nunis, Y. Hasegawa, M. Owada, Y. Tamaru, Y. Natsui, N. Sakamoto—and me.

A blizzard hit Tokyo Bay, the locale of our park, in March of 1983, during our "soft opening" month!

The president of Oriental Land Company, Masatomo Takahashi, and me.

Part of the Euro Disneyland site selection team: Eddie Carpenter, Lee Lanselle, Dick Nunis, Michael Eisner, me, Thor Degelmann, and Bill Gair.

Michael Eisner and then French president Jacques Chirac signed the first letter of agreement for Euro Disney on December 18, 1985.

The Euro Disney project was initiated and supported by the Disneyland International staff in Anaheim.

Dick Nunis was tough—and generously shared a hundred valuable insights and eternal truths.

Our Operations team, led by Steve Lewelling, got very involved in our preview attraction, Espace Euro Disney, which opened on December 5, 1990.

Peter Rummell, me, and Wing Chao. Peter and Wing supported the architectural plans for hotels and Festival Disney.

My assistant Helen Ourousseroff, Fred Benckenstein, Mickey Steinberg, and staff help me celebrate my birthday.

On my wedding day, I was so happy with my sister, Marilyn, and my brother, John, at my side.

Euro Disney opened for employee preview and testing in March 1992. The press was able to visit on Saturday, April 11, 1992, the day before the park's official opening day.

Michael Eisner enjoys the preview of the Wild West Dinner Show.

Phillipe Bourguignon, John Forsgren, Bob Fitzpatrick, me, and Fred Benckenstein.

My parents and Mimi's parents, Dr. and Mrs. Schaaf, made the trip to France to join us on our wedding day, a magical day with a magical view of Le Chateau de la Belle au Bois Dormant.

A congratulatory plaque from our colleagues in Tokyo was presented to the Euro Disney team by Frank Wells. He was a good man, a scholar, a gentleman.

Some of the key *Pocahontas* operations team gathered on the Great Lawn in Central Park to take stock.

Jim Jr's wedding day, with Rene and Michelle.

This aerial shot of Central Park in New York shows the first time Disney had a movie premiere outside a movie theater. That was quite an undertaking. The event opened to rave reviews without incident, though there were more than a hundred thousand in attendance.

My daughter Rene was living in New York in June of 1995 when we were producing the *Pocahontas* premiere event in Central Park; she came by to cheer the old man on.

A proud dad with my daughter Michelle on her wedding day.

On my fortieth anniversary with The Walt Disney Company; in addition to friends and family I had a special guest.

Luanne Wells, Frank's widow, continued to represent him and remained a good friend. She joined us for the Grand Opening of Tokyo DisneySea in September 2001.

As I participated in the Grand Opening of Tokyo Disneyland's Mickey's Toontown, my granddaughter Kayleigh was born.

Among those at my fortieth celebration was Van France. I've had a lot of guidance, and influence, and leadership in my life and career, but Van is the only guy I'd ever consider a true mentor.

When I had received my thirty-five-year service award, Jack Lindquist, Dick Nunis, and Judson Green did the honors.

Me and our daughter-in-law, Bonnie, enjoying time together with our little love Kayleigh.

The Tokyo DisneySea team from Anaheim visits The Walt Disney Studios.

Top row: K. Kato, Y. Tamaru, Jim Thomas (WDI), Ron Pogue, T. Kagami, Art Kishiyama (WDI), Hideo Amemiya. *Bottom row:* Steve Kirk (WDI), me, Mrs. Takahashi and Mr. M. Takahashi, Judson Green.

The Tokyo DisneySea Disney and Oriental Land Company project development teams.

Top row: C. Besford, K. Kato, Bob Iger, and me; *bottom row:* K. Kato, T. Kagami, Michael Eisner, and Roy E. Disney at the April 1996 official press event for the signing of the Tokyo DisneySea Park development, construction, and operation contract.

Marty Sklar, Jim Thomas, and me, just trying to figure it all out.

After two years of construction and a cost of more than $3 billion (plus another $3 billion for resort peripheral enhancements), Tokyo DisneySea opened its gates at eight o'clock in the morning on September 4, 2001.

The Disneyland International Executive Team: Lee Lanselle, Gordon Finch, Mas Imai, Jim Thomas, me, Ron Pogue, and Karl Andrews.

Enjoying the Grand Opening of TDS with Roy E. Disney, Hasagawa, Okayama, and Kamisawa.

Mimi and I take a moment together to enjoy the Tokyo DisneySea Grand Opening overlooking Mediterranean Harbor.

The original nine trainees from OLC reunited for the Grand Opening of Tokyo DisneySea in 2001.

The official ribbon cutting for the Hotel MiraCosta. C. Besford, me, Kagami, Kato, and the TDL ambassador.

Our family at the Disneyland Window dedication ceremony, April 26, 2002. Kelly, Jim Jr., Bonnie, Rene, me, Josh, Mimi, and Kayleigh.

Kagami-San presented me with a replica of my window at Tokyo Disneyland. Only three Americans have received windows at World Bazaar: Walt Disney, Frank Wells, and me.

My daughter-in-law, Bonnie, and me, with Rene and my son-in-law, Kelly. More memories from the Grand Opening of Tokyo DisneySea.

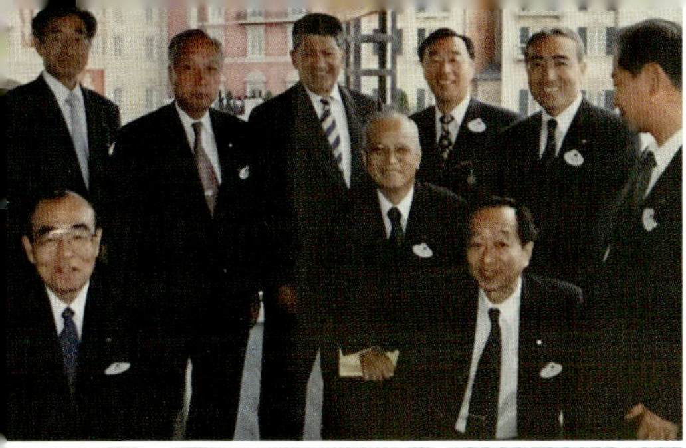

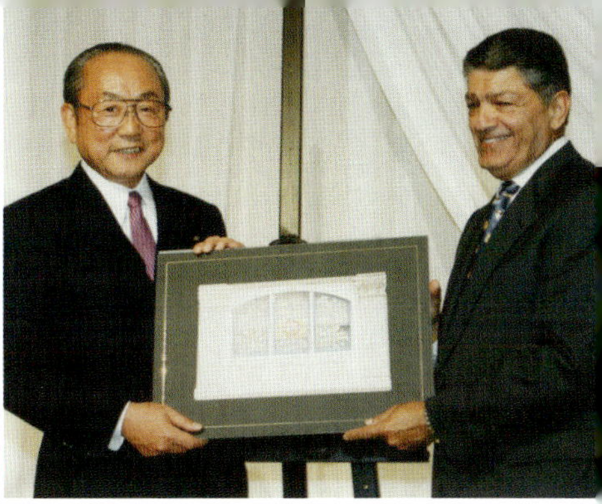

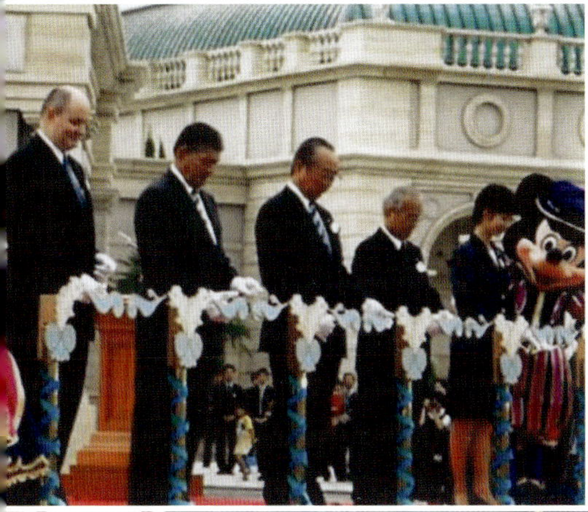

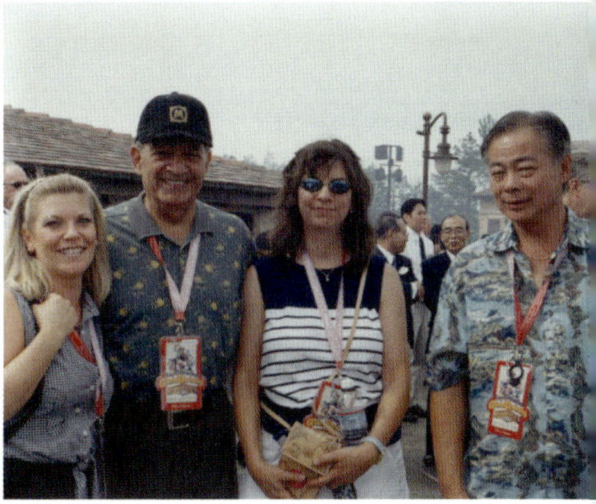

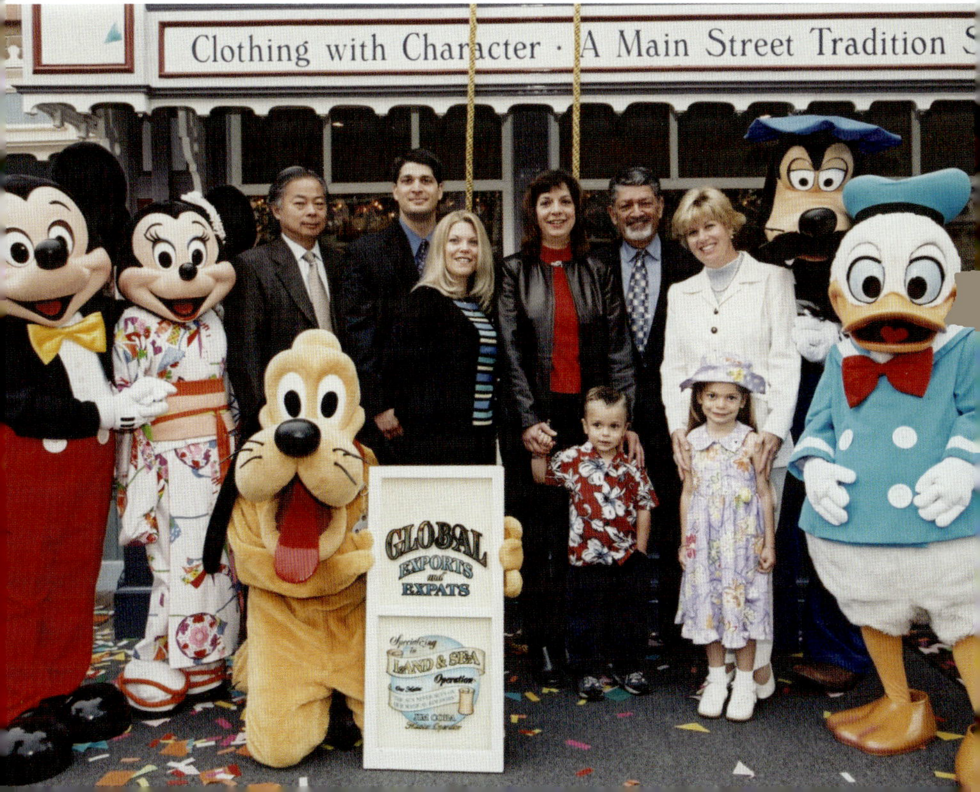

Clothing with Character · A Main Street Tradition S

A priority for a healthy retirement is spending quality time with your grandkids.

The tragic death of my daughter Michelle drove me to work to see that other families didn't suffer the same fate. I enjoyed my work as chairman of the Board of Trustees of St. Joseph's Hospital.

"Jim, you just recovered from open heart surgery—for a second time! What are you gonna do now?" "I'm going to Disneyland, of course"—for the 50th Anniversary celebrations with my dear Mimi.

Disneyland has always been a place for family. Here's mine, keeping an eye out so no one takes my window down.

The Board of Directors of St. Joseph Hospital signing the beam for the new patient tower constructed during my tenure as chairman.

A lot of people decline in their retirement because they think that it's appealing to "do nothing," but time spent with family is really good medicine.

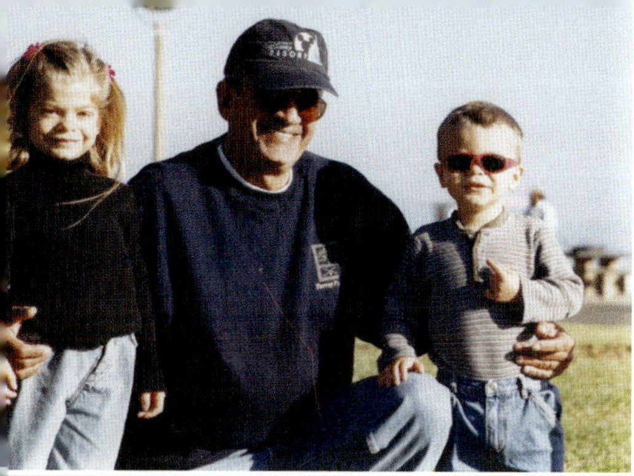

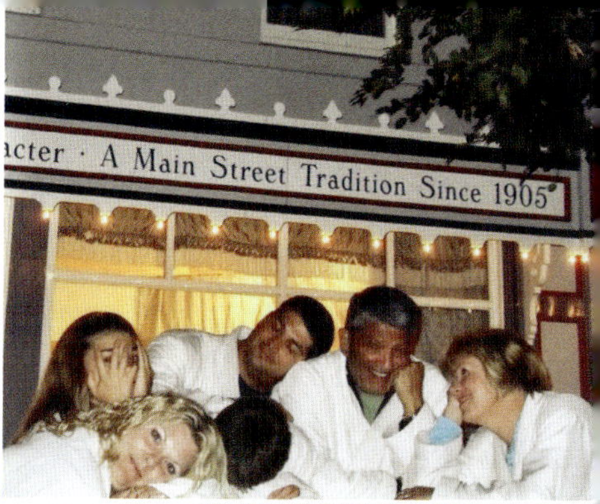
acter · A Main Street Tradition Since 1905

St. Joseph
Hospital

Herrick

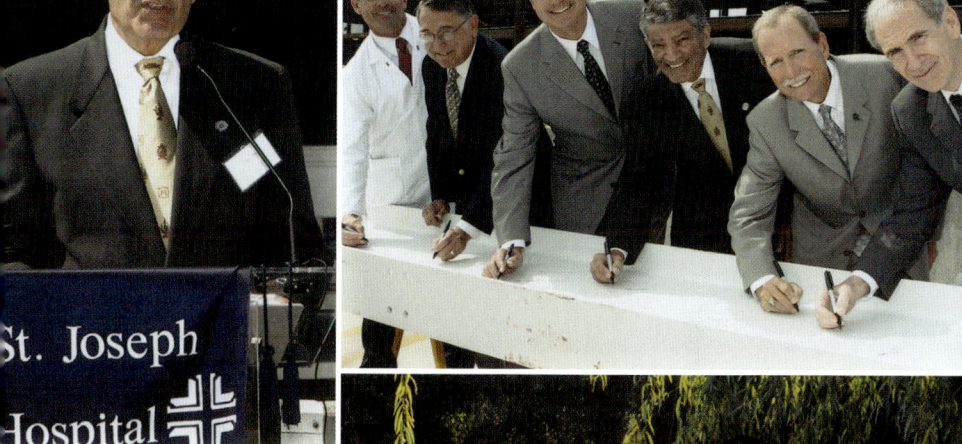

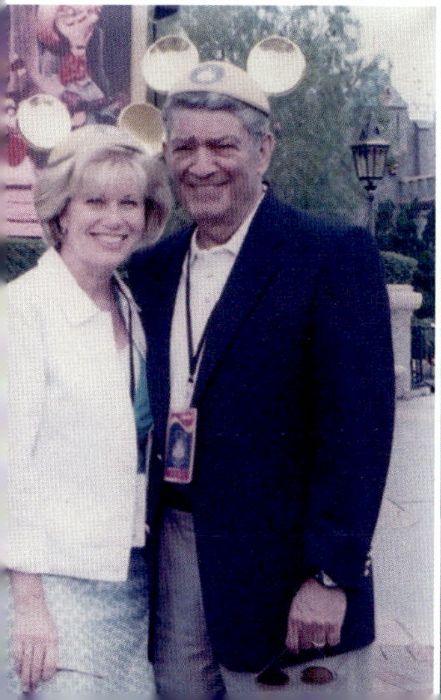

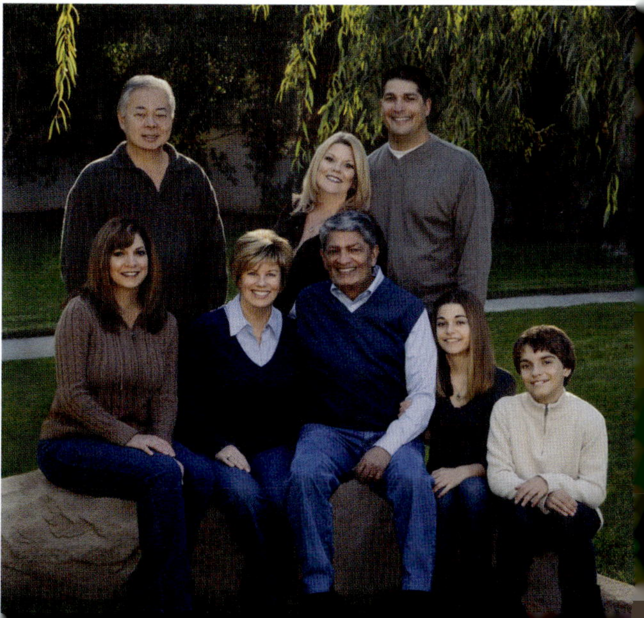

Old Disney guys: At Walt's Apartment on Main Street in 2015 for Disneyland's sixtieth. That's me, Ron Dominguez, Dick Nunis, and Marty Sklar.

Disney Legends gather during Disneyland's sixtieth birthday festivities in 2015.

D23 members gathered at The Walt Disney Studios on Friday, August 10, 2018, to have "Lunch with a Legend." I still have a little trouble believing that the legend is me.

Three generations of Car Loving Coras.

I typically find Disney fans generous. It's a culture of sharing. Disney fans tend to be my kind of people.

From the first days at Disneyland, we worked hard, and played hard. My model train setup is a relaxing hobby, and it's really fun to run with the kids of friends and relatives who visit.

In August 2018, many of those who worked on TDL, EDL, and TDS got together to share stories and lots of laughs. My co-author, Jeff Kurtti, was also with us, taking in all the historical truths and tall tales. Without this team and many others, our projects would never have gotten off the ground. I am forever grateful.

Our friends Colleen and Ray Casciari have shared many a Disney adventure with Mimi and me. Here we visit Walt's office at The Walt Disney Studios in Burbank.

During a visit to The Walt Disney Family Museum in 2018, we also had the privilege of spending time with Ron Miller. Ron and I enjoyed reminiscing about Retlaw, and those early days.

With Monsignor John Urell at the Gala Opening of the Christ Cathedral in Garden Grove, California, on July 17, 2019—a familiar date.

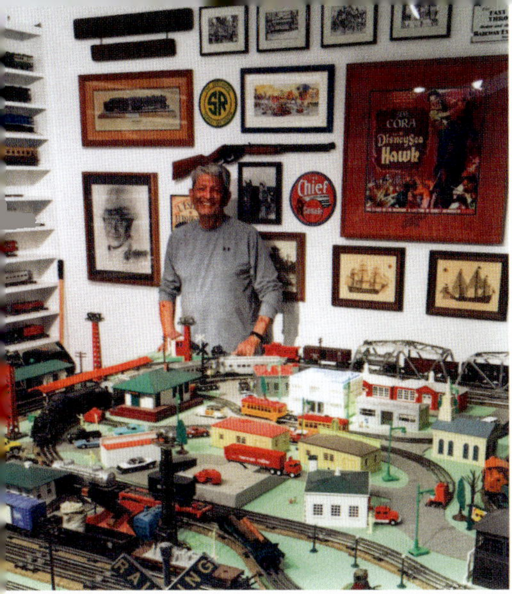
SR
CORA
DisneySea
Hawk
Chief

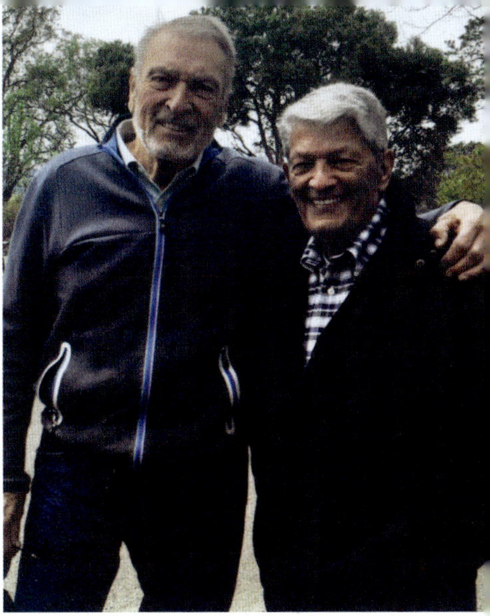

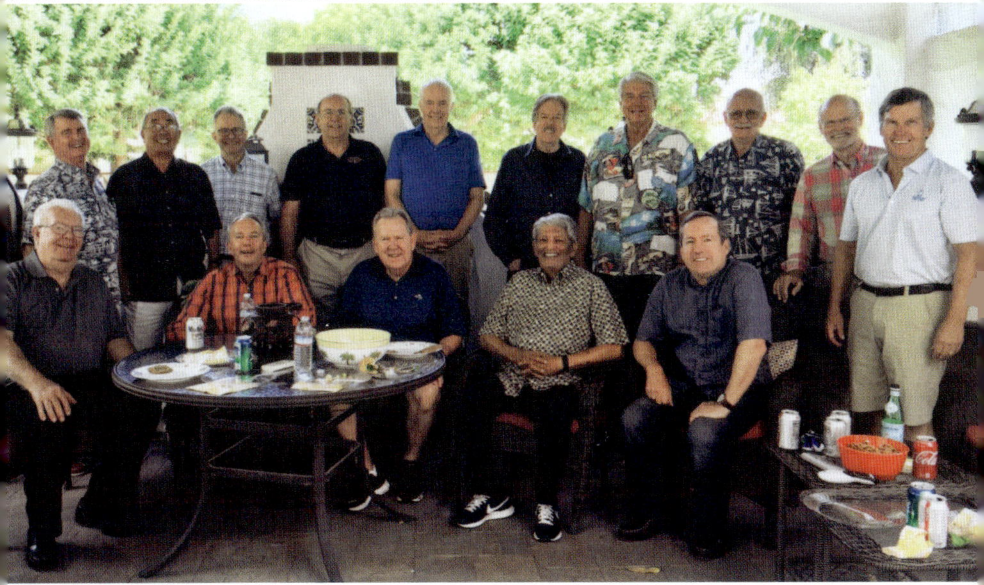

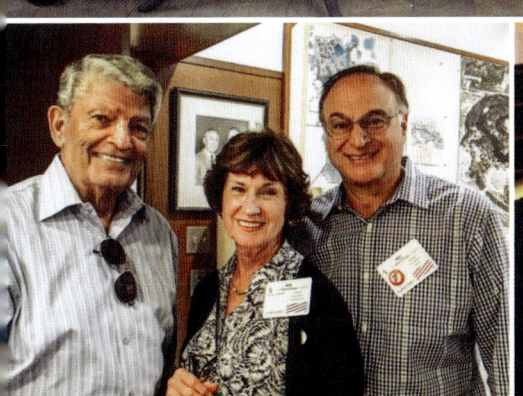

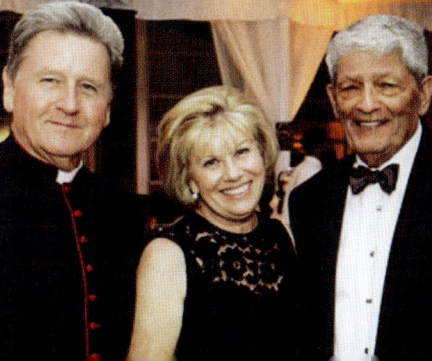

James B. Cora

Disney Legend

business- and social-practice conflicts, compromises, and lessons learned really pointed out to me so much of the intelligence, respect, and grace that is second nature to the Japanese. Our American culture and business expertise were admired, respected, and desirable attributes of ours to them. Our Disney culture brought experience and storytelling, and the bonding of community that "fit" almost seamlessly in Japan.

It all took a depth and consistency of collaboration, cooperation, understanding, education, and compromise that is rarely seen or experienced. We all wanted to succeed, we all wanted to make our projects in Japan shining successes, and examples to the world.

A Year of Lessons and Successes

That first year was, in retrospect, entertaining, educational, enlightening, maddening, hilarious, frustrating—and I think even more successful on so many levels than we could have imagined or wished for. We drew just slightly under the ten million Guests that we had projected—but we were never that short after that.

Part of that shortfall was my fault. Jack Lindquist and I had felt that this much-anticipated project, in reach of thirty-five million people within a two-and-a-half-hour radius by train or by car, would be overwhelmed by demand. We created a reservation system, just as you do for a hotel. We went to the Japan Travel Bureau, and they came up with a program. Unfortunately, at the time, nobody in Japan ever took days off from work or school just to come to a park.

We hadn't seen that, so Monday through Fridays, the place was just dead. On weekends, however, it was quite a different story, because that's when the travel agents were selling park entrance tickets, based on the recreational availability of the public. So that hurt us. We didn't hit the projections because we just weren't filling those Monday through Friday dates.

Unfortunately, the result of *that* was we got to a certain point on weekends where we'd impose attendance limits—I think it was forty-five thousand Guests that could be in the park at one time. We'd close the gates. No more people could come in. Our thinking based on capacity and square footage was that it was not safe and not a good show if more were let in, so we closed entryways.

It was something of a battle—they're so polite; people had come from afar and had to be turned away. They don't believe in turning people away, and that was really tough for all of us to monitor. (It was the same thing with restaurants. They'd let people come in, even though we had no tables for them, just to get them out of the sun, or to get them out of the rain. All the lobbies would be jammed, too—but you don't fight that. If the Guests are satisfied and they're still happy with it, then that's fine. We wouldn't do it at Disneyland, but that's a different culture.)

Unfortunately, the result of *that* was that the public thought we were sold out, because the word was out—you can't get a ticket. We kept checking Guest complaints. We started doing surveys every single day about the experience as it related to crowds, or waits, or services—and nobody ever complained about it, they were just happy to get in. I think based on that we eased our ceiling point and allowed up to forty-eight thousand in park attendance.

Celebration and Education

In order to raise our weekday population, and because in general, the Japanese would not miss school or workdays for a trip to a park, we started offering special group rates and opportunities for school groups and their teachers to come out to Tokyo Disneyland on weekdays. We then broadened that to school groups, teachers—*and* parents. Then we started picking certain towns and villages and creating "Celebration" days—a salute to Okinawa on this day; Hiroshima on this day, and so on. They would arrive by bus, or head to us via the train, and come out on those particular days. And then the word started getting around that you could go out any time. It also became an acceptable activity because they began recognizing something that us Disney guys had known a long time—Disneyland was a learning experience, and we helped educators blend a park visit with their school curriculum.

The Show Goes On Tomorrow

That first year reminded me of what the famous film director Frank Capra called "the catastrophe of success." However, for all the downside of the whole first year, we also had several tremendous triumphs, learned and invented new things, and flourished and grew. It became obvious to us that there was certainly justification for quickly getting more attractions online, and expanding things at Tokyo Disneyland.

On the tenth anniversary of Disneyland, Walt famously

admonished all of us not to rest on our laurels, that "the show goes on tomorrow" for an open-ended run, so to speak. We took that same attitude and opportunity to continue to develop Tokyo Disneyland, and start designing new attractions. We needed more capacity. We couldn't keep closing the park; that just led to lost revenue. And huge crowds at close to full capacity (however patient our Guests were) was not the optimal experience—it was bad public relations. And so WDI, our partners, began designing an expansion program, and we began planning for adding new attractions to the park.

In October 1983, just a few months after the opening, we began working with OLC making plans for new facilities and attractions, and contributing to their "first plan for new capital investment (FY 1983 to FY1987)." This became the primary master plan used as a basis for negotiations between OLC, Disney, and Chiba Prefecture.

The following year's highlights for the park were the introduction of the nighttime Tokyo Disneyland Electrical Parade and increasing attendance growth figures. The increase was due not only to the new parade, but also to the success of the Expo '85 World's Fair held in Tsukuba, Japan. According to research from the "Ripple Effect of Tokyo Disneyland on the Japanese Economy," issued by a third party in February 1986, the total production inducement figure of Tokyo Disneyland-related spending between April 1983 to March 1984 reached more than 1.48 trillion yen (which was equivalent to about $13 billion in 1984).

We also began negotiating at this time with OLC about constructing hotels (and convinced them that they should). The Tokyo Disneyland Official Hotel Program (now the Tokyo Disney Resort Official Hotel Program) was implemented in 1986. The first hotel under the program, the Sunroute Plaza Tokyo, opened July 20 of that year.

Satisfaction and Praise

Card Walker and I were in attendance to celebrate the first anniversary of Tokyo Disneyland. Card called me and a few others over at one point and said, "You guys, you did a great job, and I appreciate it; I didn't think it would go as well as it's gone. It looks great, and it operates great. Thank you very much."

Card then asked for a few minutes alone with me. We walked down World Bazaar for a while, reminiscing, and he said, "I just want to shake your hand. You all really made something happen over here—and you know I was opposed to it."

Oh, really? Were you, Card?

Home Again

I know it sounds like "20/20 hindsight," but as I said before, maybe I was just too naïve to believe we could be anything *other* than successful in Japan. I knew that I could build a team that would excel. I knew we would face challenges, but solving problems is a daily part of life. More than anything else, I just knew that the strength of *Disney* would elevate our identity and lead to success on a world stage.

We offer value. That's what we're all about—our audiences taking away something of meaning, physical, or spiritual, or educational. We provide a great story for a fair price.

We offer quality. We're clean, we're entertaining, we're consistent, and we're safe. It's not just our theme parks . . . it's publications, and products, and movies, everything that carries that Disney name.

We offer uniqueness, and a rich human element to all

of our experiences that speaks to people's individual and personal culture *throughout their lives.* That's a big responsibility, but the rewards are self-evident in the legacy of Disney.

For me personally, I'd had a long but rewarding time in the Land of the Rising Sun. I felt as if I'd prepared the soil well, and put down those grape vine shoots, and taught the people whose ongoing job would be tending to their health, and keeping them flourishing and bearing fruit.

But I already had my own vineyard back in California, and I was ready to go home to it.

Part Eight: European Tours

AFTER Tokyo Disneyland opened in April 1983, I stayed through a shakedown period, went home for Christmas, and then repatriated the following January. I returned to California and assumed the position of vice president, Disneyland International.

Susan, Michelle, and Jimmy had gone to Japan with me, but Rene had stayed at the house in Mission Viejo. (Rene was off to study at San Diego State University. Later, she was a vice president in New York for an automobile accessories company. She came back to Orange County, California, and for quite a while was in Special Events for Disney, at the El Capitan Theatre in Hollywood, and at Disneyland. She met her husband, Kelly, while managing events at the "El Cap," where he became the production manager for *Jimmy Kimmel Live.*)

I stuck pretty close to home for a while. There was just

a lot of maintenance and household things that I used to do that hadn't gotten done in a while. I spent a month or so painting and patching, reseeding and renovating, repairing and resettling—just getting back into a rhythm of homelife.

A Vine Withers

I have to admit, as happy as I was to be home, and to be together with the kids all in one place, the gulf between Susan and me had only grown wider, and hadn't lessened. To be clear, Susan was a committed and remarkable mother . . . and no doubt our children's successes are largely due to her influence—and presence. Relocating to Japan had been a hardship, for as interesting and fun as it was, there was, as you might expect, lots of disorientation and anxiety. Susan kept the kids on the straight and narrow, and was a godsend to the other expat spouses and families.

I know it sounds corny, or maybe even cold, but we'd simply married too young and had grown up into two very different people than what we *had* been. I felt selfish, and I felt guilty, but I just didn't know what to do about it—and like so many couples, I thought staying together and giving the kids a sense of stability was the most important thing. After several marriage counselling sessions, even the counselor thought we should be apart.

Sadly—and not unexpectedly—my marriage of more than twenty years was finally ending. It's not something I like to dwell on, or even talk about. That gets into all the territories of blame and regret and pain—rooms that are okay to enter if there are solutions or resolutions. But the whole truth is that, for many reasons, we simply did not make it as a couple anymore, and we did not have a marriage.

Susan and I began the paperwork and proceedings to get a divorce. I moved out of the house in Mission Viejo and found an apartment, and began my work and focus on researching in earnest the European market and Disney park prospects there.

Sometimes the shoot you plant takes root; sometimes they grow and thrive for a time, and then die—from bad soil, or neglect, or too much sun, or too little. There's a multitude of reasons a grape vine can flourish . . . or die. But no matter the cause, there are times the vine cannot be saved. It's then time to replant and begin again.

Disneyland International

I was still in charge of Disneyland International throughout this period. I had kept a core group on the team (that I couldn't let down): Ron Pogue, Steve Llewelling, Bill Gair, Lee Lanselle, Jack Myers, John McCoy, and a few others. We still had an ongoing follow-up to complete with the Oriental Land Company. We set up Disneyland International in the States to make sure we could support Japan with everything from sourcing assets to purchasing spare parts, liaising with Disney corporate and resources, and pushing ongoing training. Paricipants were working both at WDI and at Disneyland, learning new jobs at some of the lower levels that we hadn't focused on—and watching over other assignments. Support for the OLC was still the emphasis during that initial period after returning home. We began working on an "added capacity program," as we had to close the Tokyo park regularly due to popular demand and high attendance.

You've heard of postpartum depression and post-traumatic stress disorder, I'm sure. There was, for me, a kind of "post-project disorientation," a feeling of anxiety and unease, even though everything in Japan had been successful and satisfying. But my Disney career had been one of an ongoing evolution, of "going up the stairs." I don't think I was ever at my best when I was simply "maintaining" a department or a staff. I think being a "boss" was never as interesting to me as being a *leader*. I felt a need to keep growing, and keep a momentum on things we'd created and cultivated.

It was then I started thinking, *well, I've got this core team,* now *what do we do?* Dick Nunis and I talked, and he said, "You know, Walt always wanted to do something in Europe, and he had a love affair with Tivoli Gardens [in Copenhagen, Denmark]. He talked vaguely about doing something in Europe along the lines of a Disneyland, but he never described his ideas fully, or how, or where. Let's think about Europe, let's do some research."

Nothing is ever quite as satisfying to me as getting to plant some new shoots and see what vines will grow.

Storming the Magic Kingdom

Even with all the successes like the opening of EPCOT Center and Tokyo Disneyland, things were panicky and unsure within The Walt Disney Company. Disney's huge investment in capital-intensive projects had left it cash-poor and weak—thus ripe for predators. During my last days in Japan the Kirk Kerkorians of the world began making their runs at us. We were all told to tighten our belts and organize to lean efficiency to make us less attractive as a takeover object.

In 1984, financier Saul Steinberg's Reliance Group Holdings launched a hostile takeover bid for Walt Disney Productions, with the intent of selling it off in pieces. Disney bought out Reliance's 11.1 percent stake in the company, but another shareholder filed suit claiming the deal devalued Disney's stock. (That suit was finally settled in 1989 for a total of $45 million from Disney and Reliance.)

That same year, MCA (which was then the parent company of Universal Studios) actually struck a deal with Disney to buy the company—on the condition that Disney CEO Ron Miller be made MCA president. That condition didn't fly with MCA chairman Lew Wasserman, scuttling that arrangement.

In the aftermath of this, Roy Edward Disney (Walt's nephew and a powerful former member of the Disney Board) and his business partner, Stanley Gold, organized a group of "white knight" investors to fend off takeover attempts. This powerful consortium, including the Sid Bass family (owners of 18.7 percent of Disney), and the

Board, pushed for the removal of Ron Miller as CEO and president, as well as Raymond Watson as chairman, replacing them with Michael Eisner from Paramount, as CEO, and Frank Wells, from Warner Bros., as president.

The wonderful world of Disney was about to change in aggressive and drastic ways.

New Leadership

When Michael and Frank came in, there was, naturally, an initial fear of these "outside guys." Disney had been such a "family business" for so long, and our scale and intimacy didn't feel like a match for the larger and more bloodless world of Corporate America. Even on the New York Stock Exchange, it always felt like Disney was a friendly young cousin, and not really a grown-up at the big table.

With that fear, there were people leaving Disney, volunteering for early termination packages ("Let's get out before they fire us" thinking). In my opinion, the people who felt that way probably *should* have left. I wasn't really concerned about me—we'd just come off a successful project, why would they toss me out? At first I was a little worried that my *staff* didn't have enough visibility with

Frank and Michael, but as time went by, I took care of that. I set up my directors and vice presidents to meet with Frank, and to make presentations to Frank, on various aspects of the international business. Later, we had direct contact with Michael as well, especially at the Imagineering level.

I liked Michael a lot. He was an off-the-wall guy, not like any of the corporate people I'd ever seen; he'd be waving his arms and talking a hundred miles an hour about creativity and alliances and sponsorships, and bringing in different people from the outside. At Disney we'd always been pretty "inside-facing" for new projects and people.

Michael had made a huge name for himself beginning in television at NBC and CBS, and then in programming at ABC. (Eisner was a guy who saw great value in underused "real estate" like Saturday morning. He made ABC a leader in that segment and implemented other innovative programming in the early 1970s.) He went to Paramount Pictures afterward as president and CEO of the movie studio. Films such as *Saturday Night Fever, Grease,* the Star Trek film franchise, *Ordinary People, Raiders of the Lost Ark, An Officer and a Gentleman, Flashdance, Terms of Endearment, Beverly Hills Cop,* and *Footloose* were all part of his remarkable portfolio there. I wasn't sure who was going to be the driving force now—guys like Dick Nunis and Card Walker were hard-drivers, but you knew where you're going with them.

I liked Frank Wells a lot, too. He had worked for Warner Bros. as its West Coast vice president in 1969, and then in 1973 as its president, before rising in 1977 to vice chairman (until he left Warner Bros. in 1982). Frank was an avid "alpinist" and came close to achieving his goal of climbing the Seven Summits (the highest mountains on each of the seven continents!). I realized quickly that Frank was the stable "business" guy, and also kind of the "translator" for Michael. Frank could decipher and explain Michael's visions into more literal realities, and clearly share those ideas and plans about how to achieve them. He was also quite receptive, open, too—for once you laid things out for Frank, he got it. He became the interpreter *back* to Michael as to what we operational people were trying to do next.

Frank brought not only a *business* acumen to things, he was an excellent arbitrator and mediator. I guess his being a Rhodes scholar and a lawyer might have been a part of that. He made sure people didn't stab each other in the back; he would be the "conflict resolution" guy. If there was a problem, you just sat in front of Frank and told him what was going on. He'd help you correct it—or tell you to get out of his office, and go correct it yourself; that's what you get paid for. You always knew where you stood with Frank, and he'd simply help find the easiest route to get things done. Frank was a *big* influence in what we did.

Frank also trusted that I knew what I was doing, and would always come back to me and ask more detailed questions, and pretty much gave me a free hand to keep going. Michael and Frank spent a lot of time *learning*—especially in businesses they had no experience with or initially in. It may have been different on the film and television end of things, but they asked a lot of good questions and did a lot of listening about what was happening in the parks, especially at Disneyland. I appreciated that they were actually digging into the *culture* of Disney and seeing what made things tick, rather than bulldozing in with their own perceptions and ideas and making decisions before they *really* discussed things with veteran Disney people.

A lot of leadership is listening . . . and not just hearing. Hearing is physical. Listening is giving respect and credibility to what you're hearing, and finding a place for those ideas to dwell, by sharing your own experience, knowledge, and context.

Frank understood people pretty quickly, and I got to understand him. His image as a rigid attorney in wardrobe by Brooks Brothers hid a gentle humor and a humane good nature. I remember he called one morning, and wanted me to come up for a meeting at the studio midday that very day. Sheri, his executive assistant, called and asked what I wanted for lunch, since it would just be Frank and me in Frank's office.

"Oh, I don't care, anything is fine."

Sheri said, "Well, I've got to order something."

I joked, "How about pizza and a beer?"

I got there and found a pizza and a beer sitting on the coffee table in Frank's office. Frank came in and found a prim little salad that was perched next to my lunch.

"Holy smoke, who ordered a pizza and beer?"

Sheepishly, I said, "It was me, Frank," and I was about to tell him I was just joking with Sheri, when he interjected.

"That really looks great, can I share it with you?"

So the president of The Walt Disney Company and I sat in his office, and had pizza and beer together. Boy, was my life interesting.

"You want part of my salad?"

"No thanks, Frank, I'm good."

What's Next?

Through all the corporate crises, I had kept an eye on Dick's instruction to "look at Europe." Chuck Cobb was just coming on board, leading the Disney Development Company, which had been formed to coordinate master planning, development, and asset management of all of Disney's real estate "outside the berm." I met with him and his team, and they were working on doing some research in Europe that coincided in type and scale with the research we'd done in Asia. Of course, now that Tokyo Disneyland was under our belt, requests came pouring in from countries around the world, wanting a Disney park.

An International Family

The Disneyland International (DLI) market research team we assembled included Jack Myers, who had overseen marketing in Japan, and Kurt Haunfelner and Roberta Nedry. Anne Okey and Mimi Schaaf worked on reports and presentations. Shannon Lee and Nadine Felipe supported the effort. Sylvie Laffarge worked as a translator. Steven Rhinesmith and David Kanally looked at cultural aspects. Tom Eastman helped manage the effort. In

Florida, Eddie Carpenter relied on Dianne Marcum, his head of research, for analysis and financial modeling.

Since I was a "bachelor" again, or at least living like one, my DLI team also became more of a social circle as well. They gave me a sense of stability and community—we worked well together, and had fun together, too. We'd share meals, and go to screenings and events, and play softball and tennis at Tennisland, carrying on the tradition we'd started with the TDL teams.

During this time I got to be particular friends with Mimi Schaaf. She had shown herself to be a creative and accomplished member of Jack Lindquist's marketing division, where she had made several of Jack's seemingly wild ideas, such as Disney Dollars and the Children's Miracle Network Telethon broadcast live from Disneyland, come to practical reality. She had a gentle nature and a sunny disposition—she's a fine artist, and has that soul and spirit. But she was also a realist and a fearless straight shooter. I just liked her. When Mimi was around, I simply felt better.

Why Europe?

Something the Disney Development Company (DDC) had in addition to expertise in real estate and its attendant functions was a great AV/media department. DDC helped my team put together a video presentation called *Why Europe?* It talked about the countries in Europe that liked Disney a lot, based on film sales, consumer products, publications, and TV presence. The two that stood out most were Spain and France. But we also looked at England, Germany, and Italy as potential sites, and narrowed it down in this presentation to two leading candidates. We still laid out all the data, presenting the reasons why Disney should establish a resort *somewhere* in Europe.

We put together a slam-bang presentation, and printed corresponding booklets that contained additional text and data—the "leave behind," as they typically call these documents now (but in the old days called "Kirby Books," named after the posh brochures the door-to-door vacuum cleaner salesmen would carry). Dick and I went up to the studio to see Michael and Frank. We had copies of the *Why Europe?* video in both VHS and beta, our booklets, and a full carousel slide show. We were locked, loaded, and ready . . . and made the pitch like the most informed, erudite, sincere, and enthusiastic Kirby sales team you ever saw.

Frank listened attentively and simply said, "Well, it looks like a no-brainer to me. What do you think, Michael?"

"I agree, it's a no-brainer."

And that was the end of the meeting.

As we parted, Frank Wells added, "Oh, Frank Stanek [who had come back from Tokyo and had been appointed as Disney's first corporate vice president of Strategic Planning] is also working on going to Europe with a team." Dick and I both admitted that we didn't know, a little embarrassed that it might appear that the left hand didn't know what the right hand was doing. But again, Frank waved away our anxiety and simply and logically said, "Why don't you guys just work together?"

Frank Stanek, it turns out, had engaged consultants (ERA and John Robinett; Bourdais Associés with Jean-Paul Loevenbruck) and Disney executives in Europe, including Gus Zelnick in London. They were working on research analyses that covered the United Kingdom, Belgium, the Netherlands, Germany, Switzerland, Italy, France, and Spain. Luckily, all the efforts complemented each other, so the blending of the two teams worked rather well.

Site Scouting

Frank Wells asked me a lot of detailed questions about how Tokyo had come together. How did we get it going?

Who was in charge of negotiations? What were the key lessons we learned?

He asked my thoughts on things we were looking for in Europe. Was it mostly infrastructure? Was free land imperative? What incentives made sense? I told him what I knew, and what I believed in. He asked bluntly if I thought we'd be successful if we went to Paris. I said, "I think we'll be successful wherever we go, but I don't know if Paris is better than any other place." At that time, I'd never been to Europe, so I didn't really have an opinion. Frank said, "Well, you've got to go."

So away we went, and we flew everywhere: France, Spain, Germany, England, Italy. Frank Stanek and I actually went to Italy by ourselves, and determined pretty quickly that it was too hilly. There wasn't a big enough, flat enough piece of ground, and they probably would not be able to give us the incentives we wanted—and we were looking for a lot of incentives. So the countries that came out on top were France and Spain. Particularly the latter's Barcelona region; the Catalonians were great to work with. (However, the Basque separatists were not so enthusiastic, and blew up a palm tree outside our hotel to send us a warning while we were there. Dick and I were staying at a local hotel. We decided to leave and return another time.)

Following Frank Wells's announcement at the shareholders' meeting in Anaheim that Disney had narrowed down the search for a European park site to Spain and France, a Disney delegation left to meet with officials in both nations; the delegation for the initial trip was Frank Stanek, Wing Chao from WDI, Disney government relations man Bill O'Toole, and Lee Lanselle. Outside counsel in France—especially Jean-Pierre Duclos, Magali Thorne, and Bill Brown (of Donovan Leisure Newton & Irvine)—assisted with legal analysis.

I leaned toward Spain, as did Dick Nunis. It was more like Southern California—the climate, weather, geography—everything. The Barcelona Summer Olympics hadn't happened yet, and there was talk that they could turn all that infrastructure over to Disney—which would have been a big jump ahead. But the return on investment wasn't as quick as it would be in France.

When we came back, we met with Frank and Michael. We voted for Spain. But Michael really wanted to go to Paris. He liked the sophistication of going to Paris. I said, "Well, Michael, why don't we take a vote?" The whole group raised their hands for Spain.

Michael raised his hand for France.

I said, "Well, I guess we lose; I guess we're going to France."

Michael said, "That's right."

Sometimes democracy within the Disney company has its limits.

Michael signed the first letter of agreement with the French government for the site on December 18, 1985, and the first financial contracts were drawn up the following spring. (In hindsight, the competition with Paris for overnight hotel stays was a huge hurdle to our success in the beginning, and led to conference and convention space being added to the project later.)

Envisioning a Disney "New Town"

This European endeavor was the beneficiary of decades of cumulative experience from Anaheim to Orlando to Tokyo, and back again. The lessons of each of those projects fed into all of the thinking of what was at first called "Euro Disneyland" (EDL).

I fought to name it Euro Disneyland, so that it wasn't just perceived as being only for the French. As the market research was indicating, not everybody in Europe loves the

French, and I thought the name "Euro Disneyland" sent an important message. There were a lot of long debates with Michael Eisner and his staff, and the executives at corporate. They wanted to call it "Disneyland Paris." Their argument: "We called the Disneyland in Tokyo Tokyo Disneyland, so why not?" I just kept repeating, this is for *Europe*, we want Europeans to come. I won that battle, but lost the war. After opening, they changed it anyway, as they did with the ban on alcohol sales within the berm. (I still get emails today that say, "You can call it Disneyland Paris if you want, but it'll always be Euro Disneyland to me.")

One lesson that went all the way back to Walt for me was the desire for a property that far exceeded the immediate needs of a park and resort amenities. That's not just room for expansions, but also the ability to maintain *Disney Guest Standards*. It's well-known that Walt lamented his inability to buy more peripheral land around Disneyland, and hated the "second-rate Las Vegas" (his phrase) of motels and gas stations and fast food that grew like weeds all around the Disneyland borders. In Florida, "the blessing of size" (again, his phrase) guaranteed not only enough land for his ambitious dreams, but a way, like any good show, to bring the audience in to an enveloping experience, where we controlled the story.

Outside of Paris, there were large tracts of undeveloped land that were known as "new town" sites. Recognizing the potential of the future growth of urban Paris, the Paris Region Planning and Development Agency had begun in 1960 to identify growth locations, each capable of absorbing a population of half a million people, with an infrastructure design including an express rail network and five hundred miles of new roads. Presented and issued in 1975, the Master Plan from the agency called for the setting up of five "new towns": Cergy-Pontoise, Saint-Quentinen-Yvelines, Evry, Senart, and Marne-la-Vallée.

The French government agreed to sell 5,510 acres in Marne-la-Vallée to Disney, provided that the majority of it was developed in harmony with its stated vision. The land, which was originally home to farms and beet fields, lies to the east of metropolitan Paris, which gave it a huge "catchment" area—the area from which a city, service, or institution attracts a population that uses its resources. An estimated 109 million potential visitors lived within a six-hour motor radius of the projected resort's locale. There are direct entry roads to the main A4 motorway, putting central Paris less than an hour away by car. The French also agreed to extend the RER and Metro and to connect France's high-speed train network directly to the gates of the resort by 1994. A transit tunnel between England and France beneath the English Channel was also scheduled to begin construction in 1988. (The "Chunnel" was completed in 1994, bringing Guests to the resort from London in about three hours.)

In addition, the French were offering the land at well below market prices, as well as providing generous long-term credit from state-owned banks.

New Game, New Players

Thankfully, Frank and Michael decided to divide the EDL team's responsibilities up. I would focus on the theme park infrastructure and the hotel infrastructure, and negotiate all the issues it would take to support our project, and be responsible for the coordination of each entity's effort. They asked Joe Shapiro, The Walt Disney Company's general counsel, to come in and actually do the project contract with the French government. Joe had rebuilt Disney's entire legal department; he had a brilliant mind both for the law and for business.

Joe brought in a team of bright lawyers to work on it, and I sat through all of those meetings, as did Lee Lanselle and Bill Gair. They seemed to just go on and on . . .

and on, for a long time. (The legal team referred to those of us that were staying on to manage the project as "Poor Devils," and they were being very careful to check with the "client"—us—before agreeing to anything.)

Phillipe Bourguignon, under Peter Rummell at DDC, would manage construction for the hotels and Festival Disney. The outside financing and initial public offering for the project became the domain of Walt Disney Company vice president and treasurer John Forsgren, who later became the CFO for Euro Disney.

This was a big-stakes project for a company that had quickly gone from a family "boutique" to an international financial powerhouse—a *whole* different game from Tokyo, based on Disney's ownership status, and without the buffer in financial, governmental, and political issues that OLC provided. I found myself in very different situations, with very different issues, with very different kinds of players. We arranged a site tour for various Disney executives of course. That initial delegation included Frank Wells, CFO Gary Wilson, Chuck Cobb from DDC, Dick Nunis, Eddie Carpenter, and Lee Lanselle.

The Bass brothers (Texas oil heirs and investors, and the largest shareholders in Disney from 1984 until after the stock market crash in 2001) got involved. Eddie Carpenter and I met with the Bass Brothers' "dealmaker," Richard Rainwater, to review the financials for the project, and he thought the *pro forma* looked great. At some point the asset management and investment firm Lazard got involved. I remember meeting managing partner François de Combret. Business Affairs became the purview of Joe Shapiro. Peter Rummell arrived on the scene in 1985 as the new head of DDC, along with Bob Rhodes, who had become senior vice president and general counsel at DDC when the real estate company Arvida was acquired by Disney.

Everybody on this long roster of players was needed, for it quickly became apparent that the Euro Disneyland project required skills we didn't have at DLI. Luckily, I had a few things going for me, personally—I had a skill set that was transferable, and I'm a pretty smart guy . . . and a quick study. Plus, I am just humble enough to know where my skill set ends and that I need good associates; I had the trust of the key executives in Burbank—and those executives had an understanding and appreciation of the core Disney values that I'd spent a career learning, teaching, and disseminating through my work.

We were negotiating directly with the French government, but that government kept changing. When the government changed, that representative went away, and we'd have to start all over again, with a new representative and a learning curve. We would lose time every time "change" took place.

In California, I was living a bachelor's existence, and in France I resided in and out of a hotel room for almost three years, during this negotiating-process phase. I stayed the whole time as the negotiating teams came and went, as the government kept changing. Still, I thought if I *didn't* put a stake in the ground, and stay there and continue to hang on to the project, there wasn't going to *be* a project.

I was making new friends, and building a team that could go on to support us, if and when the contract was signed. But I was sure missing my home, even if my daughters would come to visit me in France periodically. (I also remained good friends with Mimi Schaaf. She and I began to form a personal bond that was very close. We saw each other when our schedules crossed in California or Paris, and kept in touch by what are "now-antiquated" methods, like handwritten notes and international long-distance phone calls. Mimi was one of those special souls that could always lighten my burdens and lift my spirits.)

We worked with a group established by the French government, called EPA France, a public corporation for territorial development, whose mission was to perform all the necessary acquisition and infrastructure operations (planning, programming), finance functions, and coordinated with local and regional governments and leadership. We brought Bill Gair over to direct facilities management; he transferred over from the Tokyo project. Bill really goes back even further than that—he was chief engineer at Disneyland, so he had quite a history working on various Disney projects. With his engineering background and experience, Bill worked with the EPA on primary, secondary, and tertiary infrastructure from the very beginning. We had to provide and anticipate electrical demands, water demands, utilities scope, sewers, and retention basins—all the things you do to operate a huge resort. (Bill later became vice president of Maintenance, Landscaping, and Construction for the project.)

Bill was the liaison for all of that; he found the information, got it from the people that knew it, and negotiated with the EPA. (Bill was actually in the EPA offices, which was in a separate locale from the EDL project field office.) *That* part of the government didn't change—the EPA stayed locally, just the way it was.

But we still didn't have a final signed contract—the government just kept changing. But we just hung in there and kept talking to them.

Some things were moving . . . incrementally. They were going to remove high-tension wires from the property and put them underground. Government reps said it would cost Disney $4 million to do that. I thought it was a good price, and so we removed them. I know when Disneyland put their wires underground it was $7 million. So I thought, "This is fine." I found out much later that in a "new town development," *they* are supposed to provide that service—free of charge. (I remember Phillipe Bourguignon saying that if the French took advantage by *not* telling me that, it was not their fault—it was mine. A lesson learned for the future.)

We had a problem with submission procedures for the contractor bids. Paul Seramy, the regional president of Île-de-France insisted he would open all the bids. I said, "Fine, we'll have a representative there with you." He said, "No, I'll open them by myself, and I will decide what contracts will be awarded to whom"—and he stuck to that. I wasn't sure that was ethical by our standards, and it ran totally against how DLI would operate. But on the other hand, we didn't have a dog in that fight. It had to be done according to our specs . . . and as long as it was done to our specs, then I didn't much care how much the French paid for it! We weren't paying for it. On the other hand, we did have to pay for tertiary infrastructure—all the little roadways *inside* the park and the resort. And those bidding processes we *were* involved in. So fair is fair, that was that—some things are just cultural, and you don't fight with them.

Ultimately, after much negotiation, the final contract to develop a European Disney resort was signed by the leaders of The Walt Disney Company and the French government (and territorial collectivities) on March 24, 1987.

This could not have been accomplished without Lee Lanselle's legal coordination, Bill Gair's input, and Joe Shapiro's legal team. Lee Lanselle was especially critical to the success of this process, providing detailed minutes of each day's decisions, commitments, and pending issues. They were slipped under our hotel doors during the night to prepare for the next day's meetings. We didn't know if he ever slept, but he was always prepared and kept us on track. At the Michael Eisner dinner celebrating the signing, I had to grab Lee by the collar when he almost face-planted into his soup. He was so exhausted; he was falling asleep. I took him outside and sent him home in a cab.

At this point, I was also promoted to executive vice president and chief operating officer for the Euro Disneyland Corporation.

Cultural Resistance

The business and political culture was certainly different from my experience in Japan, but not unexpected. We were the "owner company" now, and there was no OLC embedded in the project for so much of the liaison and relationship work on the business end. What was surprising to me to find was my first experience where a Disney presence was *unwanted* by a vocal element at the host site.

In Japan, of course, our directive from our hosts was to bring pure, unadulterated "Disney" to them. They recognized that our culture was distinct and strong and positive, and contained values of craft and quality and optimism and aspiration that were positive and desirable. But not so in France, however. The French prize academics and philosophy, aesthetics, and rigorous rationality—and in my experience, feel that they *own* absolute authority in all matters intellectual, cultural, and creative.

That's fine, I understand that. The proof to me was inherent in the successes of Anaheim, Orlando, and Tokyo. I will say, however, that the French attitude carries with it an almost comic intellectual snobbery—many of the French who rolled their eyes and threw up their hands at an inferior, fake, plastic, consumer-based Disney coming to their shores hadn't really bothered to examine Disney as either a public or corporate culture with any of the philosophical or intellectual depth they claimed to possess.

French theater director Ariane Mnouchkine famously reacted to Euro Disney (without any information about it or understanding of our project) by calling it "a cultural Chernobyl," an assessment that quickly became a catchphrase—mostly for people with only a superficial understanding of what we were doing, who we were, and our previous efforts—and successes! (She later tried to backpedal from this remark, claiming it was something said "privately." But that disingenuous deflection didn't *un*-ring the bell.)

A Cultural Figurehead

But this vocal criticism wasn't lost on Michael and Frank. Without a strong, respected, and "culturally embedded" leadership presence that was supportive of the Euro Disney project, we *did* have a missing element that we may have taken for granted in Japan—both from the innate strengths of OLC, and from any lack of "cultural resistance" we found in Tokyo. (We also relied on Japanese nationals in both Disney Consumer Products and the film distribution areas, and transferred over a former Japanese national, Hideo Amemiya, as director of administration in Tokyo.)

Michael and Frank set about to address a desire for a sort of "cultural attaché" and credible "philosophical" leader for the Euro Disney project—someone who could take the projects into the pressrooms and boardrooms and bureaus and salons of Europe, and represent the Disney intentions in a way that would make the "Disney pill" easier to swallow for a stubborn crowd. That person surely wasn't me. I didn't speak French, and had no deep understanding of the culture there, relying instead on the expertise of others that I could surround myself with. I had the "real" work of the project to do, too, the elements that called on the expertise and background and skills I *did* possess. At this point, Dick Nunis left his direct involvement in the project.

It was Roy E. Disney who responded to this pressing need. He brought in a candidate for this role to Michael and Frank: Robert J. Fitzpatrick, then-president of the California Institute of the Arts (CalArts), the arts college that Walt had founded, and Roy E. served on as a board member. (I also think much of this decision had to do with Michael and Frank's respect for and gratitude to Roy for having brought them into Disney leadership.)

Fitzpatrick was an interesting and seemingly credible choice for such a role. In 1972, he was elected as Baltimore's youngest city council member, while also serving as a professor of medieval French literature and dean of students at Johns Hopkins University. He was a lifelong Francophile, and claimed to have been awarded medals for cultural achievements from the French government. *Time* magazine named him one of its "200 Faces for the Future" in 1974.

In 1975, Fitzpatrick was appointed president of CalArts, and while in that role he also served as the director of the 1984 Olympic Arts Festival in Los Angeles. Even after being appointed to the EDL project, Fitzpatrick remained the director of the Los Angeles Festival, which had grown directly out of the 1984 Olympics festival.

"Bob Fitzpatrick brings to his new position a wide background in the arts and entertainment, as well as a thorough knowledge of France and the French culture," Michael Eisner said. "In the years I have known him through Disney's association with CalArts, I have found Bob to be a tireless worker for civic, educational, and cultural causes and a person of outstanding managerial ability."

Michael's comments and tone were optimistic, in my opinion. Fitzpatrick was fluent in French . . . and that was important. He also did have a deep academic understanding of French history, politics, and culture. He was a strong public speaker.

But Fitzpatrick did not really understand what it took to build or run a theme park or resort. Due to that and other issues regarding team effort, I felt he just did not mix well with the on-site and corporate support groups.

For the most part, Bob was pretty much enamored with the press and publicity given the project, and how many times he could be in the newspapers or on the radio or television . . . but not so much enamored with Disney. I never got the feeling that he was really a "Disney guy." His interest was mostly in the office and its trappings. He rarely, if ever, brought that "outstanding managerial ability" to anything substantially related to the creation of the project. Although he was named CEO of Euro Disney, I never found in him any of the skills or behaviors I had admired in other leaders.

Walt Disney said about all of us, "We work hard, but we play hard." My day used to start early in the morning, and it would end at night most often in some restaurant, talking to the team *again* about what we had to do the next day or for that week—the milestones and key activities that needed to be done. We never stopped.

I was not alone when it came to being committed to this work ethic; the core group of Disney management people worked under the same principles. It was difficult at times for some of the Europeans to understand or accept this practice. For the expats it was like more of a religion than it was a job. It was core to my professional identity and doctrine, one that went back to my childhood in the general store.

That wasn't Fitzpatrick's way of operating, and he frequently showed an annoying lack of curiosity about what made things tick. Early in the planning process, he simply stopped showing up to staff meetings. He was arrogant in his opinions about things in which he had no experience. He showed zero loyalty to our employees, and a tone deafness to what makes a true leader of others. (I remember when we had to cancel Christmas vacations for everybody in anticipation of the April opening, and he came down to our staff meeting with a travel bag over his shoulder and said, "Well, I'll see you in two weeks," and he went on his Christmas vacation.) He was neither generous nor a team player. In many ways, he made my job much tougher.

I was told by Frank and Michael, "You report to us, and don't worry about this"—and so I didn't. A lot of conflicts came up *because* I didn't worry about it, and Fitzpatrick *knew* that was the relationship. For the most part, I just tried my best to face forward, and do my job in the way that had proved successful before. Sometimes on a job site you find an annoying and inefficient anomaly such as a sinkhole or a rock outcropping, some impediment you simply have to work around. So we just kind of worked separately and parallel. He did his thing, and I tried to keep him posted on how the project was progressing.

One of my favorite Disney animated films has always been *Bambi*. In one famous scene, Thumper's mom responds to her son's complaints, scolding:

"What did your father tell you this morning?"

"If you can't say something nice, don't say nothin' at all."

And there ends my discussion of this subject.

Recruitment and Team-Building

Key players for the Tokyo park ended up in key positions for Euro Disneyland. Bill Gair, Jack Myers, and Steve Lewelling were a few of them; we added Thor Degelmann, as well, to the European mix—he had worked for me briefly in Walt Disney World at its opening, and had a hotel background. Lee Lanselle was another person who came over from the Tokyo project team. All of them began interviewing local people in Europe to help us fill positions. Mel Cecil, formerly director of Maintenance and Construction at Disneyland, came on board because I needed someone to "bird dog," to pick up maintenance, construction, and other jobs that weren't getting done. He kept up with the running "punch list."

The decision had been made to hire most of the people to support EDL from Walt Disney World, as opposed to Disneyland, where most of the people for Tokyo came from. This was mainly just the logistics of geography. So I also had a DLI office in Florida. Tom Eastman ran that office. He was very supportive in finding people to relocate and come support us. (He had also done a great job helping us put together the plan for Tokyo Disneyland, manpower-wise.)

Debbie Farquhar, one of my secretaries, relocated and became staff assistant. She was tough as nails and a great friend. Helen Ouseroff became my secretary in France. She had started out working for Bob Fitzpatrick, but hated it. I think he rankled her innate sense of professionalism. She asked if she could come work for me. She is half Lebanese, and half Russian. And not only is she really tough, she is fluent in English, French, Russian, and Lebanese, plus she could dictate and translate in all those languages. What a fantastic find she was, just a jewel.

International Disney Support

We found a great extended team in Disney offices throughout Europe, people who were ready and able to support our project, assisting with personnel candidates and HR issues, as well as the nuances of politics, culture, and Guest expectation not just in France, but throughout our catchment area.

This remarkable expert network included Antonio Bertini, president of Walt Disney Creations S.p.A. in Italy; veteran Disney Consumer Products executive Horst Koblischek in Germany; and Keith Bales, a consumer products executive in England. At the more local level to the project we had the president of The Walt Disney Company (in France), Pierre Sissman, and the support and strength of the legendary Armand Bigle (often called "Disney's Godfather of Europe"). Bigle had met Walt and Roy O. in 1946, and was a foundational force in establishing

Disney merchandise and publishing enterprises worldwide in Russia, Switzerland, Italy, Germany, Spain, Portugal, Yugoslavia, Greece, Israel (and other countries in the Middle East), Indonesia, and the Benelux countries. Dennis Hightower, then the newly appointed president of Disney Consumer Products for Europe, Middle East and Africa, and based in Paris, was a godsend.

Jack Myers and the EDL research team were also able to use this network to obtain the most accurate demographics for their local markets: marketing data, consumer product sales, film distribution and grosses, population statistics, local tourism connections and data, amusement competitors data. Even governmental connections for site tours and introductions to tourism ministers were set up by this resourceful team.

Finance

The toughest role to fill was finance. Eddie Carpenter was our first choice; he was part of the negotiating team at the beginning, but he didn't want to relocate. Frank Wells started looking for people, and found Judson Green at Walt Disney World. He was the CFO for the resort and hotel division, so Judson came over to Euro Disneyland as

CFO—but on the condition that he report directly to the president. I was used to getting financial reports on a daily basis. But as things developed and became more complicated, I couldn't get financial reports and the system just wasn't set up to provide them.

I brought Bob Risteen over, who was director of finance at Disneyland, and he worked on it, but he also got bogged down; I still wasn't getting reports, so I didn't know what we were spending. I know that when Frank would ask for a financial-status report, Judson would provide something, a monthly revenues statement. I don't know where it came from, and I didn't see it before Frank saw it. We were honestly both so overwhelmed by the magnitude of what we were doing, I don't think that was his focus. (They ultimately took Judson out of the process, and he became the CFO for The Walt Disney Company and later took charge of Walt Disney Attractions. Judson then completely changed careers; he returned to his roots in music and became a renowned jazz pianist, using jazz as a platform to entertain and teach lessons on leadership and creativity.)

John Forsgren, who oversaw Euro Disneyland's initial public stock offering in 1989, took over the job as CFO of EDL. (The IPO was another major project being organized during construction, so I would occasionally be torn away for the banking, investor, and analysts' meetings throughout Europe and Asia, trying to finance Euro Disneyland.)

Vacation Destination

Construction began in August 1988, and the job before me and my team was enormous. Euro Disneyland was certainly the most ambitious initial development in the history of Disney. We were overseeing the development of a full-scale, 140-acre Magic Kingdom-style park that would hold six hotels collectively housing six thousand rooms; "Festival Disney" (now Disney Village), a 190,000-square-foot shopping, dining, and entertainment complex; an eighteen-hole golf course; and Camp Davy Crockett (now Davy Crockett Ranch), a 140-acre, 595-cabin "campground" including a restaurant, swimming pool, shop, bar, tennis court, and a complete Wild West arena show and amphitheater.

The Ever-Inflating Balloon

Little by little, day after day, almost invisibly, my workload and scope of responsibility increased. There was a fight between Dick Nunis and Bob Fitzpatrick (which Frank Wells tried to arbitrate) that I should give up Tokyo Disneyland so I could focus 100 percent on EDL. Honestly, I was okay with that, I was happy to leave Ron Pogue in charge, but Dick wouldn't give in. Frank finally just said, "Cora, you got 'em both, whether you like it or not." I was the sacrifice to keep peace in the family, so I kept it. Ron did an excellent job keeping the ship straight, advising OLC what needed to be done next at Tokyo Disneyland and how to get it done. He met a lot of people in the company who could pull the strings to get what we needed. Sometimes in those days he had to beg, borrow, and steal to get stuff. He was well supported by Frank Wells, Disney management, as well as the TDL rank and file. But he did a superb job, and he continued in that role all the way to his retirement.

Resort Hotels

Fortunately, one big headache was removed from my plate pretty early on. The resort hotels were truly ambitious in scope for opening day. This was during a period when Michael Eisner collected prominent celebrity architects. He was very intent on bringing this talent into the

Disney fold, and commissioning our important buildings with them; the prestige was important to him. I heard one person joke that Michael was "The Medici of the Mouse." Gary Wilson, Disney's CFO at that time (he had come from Marriott), was also pushing Michael to create a competition of "world-class architects."

Wing Chao, at Walt Disney Imagineering, organized an "architect brain trust" to breathe some fresh air into the resort center concepts. The initial design had been created by a development consulting firm that specialized in suburban town planning. Architect Robert A. M. Stern saw these designs and felt that they looked like a subdivision in Orange County, California. He thought we could do better than what he saw as "an American subdivision in the French countryside." Wing answered the call by putting together a remarkable team of the most prominent architects: Stern was there, as were Antoine Predock, Michael Graves, Frank Gehry, Stanley Tigerman, and Robert Venturi. (WDI was at the table to monitor and integrate those architectural developments, but were not asked to be architects—except for the design at one hotel, The Disneyland Hotel at the main entrance. In my opinion, that's the best hotel on the property.)

Peter Rummell at the Disney Development Company

was a strong supporter and advisor with the hotel development push, and with it the campgrounds, golf course, and Festival Disney. Dick Nunis had brought a former Marriott guy to Walt Disney World a few years earlier, Bob Small, and now suggested we bring him and another Marriott veteran named Sanjay Varma on board to focus on hotel development and operation.

Sanjay did a wonderful job coordinating with DDC on hotels. As the chief resorts officer, Sanjay was the operations representative (a counterpart to Steve Lewelling in Park Operations). Sanjay brought in a terrific food and beverage supervisor, Lee Cockerell, also from Marriott, and he did a great job training his people. Sanjay spoke enough French to earn respect. Sanjay's wife, Hanna Varma, was a star in her own right, and by opening day had become director of operations in the park.

Sanjay was a good guy . . . and strong. He was young and smart, but could be stubborn. He got things done, but it was tough to convince him to accomplish things the way we thought they ought to be done. But at the end of the day, it's the results that matter most, and they were fantastic. All six hotels, and the campground, plus the golf course—all opened on the same day, along with

Festival Disney. The Wild West Show was managed by Ron Logan, vice president of creative show development for all of Walt Disney Attractions and his staff (along with Jean Luc Chopin, who had been hired as entertainment director for all of EDL).

For me, it was a blessed relief to have such a huge element of Cast Members being so supportive.

Increase, Acceleration, Inconvenience

In addition to retaining leadership of Disneyland International—and my role as part of the team on the public offering, site selection, and negotiations committees—all of the departmental vice presidents and directors from Administration, Operations, Human Resources, Training and Development, Food, Entertainment, Merchandise, Legal, Security, Operational Finance and Budget, and Construction Operational input reported to me. We were building an incredible team that would all eventually be training their European counterparts, just as we had done in Tokyo.

Michael Eisner had also inexplicably put me in charge of straightening out the Disney character program in Europe, because there was so much unauthorized costumed character use and counterfeit merchandise. In actuality, almost every town in Europe had counterfeit stuff. So, we put together a team that went out and just handled that—they filed lawsuits and got people to straighten out things. It also provided great opportunities for our Product Development, Character, and Entertainment teams to recruit and create their programs for the resort.

In addition to this tremendous task, I was not yet working on the site where I would have immediate reference to what it was we were building. Unfortunately, I wasn't even *close* to the site—geographically. Solely for appearances and prestige, we wound up thirty miles away, in the heart of Paris, at the Place de la Madeleine. It was small, adjacent to the Madeleine Church and its namesake square, and very prestigious (full of luxury boutiques and restaurants), but more efficient for ostentation and ceremony than getting outright business done. I didn't have an apartment yet, but was staying just around the corner from the office at the Hôtel de Crillon, on the Place de la Concorde at the foot of the Champs-Élysées (where you can get a $25 cup of coffee without much of a wait). Just the impractical *expense* of this arrangement really bothered me.

Finally, we moved from Place de la Madeleine to the Place Vendôme—we had blessedly gotten too big for the former, and from there we soon expanded operating teams to the Pascale building, both beside the A4 motorway and about halfway between Paris and the park site. (We had administration in the Place Vendôme, and the Operations and Imagineering teams over at the Pascale—but at least we were getting closer to the site.)

The first thing I asked for to be built on the project site was an office building, something that could be later turned into space for an ongoing operational use—we had to have a place for construction personnel and WDI, and the Disneyland International and Euro Disney team. We ended up with some pretty substandard trailers and ramshackle buildings—but things worked a lot smoother . . . and it was all temporary anyway.

Although in new digs, we were still perpetually confronted by all the things we had to buy—from paper clips to backhoes. We had no cars, no construction vehicles, no cafeteria. We had no skips, no scooters. We had no blueprint facilities, nothing. I reflected often on all the infrastructure OLC already had, or silently provided, that I had taken for granted in Japan. It seemed like every day was just another issue, another problem, another headache. It was just awful, and kept going downhill—in the mud—always.

The stress had me smoking more than ever. I mentioned before what a terrible mistake I made becoming a smoker, but I grew up in an era where *everyone* smoked. Walt smoked. Occasionally I slowed down, cut the number of cigarettes I was smoking, but I never quit, and now I was stress-smoking.

In Europe, wine and liquor are as common as water, and that, combined with the heavy late-night working dinners, and the ongoing anxiety was compounding things. (*Everywhere* in France there is an abundant amount of delicious food—that also tends to be rich . . . and fatty . . . and high in calories.) On top of the constant professional pressure, I was in the middle of battling a triple threat to my health.

Imagineering in Crisis

Yet another layer of discord emerged around this point: there was some bad timing at WDI just as we began our project. Walt Disney Imagineering had always been a somewhat "seat-of-the-pants" organization. Walt had founded it more as a think tank and creative laboratory than as a business; it was a cost center, not a profit center, and the way it was run and the way money was spent there created a peculiar alchemy—and a particular irritant to the organized mind of Frank Wells.

In some ways this was entirely predictable and acceptable, especially since WDI is often creating all-new experiences, and inventing all-new technology to run them. But as we began EDL construction, there was a special scrutiny and focus placed on WDI, especially due to project delays and cost overruns on a new attraction at Disneyland, Splash Mountain, and a development at Walt Disney World, Pleasure Island.

Frank was frantic to staunch what he saw as a hemorrhaging and disorganized mess at WDI, so he sent over a "fixer" who had helped streamline and cut operations and expenses at the studio, Jeff Rochlis. Rochlis had the reputation of being a bloodless "terminator," and tried (vainly, I think) to find a reliable "system" approach to projects at WDI. His "Triangle of Success" instruction books remain legendary. But Rochlis also ran afoul of the chief Imagineer, Marty Sklar, with whom he established an adversarial rather than collaborative relationship. I liked Jeff, and considered him a friend, but it just wasn't a good fit with the WDI folks.

Jeff chose an outside construction firm called Lehrer McGovern Bovis (LMB), which was embedded in the WDI EDL team, and given overarching authority in project decisions. Unfortunately, this "ED-LMB" concept was doomed from the beginning; LMB knew nothing about our type of projects, WDI was resistant, and LMB had its own internal power struggles going on at the same time. Luckily, it didn't last long.

Much Needed Upper Management

Thank God someone had the good sense to bring a guy named Stanley Steinberg on board to head up the project management and business side of Walt Disney Imagineering. Maybe the fact that the nickname he went by was "Mickey" was a good sign for us. He and Marty Sklar constituted a genuine team, and during the time that he was there, I don't think many will argue, was a "golden age" for Imagineering.

With degrees in architecture from Georgia Tech and MIT, Mickey had long been associated with John Portman & Associates in Atlanta, an internationally recognized architectural and engineering firm. They were responsible for the construction of the Merchandise Mart (now

AmericasMart), Hyatt Regency, Westin Peachtree Plaza, and Marriott Marquis in Atlanta and the Embarcadero Center in San Francisco. Portman had offices in Tokyo and Shanghai, and projects all over the world.

Mickey came into the fray in September of 1988, as senior vice president for project management for all Disney projects in the United States and Japan. With calm, intelligence, and observation, just like Michael and Frank had, Mickey made a huge effort to understand not only what our projects entailed, but what brought our unique *value* into the end product. (Early on, he had an epiphany about the level of "show" in our projects, and exclaimed, "I usually build four hundred rooms and a lobby. *All* you build here are lobbies!") He had a folksiness and a Southern drawl that was charming, but he was a pragmatic fury and brooked no nonsense. Mickey and I got along great. We understood each other's issues and problems. We'd both done things like this before. And we remain friends to this day.

As Mickey came on board, he began to observe and advise not only on domestic and Japanese projects—he actually became alarmed at what he saw on the EDL project in general, and the disarray in France. Only six months after his hiring he was promoted to executive vice president and COO of WDI, with global responsibilities. One of his tasks involved overseeing the EDL construction team. He installed an old Portman colleague, a tried-and-true expert, Fred Beckenstein, on the job site. Between the two of them (and the project management team)—plus an excellent WDI design team led by Tony Baxter—they all really brought it home.

Mickey sought constant information and involvement—and *expected* nothing less. We met on a regular basis, my operational people and Mickey's people. He sat through all of my staff meetings, and I sat through all of *his* staff meetings, to make sure everything was covered. People would report delays, or problems, or oversights. Mickey took notes—and he'd take care of things right then.

I also found early on that Mickey and I had a connection in temperament, and that we could be led away from anger by humor. When he was displeased, that sweet Southern drawl would drop down and he'd get damn mad. Whenever he "flew off the handle," people would just shudder, including my operational people who were in the room. It was so at odds with his usual easygoing persona. I'd come back at him with some sort of humorous observation. I found I could get him laughing and defuse those tense outbursts of anger. I think that's really how our friendship began. He was a tough guy when he needed to be, but he knew that you draw more flies with sugar. Mickey is one of a kind, no doubt about that. He was a cool breeze in a very hot kitchen.

Mimi Schaaf had relocated to Paris, too, and with our deep friendship—and her utterly pragmatic understanding of the project's complexities—she became an even stronger source of comfort and respite. That Christmas, she bought me a Labrador puppy (whom I named Yankee just to annoy my neighbors each time I called for her to come.)

But the Beat Goes On

As much support and relief as this relationship brought me, the project was still just a bear. Looking back on it now, I *still* don't know how we did it. It seems as if there was nothing but problems. We had divorces; some people just hated France and wanted to go back home; we had people fall in love with their interpreters or secretaries. Problems with expats with children in school arose. Transportation systems we set up to get people to and from school and work faltered. Somebody's furniture didn't arrive. Weekends of sightseeing and recreation, as many had anticipated, didn't happen.

Weekends in general typically didn't happen. Tempers and temperaments were volatile. It was all that kind of stuff. Similar things happened in Tokyo, but France was so much worse, and maybe I got involved in too much, but that was just my style.

The biggest problem was that we had a scope of work unlike any that Disney had ever known—taken on—and we all felt overworked, overwhelmed, and unsupported. Mickey Steinberg said, "I feel so sorry for you that the company's got you guys out here, and you're not getting the support you need for a project this size." And we didn't. Burbank seemed a million miles away. I don't know that they were *denying* us the people and resources we required, and I'm not sure we asked for them, because we knew they weren't available. We were constantly told, "You guys are over budget," which made us afraid to ask for another body to help. It was also unfortunate that, as I said before, I wasn't given a mechanism for understanding with practical frequency what the state of the budgets were.

In a lot of ways it had become like a military operation, a relentless slog through mud-filled trenches. Just trying to survive . . . just keeping everybody in the unit together, and taking care of yourself.

Divorce, International Style

For me, personally, through all of this, I was trying to deal with a divorce, and I was trying to get on with my life. I was reviewing documents, having meetings with attorneys, and trying to settle this whole thing via fax and international phone calls. In those days, there was no Internet or email, no cell phones, so to call the States meant international telephone calls, operator-assisted or direct-dial, on a landline, which was expensive as hell. My family all seemed so far away, and the time difference did not help us stay in touch easily. (The time zone differences were maddening. Even Frank Wells would call me at three o'clock in the morning. "Were you sleeping?" "Yes, sir, that's what we do here at three o'clock in the morning." He promised not to do that again—but did it anyway. I bought him a world clock and sent it to him, thinking it might help. It didn't.)

For a lifelong Catholic, there are other issues that added to the stresses of the divorce itself. Administratively, it's very complicated. Morally, I'd been brought up that divorce was a sin. As a person, I just felt bad about all of it, and how it was going down. This did not lessen my personal tension and worry.

It was a really tough time. I didn't sleep much. I smoked too much. My diet was a mess.

Help That Was No Help

I never missed the Oriental Land Company so much as I did during these years. We kept discovering talent deficiencies and support gaps. We just never had the staff we should have. The staff we did hire automatically got six weeks of vacation the first year of employment. We didn't have tax people there, so we had to figure out how to take care of our team's taxes here and back in the States. Finally we hired Price Waterhouse's Karen Katzbeck to assist us in tax-protecting our expatriates, so that they would not have to pay more than they would have paid in their home state.

There were staff housing shortages near the work site as well.

Frank would come over quite often and ask what the problems were—he tried to help whenever he could. Michael would also come over quite often, but he would mainly talk about design issues with the Imagineering team.

Mickey Steinberg said, "This is a huge project. I've been on a lot of construction projects and you're totally understaffed." There weren't enough people operationally that could interface with his construction teams, and there were lots of mistakes made because we didn't have operational people in the field to catch them.

Dennis Hightower was a big help. He was erudite. He knew the politics. He spoke French. He got it. We spent a lot of time together. Dennis wrote a letter to Michael Eisner, saying that I needed more help, and I wasn't getting it.

One reason for this was that lots of people didn't want to travel, because the ever-frugal Disney made them fly internationally in coach class. Which may be fine for an adventure or a one-off, but I insisted that our people had to fly in first class and business class. These people were travelling all over the world on a regular basis.

Frank finally agreed. I said, "You need to put it in writing, Frank, because you and I may not be around but the expats will be," and he did put it in writing. We had a policy with HR, and it helped me recruit at the end of the project to get more people over to France.

Another huge problem is that expatriating meant you left your Disney job in the States—and we were not guaranteeing jobs upon return! So if your job was filled while you were gone, you took potluck; they'd try to find a job for you, but if your old role was already filled with somebody else, you were done. You could get a demotion, or take whatever job was available—but it may not be what you left before heading abroad. How attractive is *that* as an enticement to relocate halfway around the world? (Frank did finally back me up on this, and would "freeze" jobs stateside for the expats. It was a major accomplishment—and redress.)

Another dilemma was that a lot of people who *did* want to relocate weren't of the caliber we needed; they lacked the significant project-based experience. Some people thought they'd be riding their bike and wearing a beret to go pick up their morning baguette. They envisioned living a life of European sophistication. Projects are not like that. They require a commitment and humility that often means your own life goes on hold. Sleeping on a sofa in the project office, working through weekends and holidays . . . it's an "all hands on deck" work style that is, in the end, oddly rewarding. But it takes a specific kind of person.

So we had a hard time! It was really a mixed bag of executives. Everybody had a different idea of what ought to be done.

One from the Heart

Given the constant inundation of problems and crises, I didn't pay much attention to how lousy I was feeling. Of course I was fatigued and felt tired and listless. That's to be expected. But I wasn't sleeping. I was having terrible backaches, which I attributed to the overall toll of the work, and ongoing, never-ending site walk-throughs. I would walk a short distance, get severe pains in the small of my back, and then stop and stretch. The pain there would actually go away. But then I started having consistent leg pain. But I reasoned that I'm on a project, I haven't got time to see anybody about that. It's just aches and pains.

I was playing golf one day with a government official. But suddenly I couldn't walk from the first hole to the second. I couldn't move. My golf partner went and got a gardener's truck, came back to pick me up, and drove me all the way to the American Hospital of Paris, where they did an examination and analysis.

The news was grim, but I still just wasn't processing the severity of it. I thought, this is really intrusive. I haven't got time for this. The project is in such rough shape, I need to get back to work. My mind had been in such a whirl this whole time, just trying to stay alive professionally, to keep a juggernaut of a project in motion, and this major event in my life seemed like an annoyance.

Mimi's father was a doctor, so I said I'd go back to the States and have it taken care of. The doctor said I wouldn't make it—as it was, there was a chance I wouldn't make it through the weekend. The iliac arteries to my legs were more than 90 percent blocked; I was lucky to be able to breathe. They admitted me immediately. I had my first of many angiograms, and was prepped to store blood for any transfusions that might be needed.

This operation, I was told, was a much more severe procedure than a typical heart bypass. This iliac arterial surgery uses a graft to create a new pathway for blood around the blockage. The graft is a synthetic tube that acts like an artery, carrying blood to the vessels that supply circulation to the legs. They have to move all of the adjacent organs to get to the iliac artery. My aorta, they said, was in especially bad shape, and would have to be rebuilt.

I asked Steven Juge, who was our project attorney, to get me a lawyer, I didn't have a will. I wanted to talk to a priest. A Jesuit priest came in and took my confession.

The lawyer came in and took my last will and testament. I called my family in California.

That following morning, they prepped me for surgery. I remember that they shaved my entire body with a blade that was used during World War I *and* II, I think—I bled all over that sheet, they nicked me in so many places. I don't have much memory after that. I'm told I was in surgery for about eight full hours, and that the procedure went well, and was successful. But the recovery would be at least six to eight weeks.

During that time, Mimi and my daughter Michelle were the first ones at my bedside to see how I was doing, to take care of things, to handle communications, and to support and encourage me. Mimi supervised every aspect of my hospitalization, with the strength and efficiency of the best project managers in the business.

Frank Wells called immediately and reassured me. "Take as much time as you need, we want you well—and need you healthy." What a great guy Frank Wells was. He *did* have a few other things going on in his life. Such a humane gentleman.

Bob Fitzpatrick came by that first night, cigarette in hand, and immediately began to ask me about work issues.

This *really* ran afoul of Mimi. I had to admire how she gave the top EDL executive a blistering piece of her mind about the inappropriateness of his entire visit. He put out his cigarette, sheepishly asked about my health, and left, never to return. (Mind you, even the nurses still smoked in the hospital in those days, and my room had ashtrays in it—today it seems crazy. Speaking of crazy, my only question to the surgeon was, "Can I continue to smoke?" He told me the damage was already done, so if I enjoy it I could continue! *Terrible* advice—and I took it!)

My staff took a picture of Mickey Mouse on a hill overlooking the construction project, and said, "Don't worry about a thing, Mickey's watching over things for you." I was touched beyond words, and so very proud of the truly remarkable, qualified, competent, and trustworthy team I'd been blessed with.

After a few days, Michelle talked to me alone. "I don't need to be here anymore, Dad," she said. "There's nothing I can do for you that Mimi isn't already handling." She said it without rancor, but rather with deep and loving kindness.

Michelle was a remarkable person. I guess all dads think that way about their daughters, especially. In high school, she was very involved with Future Farmers of

America, and she always wanted to be a Disneyland tour guide, like her mother had been. She was also proud and independent. She applied at Disneyland—and got that job—without my help, or even my knowledge.

She was also runner-up for Disneyland Ambassador two years in a row—but she was passed over because Bill Sullivan's daughter was picked at Walt Disney World . . . and having another executive's daughter would appear political. But based on that exposure, Jack Lindquist brought her into his marketing division. She married an Anaheim fire captain, and later left Disney and went on to study interior design and to work with a spatial design company. She told me she had to see if she could do well without having my last name. She did.

My health crisis was a defining moment in my relationship with Mimi . . . a relationship that had been in bloom for a while. In this dark time, we found our final mutuality. Every time I opened my eyes in that hospital room, Mimi was there—even when I found her sound asleep on the floor from total exhaustion.

And I'll never forget the way she told off Bob Fitzpatrick. It was priceless!

Hospitalization typically runs five to eight days for this sort of thing. Full recovery time is usually four to eight weeks. I had physical therapy every day while I was in the hospital, but I left after less than a week. The second week I was home, Frank flew over to check on me, and encouraged me to improve quickly—they needed me back. So, three weeks after surgery, I was back in the office.

That was another mistake I'd live to regret.

Once More unto the Breach, Dear Friends . . .

Most of the heart and health problems that plagued me later in life really are tied to the fact that I just did not take the recovery time I needed. I went back to work way too soon. But we were so busy, everything was such a whirlwind, I just didn't know what else I could do. (I also unknowingly carried with me a sponge that had been left inside by the surgeon, only to be found years later during another health emergency.)

We were now finally getting *some* additional support from the States, but unfortunately a lot of the people who came over were at the vice president level, and had quite a time in Paris, using my project budget for their expense accounts. I stopped some vice presidents from returning.

I loved it when Roy E. Disney came over. He had a lot to say, and the team loved him. It was like an endorsement and blessing from the Disney family. But my project budget would take the hit for his private plane. We were typically just a stopover as he headed on to Shannon to be at his castle in Ireland. But I'd get stuck for the $100,000 a trip.

Frank made many trips to Europe, to be brought up-to-date. At the end of each day, he'd sit down with my secretary and dictate what had happened during the day, for a memo that went directly to Michael Eisner. He really kept Michael in the loop, told him what decisions we'd made, and what progress he'd seen. He was disciplined about it, almost religious.

Michael would come over, though, and he'd have ideas and changes; the creative lead for WDI, Tony Baxter, would feed Michael ideas for design changes. We were in construction, coming out of the ground, when changes were asked for at times. There was a lot of financial impact and ripple effects as a result.

Frank encouraged me to just tell him what these creative whims cost in real dollars. "You've got to tell him," Frank said, "He's got to quit doing that." I sent Michael a note outlining the changes he and Tony had made, and their cost to the budget, asking him to help us rein this kind of spending in.

Michael sent a note back in reply, outlining *my* several operational changes.

I explained that those changes were due to revisions in safety standards and procedures, and that they weren't arbitrary.

But after that he made *very* few of those changes, and we found ways to work together to achieve his goals without a negative impact.

Thanks, Frank.

Michael was the dreamer. Frank was the doer. Walt used to say, we're dreamers and doers. That was those two.

Creative Imagination and Technical Know-How

One of the reasons Michael kept coming up with revisions and additions and new ideas was because, as I mentioned, he really connected with our Walt Disney Imagineering creative director, Tony Baxter. Tony led a group of "second-generation Imagineers," guys who'd come up through the ranks, and had been brought up with Disneyland always in their lives. They "got" the Disney show, and were all invested in creating a great park. Tony, who had started at seventeen years old scooping ice cream at Carnation Plaza Gardens in Disneyland, left his indelible mark on EDL with his reimagining of the Magic Kingdom, which resulted in one of our best parks.

Elsewhere at EDL, the show producer on Main Street, U.S.A., Eddie Sotto, was not immune to making creative changes that had impacted the budget. For instance, for the sake of a certain "look" and story quality, Eddie wanted the pavers on Main Street to be individual hand-placed bricks, rather than asphalt and concrete. He made the case not only for their visual appeal, but also the fact that—some increased labor costs aside—the bricks were a cheaper material, and in the long run, easier to maintain and repair. He was right. Eddie was a deeply informed and intellectual guy with a real flair for telling the story—but he also knew how parks *work*, and his operational knowledge informed his creative insights.

Another of Eddie's innovative thoughts was a pair of "arcades," essentially long corridors that run the length of the east and west sides of Main Street from the Town Square to the Plaza. Eddie suggested that investing in the structure and story of these corridors would gain operational efficiencies for exiting large crowds at the end of fireworks or parades, and offered an attractive sheltered alternative to the open street side in case of inclement weather. I thought this idea was both simple and sound, having seen at Disneyland how valuable this thinking would have been, and took the added cost out of the Operations budgets.

Jeff Burke was the show producer for Frontierland. A quiet, gentle, intelligent guy, Jeff understood the European taste for the American West that had come from movies and TV, and was determined to give EDL a "wild frontier" straight from the screen. He broke with Walt's own tradition about the Haunted Mansion (in EDL it's Phantom Manor). Walt had wanted a house that was pristine on the outside, and haunted on the inside. Jeff wanted (and knew the Europeans would want, and better understand) a truly spooky haunted house. A lonely mansion on a hill emerged: it was a cross between *The Addams Family* and the *Psycho* houses, one that really was a marquee for the story inside.

"Tomorrow turns to yesterday too fast," the show's producer, Tim Delaney, said. Another sharp mind, and experienced Imagineer (he'd been in charge of The Living Seas at EPCOT Center), Tim advocated, "Let's make our Tomorrowland about the visions and inventions of yesterday's futurists." So instead of Tomorrowland, Tim delivered an industrial-Victorian Discoveryland, a design that preceded the "steampunk" fad, and also got us in good with the French, because we put a lot of Jules Verne in there.

Tom Morris was the show producer for Fantasyland, appropriately because he'd begun his career at Disneyland, as a "balloon boy" for lessee Nat Lewis's helium balloon concession. This Imagineering team recognized that each of the three then-existing Magic Kingdom parks had been built by necessity on a "tabletop" ground design: Disneyland because of cost constructing on flat grove land; Walt Disney World because of a high water table, and Tokyo Disneyland because it was on reclaimed landfill. Our site in Marne-la-Vallée didn't have that restriction. Tom and the other designers created a park that has a great deal more Guest-level vertical interest—it dips into the landscape, and has hills and gullies.

Tom envisioned a Sleeping Beauty Castle (*Le Château de la Belle au Bois Dormant*) right out of the animated feature, complete with a castle that intertwined with an adjacent series of terraced hills, and even square trees! Tom did a first-pass drawing of this concept that was very exciting. He further sold it by having a concept painting done by Imagineer Frank Armitage—who had spent three years painting backgrounds on *Sleeping Beauty*!

I'm still surprised that Chris Teitz was the show

producer on Adventureland—not because our EDL Adventureland was lacking in any way, but because Chris was so reserved and quiet, not conversational, sort of a shy guy. But he clearly took the adventuresome ideas in his imagination and made them come alive in reality. Chris brought together fond Disney memories in an innovative and refreshing way—setting up attractions such as Pirates of the Caribbean, Tom Sawyer Island, the Swiss Family Treehouse, and even the old Disneyland Chicken of the Sea Captain Hook Pirate Ship and Skull Rock!

Joe Rohde is still one of the finest thinkers that WDI has ever had. Everything that he's done gets the benefit of both the academic mind of a scholar and the imaginative flair of a real explorer. Joe was with me and Michael Eisner on a research visit to a big rodeo in Cheyenne, Wyoming. Michael was fascinated with bringing a "real rodeo" to EDL. We got pretty good seats down front, and they started with bull riding. One cowboy got thrown, turned around, went the wrong way, and was gored through by the horn of the bull. After the show, we heard that he'd died. At the same rodeo we attended, they also did a wild horse event, where they let loose a dozen horses in a corral. Each cowboy had to rope, saddle, and ride a wild horse to the finish line. It's a hell of a show—but it's real, not

staged. A wild horse reared up near us and caught a cowboy underneath the chin, and killed him on the spot. After
a while everybody settled down, and I turned to Michael
and Joe. "That's why we can't do rodeos," I informed
them. It was Joe who said, "We need that excitement, but
with safety and control. What we can do is a terrific Wild
West Show." Joe is a mesmerizing verbal picture-painter,
and after he described the travelling shows that Buffalo
Bill had done in the late nineteenth century, Michael was
hooked. (But more on that show in a little bit.)

Leading the Imagineers was Marty Sklar. Marty was
a guy who also learned the "Disney Way" from Walt himself, and had been at Walt's right hand for the last five
years or so of his life. Marty was a complicated guy—he
could be vexing, he played politics in ways I didn't. But in
the end I respected him, and we shared our mutual love
and protection of the Disney culture and the importance
of quality, value, and "good show." To the WDI teams at
EDL, he was an inspirational leader, and his background
gave him an endorsement and pedigree that made his
approval worth more than any payday to his Imagineers.

Disney parks are sophisticated, expensive, and difficult. That's because passionate people deliver their best
thinking and best work in order to live up to standards

that have meaning, and create new standards with every new project.

Love Thy Neighbors

Building on landfill in Tokyo Bay meant that we had a blank page—no neighbors, no local government. Issues with the two fishermen's cooperatives in Urayasu-cho over the compensation for their loss of livelihood had been settled for decades. But in France, we were entering an established community with an existing population, covering four different sectors, containing twenty-six communes that made up Marne-la-Vallée: Porte de Paris, Val Maubuée, Val de Bussy, and Val d'Europe. The project site fell in the middle of five small communities and had five mayors. We had to deal with them at the same time, and attempt to interface with the local government officials in each community. There were all kinds of conflicts and scrapes. Local and labor issues were a constant. Strikes and construction crew fights happened. We had security officers assaulted, and project access gates torn off. Steve Lewelling and I, plus some of our staff, had many face-off confrontations with protesters. And some got violent, though all got resolved.

The mayor of Chessy, which is the closest village to EDL, didn't like us coming to his town. He didn't blame Disney, and the government had paid a very fair price for all the farmland acquired. Yet having a big resort next to the homes of the town's residents was understandably a concern. The mayor was an older fellow, and we found out later he had been a German prisoner of war, but married a farmer's daughter and decided to stay in France.

We had our security officers very visibly around, to observe and protect the construction site. In retrospect, we probably should have paid more attention to the *context* and look in our security wardrobe and personnel. The sharp khaki uniforms looked tight and smart to us—but we soon discovered that they bore an uncomfortable resemblance to the summer uniforms of the German *Waffen* who invaded and occupied France during World War II.

A lot of mornings, the mayor would come out with his shotgun, and he would take a shot at the security officers. Although the security officers were well out of range, they would still dive for cover into that Marne-la-Vallée mud.

I went over with my interpreter and my chief of security to talk to this mayor. We sat in his kitchen over a cup of coffee. After the interpreter carried the conversation back and forth for a while, the mayor's wife finally rolled her eyes and said, "Quit using an interpreter to talk to them; you probably speak English better than they do." He was putting us on, but he was really concerned about the impact our development would have on the neighboring farmland.

"Chickens are going to stop laying," he said. "Cows will stop giving milk." I tried to reassure him that the level of intrusion would (hopefully) be highly controlled and very minor.

"What about your fireworks?"

"We don't have any problems in Anaheim," I said.

"Have you any farms in Anaheim?"

He got me on that one, and of course, in Anaheim, we'd been doing those fireworks for a long time before significant residential population started encroaching on the park. Generations of locals simply accepted it as part of living in the area.

I called Ron Logan, who was then vice president of creative show development for all of Walt Disney Attractions. "Ron, I need you to bring me a fireworks show."

Ron's team came over, and they set up something similar to one of our typical fireworks displays on-site. All the surrounding villagers made an evening of it. They came out into their yards and fields with picnics, set up their blankets and lawn chairs, and looked up at the sky, waiting for dark, and the big show.

When it was all over, we could hear the cheers—everybody loved it, and thought it was terrific. The next morning, I went to check in with the mayor of Chessy.

He looked grim. "Well, we have a problem."

"Did the chickens stop laying?"

"No," he said, "and it won't bother the cows."

"What's the problem?"

He smiled slyly and said, "Why can't we do this every night?"

He was still putting me on.

That morning, he also introduced me to his son, who was going to be assuming the office of mayor. We all became very good friends over the years.

Mayors in the Magic Kingdom

We had put our best foot forward in that instance, and decided to keep reaching out. We brought the mayors from the surrounding villages closest to the park site—Chessy, Serris, Bailly-Romavilliers, Magny-le-Hongre, and Coupvray—to Walt Disney World! Dick Nunis and

I hosted them, toured the property with them, and had some nice dinners. We gave them all a gold Mickey Mouse watch as a keepsake, and I think we all had some nice times, too. When we went back to France, I think it helped a lot toward forging our future relationships with them. They understood what out project was, and they felt a part of it, not victims of an invasion.

Espace Euro Disney

Another very effective local outreach was something that was tried-and-true with our other developments—the creation of a locally based preview and information center, where travelers and locals alike could see plans, models, renderings, and get brochures and information about what was coming.

The renowned architect Robert A. M. Stern designed what was called Espace Euro Disney, located in Serris (near the exit for the A4 motorway). A two-story sorcerer's cap, like the one Mickey had worn in *Fantasia*, fronted the otherwise nondescript building.

It was designed and decorated and furnished beautifully, plus featured exhibit and display elements, including a life-sized C-3PO and a model that had been created by

Imagineering of the entire project. There was a preview theater with a special film produced for the space and, naturally, a boutique with special pre-opening merchandise. It was also possible to book hotel reservations and buy tickets for the park. This area gave us a small-scale testing ground for Park Operations, Food Service, and Merchandise, and was the beginning of our marketing kickoff.

Our Operations team, led by Steve Lewelling, got very involved in this, and were all outstanding. I could always count on him to perform at 100 percent. He brought many of the key ops players who had been with us in Tokyo, so they understood the "project mentality."

The preview center wasn't quite finished on time, but the ops team showed up after hours to bring it up to Disney show standards. It opened on December 5, 1990, and was really an attraction in itself, plus it proved to be extremely helpful in providing insights into the challenges that would lie ahead for EDL—from security to cash handling, hiring and training, food development, entertainment production and tech support, and maintenance and custodial.

It was also enough of an attraction in and of itself that we charged 15 francs per adult and 10 francs per child. (We were also opening as it turned out during a season of unusual unrest in France, so the admission charge and process not only helped with training, it allowed us a "valve" of scrutiny for visitors and safety.)

In one year Espace Euro Disney welcomed a hundred thousand visitors.

A Wild West Show—and an Impromptu Barbecue

One other unforgettable incident we had with the locals involved one of Michael's big creative ideas.

Earlier I mentioned that in Festival Disney Michael had wanted a "rodeo." Over and over he pushed the idea of a rodeo that finally evolved into a Wild West show, a kind of arena event/dinner show that is now familiar in attractions such as Medieval Times. Ours would cater to the "romanticized" notions of the American West the European cinema had promoted back in the day and focus on cowboys, outlaws, and wild animals. Buffalo Bill's Wild West Show (a version of which still plays there today) was the result. Inspired by the legendary 1882–1912 touring show created by Buffalo Bill, our show explored the lives of pioneers and featured Native American rituals, rodeo stunts, bison hunting, a shoot-out with audience participation, and even a stagecoach holdup. Live animals, including horses, a buffalo herd, and long-horned steer, were part of the spectacle.

One night after the show, a livestock pen gate was left open, and one of the longhorn steers, a very expensive "import," meandered out into the countryside.

Once his absence was discovered, the EDL security team and the local police began searching: they discovered an impromptu five-village barbecue in progress.

That local media derived a lot of amusement from the reporting of this story.

Casting a Big Show

Running the resort would require a huge cast. We predicted that we would need twelve thousand people for the hotels and the theme park. We ended up with seventeen thousand, because they couldn't work full shifts, and we hadn't understood the typical European vacation benefits. Casting centers were set up in Paris, London, and Amsterdam. Construction teams had an international mix, as we brought people in from England, Ireland, the Netherlands, Switzerland, and Italy. These people just did a great job, believed in Disney, believed in what we were doing. It was quite a challenging adventure for many of them, but they just loved being there. We knew we could expect the same with the operational employees. Disney was an international culture all its own.

During this time, the Berlin Wall came down, and Eastern Europeans were coming west through our property—and were taking shelter in our uncompleted hotels. Employees on the construction site were actually aiding these transients and refugees until the police chased them away—and we received a stern warning from the French government about "harboring."

The night that the wall came down in November 1989, Mimi and I were at a dinner with some French nationals. We were in a celebratory mood, but found that many of them were *not* happy about a united Germany. Scars from the war that had ended in 1945 were still raw.

Unlike other parks, we aimed for permanent employees instead of seasonal and temporary part-time workers. It was part of the agreement with the French government that "a concentrated effort would be made to tap into the local French labor market." The unique nature of our project and its audience brought some unique needs in qualification. Personality and communication skills are always a "plus," especially for onstage roles. We preferred applicants who spoke two European languages (French and one other, ideally). Of course, I wouldn't be me if we didn't set up Euro Disneyland with its own Disney University to train workers. By November 1991, we had twenty-four thousand applicants.

The French had promised us early on that they would build employee housing, but they didn't. That meant we went over budget to build housing for them ourselves, but Thor Degelmann still had to have his HR staff going out into the towns and villages, knocking on doors, to see if people wanted to rent rooms to our Cast Members. I think we created a whole bed-and-breakfast business around Île-de-France.

Ultimately we had them housed all over, even in the hotels—from Paris all the way down the road to Marne-la-Vallée.

The Disney Look

Since the very beginning, our parks and resorts had required personnel appearance standards. We called it "The Disney Look," and it was simply a set of grooming and dress rules that made sure our Cast Members represented a certain clean-cut and self-respecting appearance, that in turn respected the Guest and the value of their experience. There were simple regulations and limitations regarding the use of makeup, facial hair, tattoos, jewelry, and such things as smoking "onstage," in the public view.

Either inexplicably or predictably, French labor unions mounted protests against the grooming standards, which they saw as "an attack on individual liberty." We were told that Disney was being insensitive to French culture, individualism, and privacy, and that restrictions on individual or collective liberties were illegal under French law, unless it could be demonstrated that the restrictions are "requisite to the job."

We countered that in dealing with a representation of our expected and specific culture, to remove such an employment standard could threaten the image and long-term success of the park. Thor Degelmann said, "For us, the appearance code has a great effect from a product identification standpoint. Without it we couldn't be presenting the Disney product that people would be expecting." Thor noted that many other companies, particularly airlines, maintained appearance codes that were just as strict. "We happened to put ours in writing," he pointed out.

Ultimately it was all just another big public fuss about how "Disney didn't understand the culture of France," when once again, it was the French who didn't (or didn't think it necessary) to understand Disney as a viable and estimable culture of its own.

We knew of no one who had been offered a role at Euro Disneyland who had refused to take the job because of the appearance standards.

Heading Toward Opening Day

For about a year I had been out of hotels and had settled into an apartment near the Eiffel Tower. I loved that place, and my good neighbors were Mickey Steinberg and his wonderful wife, Marilyn. But as time went on, the commute to and from the project site was taking up valuable time. HR found a house for rent about twenty minutes from Marne-la-Vallée, allowing me a little bit more free time, since I didn't have to contend with the Parisian traffic. Then, about three months prior to EDL's soft opening, I moved to Camp Davy Crockett, and stayed in one of the cabins there.

My son, Jim, and his wife, Bonnie, had relocated to EDL by then. They were both working on the project and took a nearby cabin. Jim was responsible for computer installation at the hotels; he had trained in IT at

Disneyland for years prior to this new assignment. He had attended Mission Viejo High School, and due to his education while we were living in Tokyo, he was pretty advanced in the field of computer technology, and got an information technology job at Disneyland. (He's been at it now for more than thirty years—and I'm very proud of him.)

Sometimes with rough projects, you manage your way out of them, and things start to click, the machine starts to run smoothly. It seemed like every time we got one of the machines functioning, another one needed attention. Marketing was one of those.

Marketing the Magic

I felt we had a pretty strong team in place with Jack Myers and his group. Bob Fitzpatrick, however, didn't necessarily like Jack, and really gave him a hard time. I'm not sure where Bob's expertise in marketing an international destination resort came from, but he clearly didn't trust the team I'd assembled. Michael Eisner felt we simply didn't have enough manpower in Marketing, and he wasn't convinced that the marketing plans were going to work. So Jack Meyers, who I thought was a terrific guy, was out, and Mark Feary, the director of Marketing from Disneyland was in, with his counterpart, Jean Marie Gerbeaux, who came from Renault.

Then, six months prior to opening, Tom Elrod, vice president of Marketing for Walt Disney World, came over and brought a "hit team" that didn't always get along with the French, or with their American counterparts for that matter. I liked Tom, he had a great sense of humor; we'd joke and laugh a lot. But Tom treated people badly! He was just brutally hard on people. I'm not sure why . . . that was just Tom. His leadership and goals were unclear, so our overall marketing was *more* shaky because of the overlaps in who was in charge—and it was just a bad scene, so I had to spend more time with that.

Mimi, along with Nancy Valeri and her team, had been assigned responsibility for Grand Opening events, working closely with Entertainment and Operations. Mimi had lots of experience in really big and unusual "one-off" projects for Jack Lindquist—like the one where they made a huge Mickey Mouse silhouette in an Iowa cornfield that could be seen from the air to promote Mickey Mouse's sixtieth birthday (in 1988). A yearlong project in the making, Mimi had researched and found a site in northwest Iowa that had the most overhead air traffic. She then worked with the Buehjle and Pitzenberger families, whose farms and fields became the corn canvas used to create what was called the "Kernel Mickey Mouse." Mimi knew the EDL project thoroughly, having overseen marketing events tied to it since 1988 in Paris—and knew the aesthetic nature and physical qualities of the site, as well as all the players involved.

But suddenly Tom and Michael brought in Jody Dreyer, who later would become Michael's vice president of Corporate Special Projects, and put her in charge of the Grand Opening. I liked Jody very much; I'd known her from when she was an official Walt Disney World Ambassador, but now I had *two* teams in charge of Grand Opening, and we got bombarded with marketing people I hadn't asked for, and I'm not sure we needed. All good people, mind you, but then, I *already* had lots of good people in place.

I think Mimi spent as much time bringing the new people up to speed on what the embedded team already knew, and could do. Of course, because of my relationship with Mimi, I had to tread carefully. It all kind of worked, but it was really harder on everyone, and I hated the sense that we were "throwing people" at perceived problems that I didn't feel existed. Mickey Steinberg used to say of such things that it was "Doin' a lotta 'make work,'" creating things for employees to do that weren't exactly necessary, in order for people to just feel better somehow.

Security Anxiety

Judson Green got very concerned about security. He was probably still stinging because when Michael Eisner and Bob Fitzpatrick had arrived on the steps at the Paris Bourse (now called the Euronext Paris), home to the French stock market, on the first day of public trading of EDL stocks, they were confronted by protesters hurling expletives and eggs at them. Judson had no background in security, and because of the nature of our host country, we were really starting from the ground up, learning the nuances and needs of security in a nation with a very different culture. But I felt we had security covered. I had brought our best people in from the United States, and our corporate security leadership was heavily involved. But now we had to spend even more time focused on that because of what I felt was misplaced anxiety.

Sometimes these things hurt on a personal level, because it felt like such a lack of trust from corporate, as if the decades of experience my team and I brought with us had no weight.

Soft Opening and More Problems

Euro Disney opened for employee preview and testing in March 1992. During this time visitors were mostly Cast Members, and their friends and family members. We just used the soft opening, as usual, to test facilities and establish operations.

But we still weren't going to catch a break, or be treated as welcomed visitors in France, just as we had been in Japan. During the week before the opening, farmers came down and put tires covered with gasoline in front of our entrance and set them on fire, so we couldn't open the park. Even though the French police said they'd do something about it, they didn't. In fact, they sat down at card tables and played cards with the protestors to kill time. It just went on and on. Exhausting.

The custodial union rioted one night, and threw trash cans through all the windows on Main Street. Of course, there was always an added worry about the labor unions. We always knew France had a Communist-led labor federation capable of making trouble, so Steve and I met with the graveyard shift at three o'clock in the morning, calmed all that down, heard their grievances, and then resolved their problems. They were being mistreated and mishandled, not necessarily by Disney or the Americans, but by their workplace superiors. (One of my first questions, though, was, "Why hadn't the cans been *emptied*?")

The Eve of the Opening

The press was able to visit on Saturday, April 11, 1992, the day before the park's opening day. There were still ridiculous protests: villagers from nearby Meaux, for example, "demonstrated," ostensibly against the noise caused by our fireworks, though we'd already addressed, introduced, and even mitigated things by doing a special staging for them. As evening approached that Saturday, a pair of bombs damaged nearby electricity pylons, although they failed to do anything to the power supply in Euro Disney park.

There were events and festivities for the opening of the Disneyland Hotel at the main gate in the morning, and toward dusk a red carpet star arrival, with a ticker tape parade up Main Street that featured as many celebrities as studio chief Jeffrey Katzenberg could call out: Jean-Claude Van Damme, Jane Seymour, Michael J. Fox, Peter Gabriel, Candice Bergen, and Eddie Murphy among them.

A ninety-minute TV spectacular was broadcast world-wide, hosted by Don Johnson and Melanie Griffith. It featured Spanish singer José Carreras, Cher, champion French ice dancers Isabelle and Paul Duchesnay, Gloria Estefan and Miami Sound Machine, the Gipsy Kings, Angela Lansbury, the Four Tops, the Temptations, and Tina Turner. (It was a *very* peculiar talent lineup, and in looking at it today, a *very* 1990s TV show/special.)

The first Euro Disneyland Ambassador, Sabine Marcon, introduced Michael Eisner for a ceremonial castle lighting, featuring a specially formed children's choir singing "When You Wish Upon a Star" (in French). There were live musical performances, other special guests, and a European "premiere" of *Captain EO*. A few remarks by Michael Eisner and Roy E. Disney preceded the ceremonial ribbon cutting, accompanied by all the fanfare and fireworks that you would expect.

As I watched from the Main Street Plaza—still going over in my head everything that still had to be done for the next morning's Grand Opening—I saw members of the press standing in the planters, trampling the newly planted flowers in order to get a better view of the show. I told one man to get out of the planter, and he rudely replied, "Say it in French, *monsieur*." So, I very loudly told him to get out of the planter as I reached for his collar to drag him out. Fortunately, security stepped in before I lost it.

The next morning, Sunday, April 12, Euro Disney Resort and its theme park, Euro Disneyland, officially opened. As had been the case with Walt Disney World's opening in 1971, everyone was warned to expect chaos on the roads. A government survey had indicated that half a million people—in ninety thousand cars—might attempt to enter the property. There were radio broadcasts warning vehicle traffic to avoid the area. A strike (ostensibly protesting a traffic overload) closed the extension of the RER, the suburban railroad that normally makes the commute from the park site to Paris in forty-five minutes.

Déjà vu. As it had been with Walt Disney World, the fear of overwhelming Opening Day crowds kept away the expected Opening Day crowds. The weather indicated there'd be scattered showers throughout the day, and by midday, the parking lots were only half full, suggesting an attendance level below twenty-five thousand.

The sky was gray and the air was heavy with the feel of impending rain. Nevertheless, a welcome speech by Michael Eisner took place on the balcony of the Main Street Station, with EDL Ambassador Sabine Marcon in attendance. They then hopped into a Main Street fire truck and rode to the castle for the Euro Disney dedication speech, just as the clouds parted and the sun shined brilliantly upon Sleeping Beauty Castle for a truly "Disney" looking day.

> *"To all who come to this happy place, welcome."*
> *Once upon a time . . .*
> *A master storyteller, Walt Disney, inspired by*
> *Europe's best-loved tales, used his own special*
> *gifts to share them with the world.*
> *He envisioned a Magic Kingdom where these stories*
> *would come to life, and called it Disneyland. . . .*
> *Now his dream returns to the lands that inspired*
> *it. Euro Disneyland is dedicated to the young and*
> *the young at heart, with a hope that it will be a*
> *source of joy and inspiration for all the world.*
>
> *—Michael Eisner, 12 April 1992*

My daughter Michelle had come over for the opening ceremonies. We stood together while we watched it all unfold. All the problems aside, it was really something to be a part of a moment this grand, this important, in the

history of The Walt Disney Company—and its culture—
and international travel and tourism. But Michelle
whispered something in my ear that was far more rewarding than anything else: "I'm so proud of you, Dad."

But Troubles Continue

Even after opening, though, we were still subject
to the whims and opinions of Johnny-come-latelies and
freshly minted experts. Disney Studios chairman Jeffrey
Katzenberg was asserting his presence much more forcefully as time went on. I was in meetings for Euro Disney
that he attended, and I thought his input was sound, but
I remember saying to one of my peers at the table, "This
room is not going to be big enough for Michael Eisner
and Jeffrey Katzenberg." We could sense a building tension between mentor Michael and protégé Jeffrey. Both of
them were bright, experienced creative people.

During the opening week of Euro Disney, Jeffrey's
wife, Marilyn, went through the park, and decided that
she didn't like our merchandise. Our initial strategy
had been a higher level merchandise mix, a more luxe
assortment—we perceived that our audience (and our
research had backed this up) would not be as interested

in just plush and toys, key chains and trinkets, sweatshirts and T-shirts. So we had some really "upscale" boutiques and clothing shops, stylish stuff, but with a Disney twist.

It was clearly "Disney," but it was a whole different level than what we were used to selling at the time, especially in the clothing and accessories lines. Yet for uncertain reasons, Jeffrey went to Michael and talked about merchandise. Then he came to me; I brought along Sam Hutchins, who was my merchandise director. He had done a great job—and a lot of research—to arrive at a merchandise mix of souvenirs *and* sophistication. (Remember, too, we had the extraordinary combined experience of Armand Bigle and Dennis Hightower involved in this strategy, too.)

Although we were already open, and had stock that was displayed and selling well, Sam and I had to sit down with Jeffrey, and reformulate the whole merchandise assortment—based on the inclinations of someone who hadn't done the research, without expertise . . . or without an understanding of our consumer—seeing our merchandise after a day or two, and assuming an inexplicable expertise. We'd been working with this project for years, two years negotiating, five years in construction and design, and pretty much thought we had its needs and nuances locked down. Instead, we were told to comply with the whim of someone that in my mind offered no real improvement either in operations or Guest satisfaction.

June Wedding

I will be fully corny now, but utterly truthful, that during this time (and ever since), Mimi was my rock. In every aspect of my life's circumstances, she brought level-headedness, loyalty, love, erudite observation, grace, and good humor whenever needed and always in an appropriate way. I was grateful every minute that she saw qualities in me that she valued . . . and I was delighted and blessed when she agreed to be my wife.

Steven Juge, the Euro Disney lawyer who had done my will, was a big help getting things handled legally and properly through the U.S. Embassy. Remember that mayor in Chessy, the one with the shotgun? He had introduced me the day after our "test" fireworks show to his son, and we all became good friends. The son had become mayor, and handled our marriage legalities locally, so we got married in his city hall—a requirement of French law, which didn't exactly live up to the ideal of a ceremony suitable to both my and Mimi's families coming all the way to Paris. We wanted something that was a little more, I don't know, "Disney."

We were married in June of 1992, first in Chessy's town hall, and then again in the Founders' Club in the Disneyland Hotel, overlooking Euro Disneyland's Magic Kingdom and that picture-perfect castle. ("You're making an actor out of me," the mayor faux-objected. "But I'll do the wedding twice.") We were both extremely blessed to have our families join us that day—including both sets of parents. My son and brother were my best men, and Mimi's sister was her maid of honor. It was a time for celebration . . . of our many years of hard work.

Shakedowns and Shake-ups

As I had with Tokyo, my intent was to stay with EDL for about a year. The project had been beyond tough, and the shakedown time afterward was proving similarly difficult. Many of the expats were exhausted and ready for their counterparts to take over.

Although we had been successful in staffing and training our Opening Day Cast Members, within the first nine weeks a large number of them left Euro Disney. The not-so-sympathetic press said it was five thousand; we estimated that it was about a thousand—still nothing to be proud about, but not unexpected. We had seen it in Walt Disney World: people who wanted to be part of the historic moment, to be "on the ground" for all the events and ceremony, had dreamed of a nebulous "Disney" job for a long time.

But once the work became "somewhat routine," they were done. It was mostly on the hourly Cast Member level, but supervisory people, too, were departing—for everything from homesickness (they came from all over Europe) to it just wasn't what they expected. Or some didn't like the regimen, or didn't like the product, or didn't like having a million people step on their feet. Or who knows . . . but we were prepared for it. We had kept our recruiting staff on board, and had continued to interview.

Unfortunately, it was as if the difficulties in getting Euro Disney off the canvas would continue as its cultural identity was being questioned by some. There were several issues that contributed to the difficulties Euro Disney experienced at first. Along with its $4 billion debt, there was a severe economic recession in France at the time. Then unfavorable exchange rates and high interest rates—doubled the estimates. This caused, among many other things, little or no sales of property and hotels (due to the collapse of the French property market) and lower Guest spending. Everyone did their best, and much of it could be mitigated, but it was a foundering ship, one which unfortunately had a captain thoroughly unqualified to sail her.

It was interesting to recall that Jeffrey Katzenberg that week in April when we opened invited me to breakfast. He said, "Anything you need, any problems you have with this project, I want you to call me." I didn't report to him, of course, but I appreciated the support, and gratefully agreed. But I'll never forget his prescience. "You're going to have real problems here. We're leaving this project in [the] hands of somebody who's simply not going to be competent. When you go back home, Jim, there's going to be problems."

I knew what he meant—and he knew that I knew what he meant—and he was right.

Well, I still had lots of issues and lots of problems, and Frank Wells knew what the issues were. And I would not go to Jeffrey, when I had a long alliance with and support from Frank. But ultimately, breaking points just happen.

In August of 1992, after yet another frustrating, maddening head-butt flare up with Bob Fitzpatrick, I had finally hit that boiling point. Frank was there, and watched me blow up, concluding with my proclamation, "I'm packing my bags, and I'm out of here. Good luck."

Fuming, I turned to Frank. "Is there any problem with that?"

Frank, as usual, the soul of calm and reason, said, "I'm surprised you put up with it this long."

I began making my plans for repatriation that evening.

Going Away

In September of 1992, Mimi and I said a final good-bye to our friends and project family in France. We'd been through a kind of hell together, and although much of the EDL project was difficult and unpleasant, we got through it, and created a beautiful project that I'm still proud of today. I survived a medical crisis that probably should have killed me. I fell deeply in love and got married to a truly wonderful woman. I have happy and grateful memories of so many people. The big projects are a bonding experience: you form friendships, share memories, forge a common culture that lasts a lifetime. It's like war buddies who have nothing in common, but who can sit up all night talking about their shared service. I made good friends on EDL. They still are.

Shortly after our departure, Jeffrey's prophetic words from April proved accurate.

Phillipe Bourguignon was a French businessman who had spent fourteen years with the Accor Group, a French multinational hospitality company that owns, manages, and franchises hotels, resorts, and vacation properties. Disney had recruited him as the head of real estate development for DDC in 1990. He was heavily involved in the resort developments in EDL, and in October 1992 he was named the new CEO of Euro Disney, a position he held for five tumultuous years afterward.

Euro Disney's projected attendance for the first year was eleven million visitors, and projected operating income was predicted to be $373 million. In the end, Euro Disney attracted ten million visitors that first year, and declined to 9.8 million in 1993. Subsequent attendance growth was projected at 2 percent annually for twenty years, compared to 3.8 percent at other Disney parks. However, the park did not meet its projected operating income.

It was not the success story in that sense that Tokyo had been, or that might have happened if not for the serious financial issues that were essentially out of our control. In some ways, we took on a project that was too big and complex, and I think would have benefited had we left more Disney veterans in major roles. We did that in Japan—and Walt Disney Attractions Japan still exists to liaison and support the local management. Perhaps that approach might have made things run much more smoothly.

I was proud to be a part, again, of exporting such a treasured and valuable culture to another part of the world. I was exhausted, and not just a little bit scarred, physically and emotionally, but I remain proud of that work, still.

Some French intellectuals just wanted to prattle on how "the industrialization of fairy tales crushes the imagination of children and turns them into consumers and spectators," and that's fine—that's what intellectuals often do. That's not what *we* do, and not what we believe.

Philosopher Michel Serres contradicted, "It is not America that is invading us. It is we who adore it, who adopt its fashions and above all, its words." Something the French seemed frequently embarrassed to admit, so they covered it in bluster.

When writer and journalist Jean Cau dismissed the entirety of our efforts as "a horror made of cardboard, plastic, and appalling colors, a construction of hardened chewing gum and idiotic folklore taken straight out of comic books written for obese Americans," I truly questioned whether he had actually visited the park.

French political scientist Patrick Wajsman said France was in trouble if it felt threatened by Mickey Mouse and Donald Duck. "A child's laughter has no nationality, no passport, no ideology," he said. "Any moment of happiness is there to be enjoyed."

It reminded me of Ray Bradbury's informed, and intellectual, and emotional embrace of Disneyland. "No beatniks here," the famed author wrote. "No cool people with cool faces pretending not to care, thus swindling themselves out of life or any chance for life . . . Disneyland causes you to care all over again. You feel it is that first day in the spring of that special year when you discovered you were really alive."

I was glad to go home. Mimi and I had just planted our own grape shoot. I was happy to sit in the garden and watch the vine grow, and see what fruit would flourish.

I wanted to keep those happiest moments from Europe, and leave the harsh memories behind.

It had been seven years. I wanted to look ahead. Don't look back. We're not going that way.

Part Nine: Home Again

O F COURSE "coming home" was also actually coming into a whole *new* life. It was just in a lot of the same places where I'd already been, with many of the same faces—and my growing family, too. But it was a new beginning, both personally and professionally.

I returned to my Disneyland International offices at the Plaza Alicante office tower, about a mile from Disneyland. (We'd had to vacate the old offices in New Orleans Square when the Disney Gallery was created for that space.)

Shortly after that I was off to Japan, getting back in touch with my colleagues there, and beginning some tentative discussions about a second theme park for the Tokyo site. (I say tentative because Frank Wells had been trying to push for a second park almost from the day he arrived at Disney, but couldn't even get a spark, let alone the necessary flame.)

It was a great reunion, and after the difficulties of Euro Disneyland, it was refreshing to reconnect with old colleagues, meet new ones, and revisit something that had been such a pleasure and such a success.

Within weeks after my return to the States from Japan, though, my first heart catheter failed, and I was back in what would be a maddeningly repetitive series of hospital stays grappling with medical issues that plague me to this day. That December, I suffered a heart attack, and required quintuple heart bypass surgery. In January of 1993, my dad had a heart bypass procedure, too. He never fully recovered from his surgery, and passed away about a year later.

When we returned, Mimi and I finally settled into a house in the hills of Yorba Linda, California. It was good to be home and spend time with our families there. We planted a grape shoot in the back, as had become the tradition. Soon, I went back to tend my professional vineyard, but Mimi decided to stay home and tend gardens there. She took a sabbatical for a year—there were too many details and tasks; she wanted to focus on our home and on her art, and both of our mothers lived locally and were getting on in years, and certainly benefitted from her skills at caregiving.

President of Disneyland?

Meanwhile, at Disneyland, Jack Lindquist was retiring. Jack and I had been friends for a long time, and would be until the day he passed away. One of Jack's last acts before he retired was to come to France. He made a special trip shortly after we had opened.

We sat in one of the restaurants and Jack said, "Do you know what your next project's going to be?"

I said I didn't. Frank Wells had talked to me about wanting to do a second gate in Japan, but was determined to negotiate the deal himself, and I knew he wasn't getting anywhere. So I told Jack I imagined that at some point I'd go back and do that.

Jack said, "I want you to take over Disneyland."

I said, "Jack, I don't think you have the authority to offer that."

Well, by this time, Judson Green had been promoted to lead Walt Disney Attractions globally. He led the push to add new parks, hotels, and retail and entertainment zones, and I had, of course worked closely with him on EDL. So I gave him a call.

Judson was pretty angry that Jack had offered such a thing. Well, of course he was! Jack didn't have any conversations with Judson first—and it put Judson in an awkward position, because he didn't want to make that offer.

Judson may simply have known that Paul Pressler was who Michael Eisner had in mind to replace Jack. Lines of ascendancy within The Walt Disney Company were changing, and corporate executives were being shuttled *between* leadership in business units, instead of ascending in a single unit and staying there. This is an understandable strategy in a big (and getting bigger) company, and ideally you get a corporate executive force with a broader experience and understanding of the company—if those execs are inclined to listen and learn, rather than "make their mark" on a unit and then leave for greener pastures.

But I also noted a growing cultural tendency that was much more "corporate," and a lot less "Disney," a sense of rivalry and competition between and among executives. Everything from a "friendly game" of basketball to the presentation of a new project concept became a way to show off for the big boss, get noticed, or "climb the ladder." Many of these new-generation executives had their "eyes on the prize" of one day ascending to Michael's or Frank's job—and many of them dropped out when they realized they weren't going to get it.

Paul Pressler began in 1987 at Disney Consumer Products, and was being groomed as a junior Michael Eisner. He was soon put in charge of the fledgling Disney Stores retail rollout, where he further impressed Michael. Judson and Michael had decided that Paul's approach in the Disney stores could have significant positive impact on the profitability and operation of the park.

Jack had to circle back to me.

"I got in trouble," Jack said sheepishly.

"For offering me your job? I told you at the time I didn't think you had the authority to make that decision," I told him.

"But I'm the president of Disneyland!" he said with a wry smile.

I laughed. "I guess you know how much authority you have now."

For a while I had really felt elated. I'd started at Disneyland, and I'd love to do that. I think I'd still love to do that, and I've been retired for twenty years.

Of course, looking back on it now, those were really changing times at Disneyland. The reasons Paul Pressler was put in that position were not necessarily about Disneyland itself, but rather about creating lines of successorship on a corporate level. I'm not sure I could have handled the close corporate supervision after I'd been largely autonomous and left on my own for two major projects. It would have been tough to go back into a corporate life.

Plus, they were asking for stuff that would have rubbed me the wrong way, choices I felt sacrificed Guest experience and show quality for financial gains. The shopping mall model of return on investment per square foot was not a comfortable fit with our storytelling at Disney. Streamlining of product acquisition and manufacturing diluted the shopping experiences in the park. Everywhere you looked was the same merchandise. A lack of variety in designs, and in quality levels, and in price point dulled the uniqueness of the overall merchandise mix.

Sometimes it's the attractive opportunity that's *not* given to you that saves you from a big mistake.

I went back to work with a terrific and proven team, and great big colorful and exciting maps of the whole world.

International Research

There was still a fairly intense international desire for Disney parks. Many of the inquiries were from locations that were simply and obviously unable to support such a development, for reasons ranging from weather, to political instability, to suitable-land availability.

We kept a big map on the wall in our offices, with dozens of little red dots marking all the locations that had made inquiries. I remember showing that to Michael and Frank. Frank turned to Michael and said, "It looks like you'll be with this business for a long time." They were unaware of, and really impressed by, all the people wanting to do something "Disney."

I still remember one of the sites I was most interested in; it was long before we even imagined that mainland China was a possibility. That was never on my five-year plan—but South America was. We had found a site outside of Rio de Janeiro, Brazil, as a prime spot to develop a Disney resort. I believe that later a large number of the venues for the 2016 Olympics were built on the site we had uncovered. I thought that it checked a lot of boxes for us in terms of available acreage, government underwriting and support, convenient infrastructure, construction expertise, and available labor for building and operation.

The South Americans were nuts for Disney, and had been for decades, ever since Walt and a corps of his artists had visited the continent (they referred to themselves as "El Grupo"), and created popular film projects based on those

visits, including *Saludos Amigos* and *The Three Caballeros.*
Our research also showed that South Americans were the
number two nationality of visitors at Walt Disney World,
and Brazilians the largest figure among them. Larry Murphy, Disney's executive vice president and chief strategic
officer, saw a location in Brazil as "too close," and feared
that those Brazilian tourists who flocked to Walt Disney
World would stay away if they had a Disney resort closer
to home. I still think it's an untapped market for a Disney
development.

Look Globally, Think Regionally

The performance of Euro Disneyland may have briefly
cooled the enthusiasm for international development,
but Disney parks in general were performing extremely
well, and expanding and enhancing this business segment
seemed to be an excellent strategy.

There was an initiative to examine the idea of smaller
domestic parks, situated regionally, as a supplementary
experience to our key destinations on the East Coast and
West Coast.

The Disney Store concept had been successful, even
though there was much discussion and disagreement about

whether a retail presence would "cheapen" our name, or create some sort of competition with our parks. We found that these "frontline" presences actually *strengthened* our identity, and the experiences within the stores were treated with a lot of care and attention to show value.

Disney's America

DDC and WDI at this time were working on a unique stand-alone park concept for a three thousand-acre site near Haymarket, Virginia—not far from Washington, D.C. It was intentionally and specifically *not* a "Disney" experience, in the sense that characters and stories from the Disney culture were not going to be its storytelling foundation.

This was conceptually a strong idea. This park, to be called Disney's America, would be a Disney-quality, but smaller experience, one that drew its stories from, and supplemented, the historical experiences of the region. A new Hall of Presidents was part of the plan, along with a State Fair section, a "Family Farm" area, a Lewis and Clark-themed white-water rafting ride, a Native American village, Civil War fort, and an "Ellis Island" locale. It was clear that the company thinking was enthusiastic about the market's ability to support and sustain regional destinations, and that the reliability on Disney quality and value would permit creating unique original thematics.

Disney Regional Parks

At Disneyland International, we began to research and study the implications of taking our proven park concepts into a regional market. Small parks, working around a concept of an "E Ticket" attraction such as Pirates of the Caribbean or Haunted Mansion, surrounded by public space, themed dining, retail, and entertainment venues was truly being explored. We started working on regional theme parks. We truly were thinking of locations between Disneyland and Walt Disney World in Ohio or Oklahoma or Utah, places that didn't have adjacency and access to Disney. We researched sites and developed several plans like that.

Ultimately, all of them were rejected, as was the entire "regional parks" concept, because of the fear of cannibalizing Walt Disney World (primarily) and Disneyland. I still think it's a good idea. I think regional Disney parks would only whet Guests' appetites for seeing something bigger and better, making a pilgrimage to "the real thing."

Closer to a Tokyo "Second Gate"

One evening in the last week of March 1994, I had a conference call with Frank Wells and Ron Cayo, former chief counsel at The Walt Disney Company, and the guy who had been the lead negotiator on our contracts with OLC. My visit to Tokyo late that past year, before my several health and heart issues, had convinced me of something I'd suspected for a long time. As I said, Frank had been trying to get OLC to commit to a "second gate," an additional theme park at the Tokyo site, which in turn would leverage more ancillary hotel and resort business.

After all that time, Frank still wasn't getting anywhere, and I told him bluntly, "In my experience in Japan, they're not used to presidents dealing with presidents. It doesn't work that way. You need me to get in there, and Ron to get in there, and take all of the information, project logic, and design possibilities through to the *lower* levels. Once they're convinced," I said, "they'll elevate it from within, and be able to talk up the project with enthusiasm and authority, all the way to Masatomo Takahashi, the head of Oriental Land Company." It's called [the] Ringi System. It's like "passing the buck," upwards.

Frank said, "Fine. I've been working at this now for

years and I haven't gotten anywhere, and I doubt you'll get anywhere either." But he did encourage us to try a different strategy, and see if we could make it work.

Tragedy and Transition

On Sunday, April 3, 1994—Easter Sunday—my phone rang at home. It was Ron Cayo. Odd to get a call like that on a Sunday, especially Easter, I thought. Then I heard the terrible news: Frank Wells had been on a skiing weekend trip in Nevada's Ruby Mountains, near Elko. While leaving the area in a chartered helicopter, poor weather had caused an engine failure. Frank Wells had been killed in the crash that followed.

Not only were we all stunned at Disney, but the entire entertainment community mourned this tragic loss. I don't think I'm overstating that the Disney organization would never be the same. In his decade at Disney, Frank had been transformative. The soul of reason and the rock of constructive thinking, he'd been the dealmaker, the arbitrator, the peacemaker. He'd been a thoughtful listener and a sound, careful, and informed strategist. He was a really good man, a scholar, a gentleman. For all his success, he still *aspired*, and that philosophy inspired those of us who worked with him.

A memorial event was held at the Studio in Burbank on Monday, April 11, 1994. Attendees filled the biggest soundstage on the lot to capacity, and the adjacent stage airing a video simulcast was also overflowing. Dozens of additional people stood outside the open "elephant doors" of the stages, listening to Michael introduce speakers such as Clint Eastwood, Robert Redford, Roy E. Disney, and Candice Bergen. A choir from the First African Methodist Episcopal Church of Los Angeles sang. More than two thousand people came together that day for this three-hour remembrance to honor Frank.

As we headed home, I reflected on all that Frank had done—for Disney, for me, and for so many others. I remembered a slip of paper Frank always carried in his pocket. He told me he'd carried it for thirty years. It read, "Humility is the final achievement."

More Transition

The loss of Frank hit Michael really hard, too. A mentor, guide, protector, and friend—the left brain that tempered and supported Michael's right brain, was pulled out of his life. Certainly the stresses of the job can affect the health of any person, but I think this event pushed Michael even harder. On July 16, 1994, Michael was taken to the hospital and underwent quadruple bypass surgery. (Even with such a crisis behind him, Michael still called on me frequently about his own heart issues. He'd ask me about symptoms and pains, what treatments or drugs had they tried, what the medical experts thought about this or that, as well as other issues. I was happy to share my war stories and what I'd learned, but I kept worrying that Michael was relying on my words, and I told him, "You really should talk to your own cardiologist about this stuff, Michael. Are you getting these things checked out and taken care of? Don't make my mistake and brush off what your body is trying to tell you—don't ever be 'too busy' for that.")

Tensions between Michael and Jeffrey Katzenberg boiled over around this time, and with Michael still recovering from his heart surgery, Katzenberg resigned from Disney on August 25, 1994.

The company was in a period of uncertainty, and there was a tentativeness setting in that I hadn't felt since Michael and Frank had arrive a decade before.

Mimi also decided at this point not to resume her Disney career. She wanted to focus her energies on her skills as a fine artist. This was a decision that I supported wholeheartedly.

Disney's America Abandoned

With all of these shake-ups, many projects were put on hold. Disney's America had never gotten any traction; it was immediately opposed by some of its wealthy and influential potential neighbors in Virginia's Prince William County. And the project site, only miles away from historic locales such as the Manassas National Battlefield, riled up many historians and politicians.

Financial projections also came back less positive than expected. A four-season location would have low attendance and more closure days due to weather. The park had announced a 1998 opening, but the whole thing was abandoned thirteen months before the scheduled groundbreaking.

Our Regional Parks concept had likewise gasped its last breath—the failure of a "Mickey's Kitchen" restaurant pilot program in Montclair, California, and Schaumburg, Illinois, had convinced more people internally that Disney and regionality were not going to work (even though I think these were bad metrics from which to draw that conclusion).

In spite of all the unsteadiness, I was promoted to president of Disneyland International, where I became responsible for the development and creative direction of Tokyo Disneyland, in addition to directing the strategic and creative development of the site's second gate.

A Premiere Project

The head of Disney's film distribution company at this time was a fellow named Dick Cook. Dick had started at Disneyland working for Retlaw in about 1969, just as I was leaving it. He had also been a conductor on the Disney Railroad and on the Monorail crew. Dick moved to the Studio in Burbank in 1977, to manage pay television and nontheatrical releases; in 1980, he moved to the film distribution department, heading both distribution and marketing. Years later, in 1994, Dick had been made president of Buena Vista Pictures Distribution. (He was a ride operator who would move up to chairman. I was a ride operator who would move up to chairman. We're the only two in Disney history I can think of that did that.)

Dick came to me at an opportune moment with an interesting (but not totally unfamiliar) special project. I was still leading DLI, but certainly was "between projects"—still doing R & D on future possibilities, and I had only just begun negotiations with the Japanese for the second gate proposal at Tokyo upon Frank Wells's passing. Dick asked if I would head up a project team that was going to do a lavish world premiere for the animated feature *Pocahontas.*

Poppins *Precedes* Pocahontas

Since I'd known Dick since we were "kids," he knew who I am and what I do. Coming up through the ranks, he understood Disney parks and resorts I think better than anybody did at that corporate level. We'd also worked together a couple of times through Jack Lindquist on events where pictures marketing and parks had intersected.

Dick also remembered that in past efforts with movie events, a couple of standout campaigns had been handled mainly by the teams from Disneyland. I'd been a part of one of the most famous: the August 27, 1964, benefit premiere of *Mary Poppins* at the legendary Grauman's Chinese Theatre in Hollywood. Just the statistics should have been daunting and intimidating to our Disneyland team back then. There were some 1,500 total theater-goers, celebrities, and VIP guests; street-side bleachers to accommodate two thousand onlookers; valet parking for six hundred to seven hundred cars; support staff consisting of a couple of dozen Disneyland tour guides and security officers (the security men were dressed as English bobbies), twenty-five Disney characters, a twelve-member Pearly Band, Disneyland's Dapper Dans (dressed as chimney sweeps), thirty-eight theater ushers (dressed as Mary Poppins and Bert), and every Publicity staffer from Disneyland and the Studio.

The head of Disneyland Entertainment, Tommy Walker, had been put in charge of coordinating the event, a benefit for the nascent California Institute of the Arts (CalArts). Walker's goal was pretty simple: "Walt wants this premiere to be the finest, best-organized one in our company's history."

Dick Nunis oversaw a group of us that focused on crowd control and valet parking. I worked with Ron Dominguez and Bill Sullivan. Ron recalled, "We were pros at it. That was our business—moving people and handling people, making sure they had an enjoyable stay at Disneyland. So we just transferred that philosophy to the sidewalk there at the premiere."

For those of us from the park, we'd pretty much had a single two-hour overview and briefing on what we were going to be doing, which wasn't enough after we actually got there. It was intimidating, because it was well outside the kind of operation we were used to, and we were a little nervous because we'd heard this long list of stars who were going to be there—and the fact that Walt was going to be there was enough to make us assistant supervisors pretty nervous to begin with. It was "outside the berm," and out of our comfort zone.

In those days, you never got out of the park to do anything, except go home. So, we were all kind of apprehensive—wondering how's *this* going to work?

Our brief pre-planning session helped, but once we got up to the site and on the ground, we relied much more on common sense, thinking on the go, and adapting to immediate needs and situations. We were in constant communication with each other on the ground, but we all didn't see how the other pieces were working, until we saw TV film footage later. It seems as if we were just cogs in this wheel and never got to stand back to really see it in motion. I think Ron Dominguez was opening doors for some of the celebrities while I was sending cars out front: he never saw what I was doing, I never saw what he was doing, until we talked later and realized what our jobs had been.

But we again showed that Disneyland was a good team and could handle what was thrown at us. (I hadn't been a part of it, but a similar "all Disneyland hands on deck" push had made the 1960 Winter Olympics in Squaw Valley a huge success.) Reporter Eddy Jo Bernal of the *Los Angeles Herald Examiner* wrote, "With such a large delegation from Disneyland—and all wore badges from that country—one could only wonder: 'Who's minding the shop in Anaheim?'" Nobody really seemed to care much who was going to run the park while we were gone, because this was *so* much more important than running the park at the time—this was *the* premiere for *Mary Poppins*, and, of course, everything that went along with it. That was our number one priority.

I have a terrific letter that Card Walker sent to us after the event. It says, "We all know the Disneyland name is magic around the world. But to every one of you who participated in the staging of the *Mary Poppins* premiere at the Chinese Theatre last night, that magic was turned into the greatest team and dedicated effort Hollywood has ever seen."

Publicist Thomas Wilck wrote to Tommy Walker, "I'm sure that I've never seen before, and probably never will again, an event of this magnitude, requiring so much cooperation and coordination, in which every single participant handled his assignment so well. It was a beautiful thing to watch."

Pocahontas *in the Park*

There was certainly precedent and pedigree with large-scale-events production in Parks and Resorts, so when Dick Cook approached me about a *Pocahontas* premiere, I thought, "Well, we did well at Grauman's Chinese Theatre with the *Poppins* premiere, and then followed that a couple of years later at the Hollywood Pantages with the premiere for *The Happiest Millionaire*. There's a kind of template in place for this sort of thing."

That wasn't what Dick Cook and Michael Eisner had in mind. At all. They wanted a spectacular Event with a capital "E," with musical performances and live entertainment, and a movie screening. Outside. At night. In the middle of New York City, on the Great Lawn in Central

Park. And they anticipated an audience of sixty thousand people!

I formed a triumvirate leadership unit with Bob Gault, then-director of Disney Special Events, and Lyle Breier, who was Dick's special events vice president. I didn't really have a "team" that does that kind of thing, but I knew we had nothing but talent, and we all knew how to learn quickly. Skill sets and lessons learned over decades tend to translate pretty well.

"The Great Lawn in Central Park is usually associated with softball on languid afternoons or summer concerts by the New York Philharmonic," the *New York Times* wrote about our event. Our plans were much bigger, and much more invasive than any New Yorker was used to.

Michael liked to describe the event as "the family Woodstock of the '90s," and he felt a communal outdoor screening seemed appropriate to the themes of *Pocahontas.*

Most people in New York were supportive of our efforts to make this one-of-a-kind event a reality. Some people groused about "commercializing" the public space, with the *Times* reporting, "They insist that it looks more like Disney is transforming the park than celebrating it, that the premiere is more commercial than previous large concerts in Central Park, and that its physical scale seems inappropriate."

But they were wrong, and our event was free (the majority of the tickets to the event were given away in a random national lottery a few months before the premiere). We weren't the first "commercial" event staged there, nor was ours even the largest in terms of anticipated audience. More than two hundred thousand people (and up to eight hundred thousand!) had attended concerts by stars like Barbra Streisand, Simon & Garfunkel, Elton John, Luciano Pavarotti, and Diana Ross. Those artists also created television specials and top-selling audio recordings of their shows.

Our premiere *was* the first event in the park to require tickets—previous concerts and other events were opened to anyone, first come, first served. We wanted to maintain crowd-size control for safety, mainly because we expected many in our audience to be children, and we knew our equipment would fill up a lot of space on the Great Lawn. And we're Disney: safety and Guest experience are always paramount and fundamental concerns.

"I don't believe in the overcommercialization of public parks," Deputy Mayor Fran Reiter said. "But I do believe these kinds of gatherings, if they are free, can be very beneficial to the city. We want New York seen as a place where sixty thousand people can come together and have a good time."

Most of our critics in the city leadership didn't speak on the record. Disney was at the beginnings of an agreement to take over the derelict New Amsterdam Theatre on Forty-Second Street, and no one in local government wanted to foul that feathered nest. And a good thing, since that project sparked a revitalization that reinvented the heart of Times Square and Broadway.

Michael Eisner, New York born and raised, saw it as a huge gift to, and a celebration of, his hometown—a historic event that could only happen in New York, and one that would be remembered for decades to come.

Moving to Manhattan

Mimi and I relocated to Manhattan for a period of several months shortly after the new year of 1995 began. The event planned also began to take shape around that time. It was enormous, and would definitely be the monumental happening that Michael envisioned. Thus, it would also require a 24/7 kind of commitment—just the kind of thing that would recharge my batteries. As I've said, I'm not best at just managing a stagnant entity, and feel much more "in my element" when I've got something with a beginning, a middle, and a tangible end.

In my mind, it was Bob Gault who was really the leader of this huge project. I think maybe Dick wanted me there as security, and I certainly had the experience with things such as Guest Relations, Security, Merchandise, and Food Service that maybe Bob wasn't as well versed in. I'd also been in leadership on a few large-scale construction sites, so that stuff didn't make me nervous at all.

We really looked at the area in Central Park as our "attraction," and given the size of the square footage and the viewing angles from the ground, we realized that not only were multiple screens necessary and desirable, but they'd have to be of an unprecedented scale—we'd need to design and fabricate four "screen towers," each eight stories tall. Given the wind rate across the Great Lawn, these had to be superstructures, not just screens. Bob Gault brought in heavy-hitting engineers from the corporate side to create viable temporary buildings for the premiere. Six construction cranes hauled huge red steel cargo containers into the sky, stacking them until they were piled ten high. Work crews unloaded truckloads of crowd barriers, while forklifts shuttled building materials and supplies back and forth across our "construction site." One of the papers said the Great Lawn looked like Port Newark across the river in New Jersey.

We probably did look more like a container-ship terminal, and there were those who naturally worried that we'd do permanent damage to a beloved New York City site. But we also knew that there had been plans for some time to reseed the entire Great Lawn in late August. (It was later postponed until after a visit by Pope John Paul II set for October, since there were plans to celebrate a Mass in the same locale.) But to mitigate damage to the grounds themselves because of our building and the hundreds of thousands of feet and stroller wheels and the like on the lawn expected, we laid down 120,000 square feet of synthetic turf for our premiere.

The head of the city Parks Department said it was like building the pyramids in a week and then taking them down again.

Premiere Night Approaches

Of course, there were bumps. There was a rainstorm that threatened some of our equipment. Police and a parks official found someone trying to steal projection equipment from our specially constructed projection booths. There were charges that hundreds of tickets had been unfairly distributed to city employees and assorted big shots (not sure about "unfairly," there's always some comps and thank-yous to important project people). And there were constant forecasts of even heavier rain for Saturday.

As the week wound down, we were continually under overcast skies with scattered rain. The weather wasn't typical for a New York June, and there were even some storm warnings. And the night before the event, wouldn't ya know it, we had a thunderstorm. The fire marshal showed up and said he thought the premiere the following night might have to be cancelled. Too much lightning, too much wind, too much thunder was predicted and he claimed that the screen superstructures weren't secure enough.

Bob Gault called on me to intercede. I said, "Well, they've been secure enough. You guys have had people out here almost every day while they were welding these containers together, and thought it was fine. What's the problem now? What do I have to do to make the problem go away? We've got to go on tomorrow, it's a *premiere.*"

"Well, you guys have been working out of the police station, right?"

I said, "Sure." The city had given us project space in the Central Park Police precinct station house, the oldest station house in New York City.

He said, "You know those stairs, how they're all beat-up? If you guys brought carpenters here, if they could repair those steps, that would go a long way toward making things a little bit better."

I love New York.

"And all those interlocking barricades you guys brought in from California? If those got left behind when you're through, we could sure use those for other events."

I smiled and said, "I'm sure we can do all that. What else?"

He smiled and said, "That's it, see you at the show."

The Premiere in the Park

The weather remained gloomy on Saturday, June 10, 1995. We were ready, though. Entry access, crowd control, and merchandise and food locations were in place. Hundreds of portable toilets lined the perimeter of the site. Our eighty-foot-high screens were silhouetted against those gray overcast skies. Rain or no rain, we were ready for the biggest movie premiere in history.

Because thousands of people had thronged into Central Park by early in the afternoon, waiting to get the best "blanket spots" on the Great Lawn, we opened the gates early, at least an hour before the festivities were scheduled to begin. We had originally expected sixty thousand people. After ticket distribution in the spring, that number went up to one hundred thousand. But on the day of the premiere, more and more people kept coming in. It turned out that Lyle Breier had given out more tickets than we had thought were going to be distributed. You also factor in a percentage of no-shows, especially for free events. I'm guessing our no-show percentage was *nil*. As Bob Gault and I were driving around in a golf cart, checking the perimeter, we also saw that police manning the entry points kept allowing in family, and neighbors, and holding the ropes open, waving all comers to head on in. I'd guess we ended up with 120,000 to 125,000 people.

Despite the massive numbers, the people in attendance were low-key and friendly. People had come from all over the country to be a part of this, and as more people arrived, those guests already in place adjusted to make more space. People moved their blankets over to make room for strangers. It was truly a nice crowd. I remember we had two "incidents": a stroller bumped into the back of a lady's heel and she got very upset about it . . . and one person lost their wallet. And it was turned into our Lost & Found—with everything still in it. It was really a well-behaved group.

We had built a gigantic outdoor stage, with every amenity even the best concert amphitheaters featured, for an afternoon of live shows and music concert programming, to keep people energized and entertained while we waited for dusk. It was June, so dusk wasn't until 8:26 p.m. Our show probably wouldn't hit the screen until close to nine o'clock.

As dusk drew near, we had fifty-six thousand watts of light set to illuminate the night. That was enough electricity to power the World Trade Center. The audio wattage we used was equivalent to five high-end rock music concerts. Forty miles of cable were laid down, and eight projectors were used for nearly sixteen miles of film. Because of the throw distance from projector to screen, special wide-gauge 70mm prints of *Pocahontas* were made—eight of them to be precise, so each projection booth had a backup running simultaneously. The picture audio was even intentionally offset "out of sync" by twelve frames, in order to compensate for the sound travel time around the Great Lawn.

The show started with the nightfall, and everything went off without a hitch. The crowds were loving every minute of it, and many on our teams were actually moved to tears when the Walt Disney Pictures logo flashed onto the giant screens. We'd done something utterly unique. It was above and beyond our standards for Disney show quality. We'd worked hard and challenged ourselves. And we'd grown and succeeded. As the end credits rolled, we naturally "plussed" the whole evening with a surprise fireworks display to send people on their way home.

Plus, as a final gesture of gratitude and goodwill, Disney gave New York a million dollars for the use of Central Park.

Mayor Rudy Giuliani said that the city had certainly incurred costs from our premiere, but they would not be even close to a million. He also estimated that the event had a wider economic impact, bringing tens of millions of dollars to the city in direct and indirect revenues like food, retail, hotel nights, and the like.

Michael took me aside and offered me such a sincere and personal congratulations and gratitude for being a part of this. As a native New Yorker, he admired how easily I'd interacted with the politics and infrastructure of the city. I gratefully accepted his compliments, but I also told him about the efforts and sacrifices and skills of this great internal Disney team. "It's a big job, because there's a lot of them, but a note from you would mean the world to them."

Within a couple of weeks, Michael had sent every team member a specially created commemorative print celebrating *Pocahontas in the Park*. The art piece had everyone's name on it—and each came with a personal note signed by Michael.

It's amazing, what remarkable things you can do with remarkable people. Nobody ever said, "We can't do it." The possibility of failure never crossed our minds. Through my entire career, all I've ever heard is, "Yeah, we'll figure this out. Let's just go do it."

Planting shoots. Coaxing vines to grow and bear fruit. Harvesting. A cycle of satisfaction.

A Terrible Parting

My daughter Michelle was pregnant at the time I went to New York. She was such a dear-hearted person, and single-minded about two desires in her life: one was she wanted to be a Disneyland Ambassador, a dream unfulfilled. (I often still feel that my employment status prevented that dream.)

She also wanted—more than that, however—to be a mother. She had miscarried once, but she was pregnant again, and we were all thrilled for her. I talked to her on the phone during my relocation to New York, and as time went on I got more and more concerned. She kept getting sick, not feeling well. After a while that general malaise turned to nausea and vomiting. Her doctors were stymied. I was far away and kept prodding her to keep going to the doctor and find answers.

When I got home, it was worse than I expected. She couldn't hold down any food. She should have been hospitalized, but wasn't. Her health problems just continued, and on August 28, 1995, Michelle and her baby died. We learned later that her problems had been caused by an extreme thiamine deficiency (it was known in the past as beriberi), a lack of vitamin B-1. It's a rare disease, and if she'd had better medical care, she might have been diagnosed and treated.

I'd just come home from another professional accomplishment. I'd spent a whole career fixing things. I couldn't fix Michelle. That was a kind of agony I can't describe.

A father holds his daughter's hand for such a short while, but he holds her heart forever.

Our world was thrown off-axis. We'd spent so much time with Michelle and her husband at the Yorba Linda house—there were so many memories there. It felt so haunted. Mimi and I sold the Yorba Linda house and found a somewhat secluded "horse property" in an equestrian area of Orange Park Acres in Orange, California. (Mimi's mother and my mother both lived in the southern part of California's Orange County, so being closer to them was another advantage.) We didn't have horses, so the paddock became tennis courts, the stables became a garage for my antique cars and collections of career memorabilia, and the stalls each assumed individual roles: Mimi created an art studio in one, and I used one for my model railroad setup.

The property also had a pool and a large back patio, where we would spend a lot of our lives to come. Alongside that patio, I found the spot, and planted our grape shoots. This was more than seven decades after Sitte had secreted them into the United States. The vines from the "Old Country" continued to propagate, and to remind me of the fruits of every aspect of life.

Two Debuts

In my role with DLI, I kept in close touch with the ongoing development of the Tokyo park and property. In April 1996, we debuted Toontown, a version of Mickey's Toontown, which had opened at Disneyland in 1993. The same day Toontown opened, my son, Jim, and daughter-in-law, Bonnie, debuted our first grandchild. I had flown back from Tokyo just in time to welcome a beautiful grand-daughter, Kayleigh, into the world. I will always be grateful to Bonnie for waiting for me to arrive at the hospital.

We welcomed our wonderful grandson Joshua into the family three years later. I suppose being born into a "Disney Family" brought some extra fun with it, but the two of them spent many fine and fun hours throughout their youth with Mimi, exploring their creative nature and artistic talent in her studio.

Kayleigh recently graduated from Point Loma Naz-arene University in San Diego with an art degree; Josh studied photography at California Baptist University in Riverside. He's now a professional photographer.

These two kids are the joy of our lives, and we're so proud of the adults they have become.

Floating Disneyland

Every couple of years, Michael Eisner hosted a huge Executive Summit in Aspen, Colorado. All the leadership and key executives gathered away from Burbank, and were given presentations and lectures that were felt to be leadership-inspiring and team-building, and there were many wide-open and fearless discussions encouraged about the state of the company, future directions, and the imagining of new efforts.

I remembered Jack Lindquist talking years ago about "phantom boats"; well, Jack called them phantom boats. They would take the elements of Disney attractions and experiences from country to country by means of an ocean liner—not a cruise ship, but a ship that would show up in port and offer little preview centers and maybe an attraction or two, to whet people's appetites and encourage them to come to our parks and resorts. I kept thinking, *well, why not take a whole Disney park around the world? Maybe on an aircraft carrier?*

So during this Executive Summit, a couple of us got on the phone with the Department of the Navy and ended up talking to an admiral who knew about surplus and decommissioned materiel, including ships. He told us they had a medium-sized aircraft carrier they were going to destroy, sink as a training exercise, and use it to create a coral reef somewhere. I asked if they'd sell it to a private corporation, and I got a price. (Of course, the carrier would be stripped of everything except its superstructure and propulsion; there'd be no armaments or secret stuff, but since we would have to gut the insides for our purposes, this was fine.)

The navy had provided us with all of the dimensions and information we needed on the aircraft carrier, and the WDI guys, with the operational guys, sat down and started imagining what we could do with a ship this size. We developed some immediate ideas of a Fantasyland and a Tomorrowland on the aircraft carrier, with a Downtown Disney kind of a thing on the upper deck, and a big Ferris wheel to "marquee" the thing.

We also looked at oil tankers. There was more room inside oil tankers than in aircraft carriers. Two huge oil tankers would take a whole park. You could have all the lands that Disneyland has. But oil tankers are pretty boxy and ugly, and you wouldn't have that big top deck to do big marquee elements. I liked aircraft carriers because they look kind of sexy. Some people in the company were against the militaristic overtones. I argued that turning swords into plowshares was about as purehearted as can be—I mean none of us wanted to appear militaristic.

I added the concept of having a "preview boat," sort of a seafaring "advance team," a ship that went out ahead and sold tickets in advance for the "Disney Ship" that was coming to town. Kind of like what the circus used to do.

The Disney park ship would just follow the sun, wherever it was summer or spring, you'd chart a course and make a marketing plan and go with a Disney park from port to port, all around the world. This was before anybody thought about doing anything "Disney" in China or Hong Kong. People who would never see Walt Disney World or Tokyo Disneyland would get to have a Disneyland sail into port and visit *them*. Michael absolutely loved this idea, so we started working on it in earnest.

Tony Baxter at WDI, who had led the WDI team on EDL, and was now a vice president of creative, was the lead designer, and an Imagineer named Bruce Gordon did a lot of work on it. They created an entire concept, several iterations as I recall, showing the dissected deck plans and what attractions could be accommodated. A Rocket Jets "conning tower" and train ride attraction were on top, along with that "iconic" Ferris wheel. Other attractions thought about were Star Tours and "it's a small world," plus a Jules Verne deck with a full-sized Nautilus submarine, a

Mickey's Toontown, an Indiana Jones attraction, theaters for live performances, restaurants, and merchandise. They built a beautiful model at WDI Dimensional Design, and began to refine and develop the creative ideas and research the practicalities of such a vessel—and even christened her the SS *Disneyland.*

At this time, however, Disney had committed enormous resources—and more than a billion dollars of capital—to their first entry into the leisure cruise industry, with the founding of the Disney Cruise Line division. The maiden voyage of the first ship, *Disney Magic,* was scheduled for March 1998. (It was delayed, however, and didn't set sail till that July.) The fleet's second ship, *Disney Wonder,* was slated for launch later that year, in December.

Up in Burbank, Larry Murphy, executive vice president and chief strategic officer—and really the driving force in the cruise business—was deeply trusted by Michael. Larry disliked our "Floating Disneyland" project on a couple of fronts. The Disney Cruise Line was seeking their registry and maritime permissions on so many levels and with so many authorities by this stage, and they worried that if our "ship" started doing the same, it might lead to crossed wires and cause confusion.

Larry also thought that two seafaring entertainment

enterprises launching too close together would trigger a great deal of confusion not only with sanctioning boards and in the corporate ranks of the industry, but also with consumers and tourists. One would have the potential to sink the other because of it. Why not enter the leisure cruise market and test the waters, learn the ropes, and then use that knowledge to expand into this other enterprise with expertise?

So the SS *Disneyland* was put into development dry dock. It's still there as far as I know.

A Return to Tokyo

I enjoyed the process of creation and collaboration that we had with our floating park project; I still think it's something worth examining for regions underserved by available Disney parks. I was disappointed to see it founder, but as the gathering was wrapping up there was finally, blessedly, movement in Tokyo with OLC. They were ready to get moving on the second gate and developing their overall resort strategy.

I was ready, too. There were too many vines that had not taken root since my return from Europe. It was time to plant again.

Part Ten: Another Sunrise

IN A 1983 article in the *Los Angeles Times*, shortly before the opening of Tokyo Disneyland, an Oriental Land Company (OLC) representative predicted that it would be seven years before their investment would be paid back. That initial investment was returned *in full* by the end of year four.

Tokyo Disneyland was an ongoing success story. Even after the fifth anniversary, in 1988, the attendance for Tokyo Disneyland continued to rise, thanks in part to the introduction of new events and attractions. In fiscal year 1991, the park welcomed its one hundred millionth Guest.

A decade after opening, OLC saw a pre-tax profit of $202 million in the fiscal year that ended March 31, 1993—in the middle of the worst recession in Japan since the end of World War II. The annual attendance has averaged between seventeen and eighteen million Guests.

Tokyo Disneyland was an ongoing financial success because the connection and interweaving of Japan and

Disney created something that brought strength—and appeal—to both. The park is like a traditional Japanese garden, a highly designed version of nature that the Japanese see as more satisfying in its perfection than nature itself. It is so precise in its depiction of an unthreatening, fantasy America that, in an odd sort of way, the park has become totally Japanese. And that, of course, is just the way the Japanese wanted it. It's what OLC asked for. When the Japanese come to Tokyo Disneyland, according to Masako Notoji of Tokyo University, "they are enjoying not the 'American Dream,' but their own 'Japanese Dream.'"

"The 1980s was a decade of great economic affluence and an era when Japanese society started to feel a part of world culture," Notoji pointed out. "Tokyo Disneyland really became a symbol for many people of Japan's entry into world culture."

In December 1988, the JR Keiyo Line train service opened its Maihama station, located just adjacent to the park's main entrance—making Guest accessibility to the park far more convenient now. (Before this, mass transit access to the park was bus service from the Urayasu station on the Tokyo Metro's Tozai Line, about twenty minutes away. We found out later that OLC had owned and operated these bus lines, so they undercut their own profitability in order to add convenience for their Guests.)

At the time, the JR Keiyo Line was running temporarily between the Soga and Shin-Kiba stations. In March 1990, the line was extended to the JR Tokyo Station. I think this widened our audience, too—everyone from young "urban explorers" to multigenerational families could simply get to the resort with greater ease.

A Culture of Family

At the time we opened Tokyo Disneyland, it wasn't really common for adults to enjoy amusement parks. Grown-ups just waited around while the kids enjoyed themselves, because they felt theme parks were for kids. (In fact, leisure itself was not always a part of the Japanese lifestyle. Fathers used to see family outings as a duty.) This was along the lines of what people had thought when Walt opened Disneyland, and one of many reasons Walt built it. "I felt that there should be something built, some kind of an amusement enterprise built," he famously said, "where the parents and the children could have fun together."

As Disneyland had in the United States, Tokyo Disneyland wrote a new chapter in Japanese social history, with the simple idea that family outings can be fun. Families now account for about half of the park's visitors.

In addition, it's been noted that Tokyo Disneyland, and the way that OLC completely embraced the ideas of *Disney Quality*, changed their national culture of customer experience. "Before Disneyland, [the] Japanese were without standards to judge service," said Hidehiko Sekizawa, a specialist in the leisure industry at the Hakuhodo Institute of Life and Living.

One of the OLC executives told me, "We Japanese are not really good at creating something from the beginning, but we're very good at making something better. TV sets, electronics, cars. You make it, you invent it, we'll make it *better* than what you made it." I think that's how they looked at Tokyo Disneyland. *You make it, we're going to just make it better as time goes on.*

I have to say, I don't know if it's better, but they have spent an enormous amount of money and time enhancing what we first built. They're also putting in new attractions much faster than we would have, including thrill attractions, which we didn't have much of when we first opened, to appeal to a broader public. They're just making it *better*. (This was mainly due to our pushing for greater in-park capacity since we were "selling out" the park regularly.

We continually proposed new attractions and venues and had to sell them on each idea. We developed an "Added Capacity Program," where we pitched one attraction at a time.)

We started looking into the idea of creating a second theme park for Japan soon after the opening of Tokyo Disneyland, along with holding discussions about the development of the area around the park. These deliberations went on between OLC, Disney, and the Chiba Prefecture. By 1987, Frank Wells was leading these talks, evaluating the idea of a second theme park. There was joint research conducted between the OLC and Disney on what the public reception would be toward a second park. Although OLC announced plans for a second theme park in 1988, it took almost eight years to solidify and set a contract for that deal.

Using the Ringi System to Move Ahead

Based on Frank Wells's encouragement shortly before his passing, Ron Cayo and I went ahead with moving the Tokyo Second Gate concepts into the bloodstream of OLC via the Ringi System. At the same time, Ron brought on a guy named David Thompson, who was then part of legal counsel at the Studio. Frank had set the whole thing up. He had made it easier for us. He explained it to the Japanese why they needed it, what it was going to do for attendance, and how "the whole will be greater than the sum of its parts." We just picked up that ball and ran with it.

Finding a New World

A concept and name for the second park proved just as elusive as the "deal" itself. Initially, there was some interest in a Hollywood- and movie-based park similar to Disney-MGM Studios, which had opened in Florida in 1989. "Disney Hollywood Studio Theme Park at Tokyo Disneyland." Some concept work was done with this idea, but I don't think the Japanese were much impressed by the Florida park, and how it might "translate into Japanese." We took the OLC brass to Walt Disney World, and they simply did not like the studio-themed park.

The announcement that Universal was bringing their highly successful, tried-and-true movie studio park to Osaka further dampened enthusiasm for a "Disney version" of the movie park, so research and development for a whole new theme was begun in about 1992. In the second theme park, the Japanese outlined to us that they were searching for a plan that would "create a new market by providing a completely different experience from Tokyo Disneyland" and that "is suited to the Japanese people, making them want to return to it again and again."

Our overall marching order was that it had to be better than TDL. Experience quality was so much the priority that they wouldn't establish a budget. Much in the style of the Added Capacity Program, we just kept designing, shaking down, costing out, and then presenting each component as we went. OLC paid for all the R & D, design, and implementation—and I don't recall them ever turning anything down. I established a budget in detail as we went along, so I could monitor our own process and discipline.

A Completely Different Experience

Japan is an archipelago made up of thousands of islands, surrounded by the Pacific Ocean, the Sea of Okhotsk, the Sea of Japan, and the East China Sea; Japan's coastlines stretch more than 18,480 miles—and no point anywhere in Japan is more than ninety-three miles from the sea. Not only does the sea play an enormous role in Japanese culture, history, society, art, food, and identity, the Japanese believe that Japan itself was a "gift from the sea" to the people of Japan. "The seven seas" as a thematic foundation gave the Imagineers an incredible global wealth of history, folktales, fantasy, adventure, and science fiction stories upon which to draw for environments and stories.

I think that during the 1980s and 1990s, there were those in corporate leadership at Disney who had gotten fixated on the idea that new Disney park attractions had to be based on some contemporary property or feature some popular star. There was a notion that somehow the stories contained within the Disney canon weren't appealing enough for modern audiences (even though thousands and thousands of people who have never seen *The Adventures of Ichabod and Mr. Toad* continued to queue up at Mr. Toad's Wild Ride at Disneyland) . . . or that the Imagineers were somehow incapable of creating attraction stories that could have popularity without relying on what we now call existing "intellectual property"—never mind Pirates of the Caribbean and the Haunted Mansion and Big Thunder Mountain Railroad.

In creating a wholly "Disney" park themed to the sea, a large portion of the storytelling and place making would lean heavily on the *original* ideas of the Imagineers.

While resources and inspirations for many of the areas and attractions may have touched on ideas that had been used in other Disney parks (Port Discovery has a philosophy of "past future" not totally unlike EDL's Discoveryland, for instance), it was an exciting challenge to see if they could come up with an experience that might come close to Magic Kingdom park, but that didn't largely rely on well-known experiences and characters and stories.

The Imagineers began their typical deep research and lofty dreaming around stories of the seas—in fact and fiction and fantasy. A series of "ports-of-call" began to take shape, such as a Mediterranean Harbor, an American Waterfront, the Arabian Coast, a fantasy Mermaid Lagoon, Lost River Delta, a Jules Verne-like Mysterious Island, and the retro-futuristic Port Discovery.

Lots of people think our seafaring thematic was an outgrowth, or even a "design lift," from a park design proposed adjacent to the retired *Queen Mary* in Long Beach, California, in 1990. Not true. None of the elements that were proposed in Long Beach ever ended up in Tokyo. It wasn't one that triggered the other. We were independently thinking about a second park.

"And so, slowly but steadily," the official OLC history reads, "the second park began to materialize. And at the base of all these efforts was the boundless enthusiasm and staunch determination to create a unique park that cannot be experienced anywhere else in the world."

Sometimes, that "boundless enthusiasm and staunch determination" came with an overabundance of caution from our Japanese partners. Many still didn't think there was enough demand to be able to fill two parks—even though we were turning Guests away daily at Tokyo Disneyland. Some didn't feel there was going to be enough demand to operate both parks. We did our own studies in concert with them, and proved that the demand was there, that "if we built it, they would come."

Even though the creative development, being led by Bob Weis (who is today the president of Walt Disney Imagineering), was bowling everyone over, we were still showing them things that were really unfamiliar . . . and untried. Some of the first designs had a large lighthouse as an "icon" structure, a central focal point as Guests enter the park. It was chosen and designed for very American ideas—a "beacon of hope," a happy homecoming, a guiding light for adventurous seafarers. But for the Japanese, a lighthouse brings up ideas of loss, of melancholy and loneliness.

Bob Weis had a good relationship going with

Masatomo Takahashi, the president of OLC. Bob discovered through some conversations that Takahashi was an iguana-fancier, and managed to bring an iguana through Customs in Tokyo, and then present it to Takahashi in his office—along with some new designs for the proposed new park icons that Takahashi liked.

We kept looking for a "castle," an icon at the visual center of the proposed park that communicated the international character and the sense of a maritime adventure that was the heart of our storytelling. Steve Kirk and the Imagineers kept tossing ideas around. What exists all over the world? What would you see if you were in a ship?

I remembered going to Knott's Berry Farm when I was a kid and being fascinated by a "volcano" made of lava rock. It was probably only about twelve feet tall, but it had lights, sound effects, and even steam that (well, to a kid anyway) was pretty impressive. I wondered if Steve and his team could create a "real" volcano, and the result was Mount Prometheus, an "active" volcano with bursts of fire, steam venting from cracks in its sides, and water blasts from the "ocean" that it rises from.

The lighthouse was gone for good, too—replaced by a global symbol presenting the entire Earth as a "water planet," rising from a kinetic fountain: the AquaSphere.

This icon set a mood for a seafaring visit around the world in a much better context for our Japanese audiences.

Sign on the Dotted Line

In the spring of 1996, only a few months after we'd begun our contract work in earnest, we had finally gotten to the final stages of the contract negotiations with OLC. (See, Frank? I told you we could do it!) But then there was hesitation. Still such an abundance of caution. More time was passing without the commitment. Taking advantage of a Japanese cultural predisposition to avoid any embarrassment, we kind of *pushed* them over that last hurdle.

You've heard the expression "losing face." We finally got that deal done when I said, "You know, Michael Eisner is on his way over here [which he wasn't at the time]. He thinks you're going to do a second park—so we should have a press conference while he's here." Up to that point, they just couldn't seem to "close the deal," so I called Michael, and he said, "I'll get on a plane and come on over."

When they heard Michael Eisner was on his way, they put together a press conference. We had it when Michael got there (along with me, Bob Iger, Roy E. Disney, and

Tetsuro Sato and Toshio Kagami from OLC). Our second gate became a reality, because our counterparts didn't *want to lose face.*

In April 1996, Oriental Land and The Walt Disney Company signed the "Tokyo DisneySea Park Development, Construction and Operation Contract" and the "Tokyo DisneySea Hotel Development, Construction and Operation Contract."

So we had our agreements in place, and we had a wonderful project name: Tokyo DisneySea.

Even this name, however, turned out to be somewhat controversial because *sea,* if mispronounced (and pronounced "shi"), could mean *death* in Japanese.

Leading the Second Gate Team

Many years before this, a group of us were flying to Europe to look at another site for EDL. Frank and Michael were on board, along with then-president of WDI Carl Bongirno, Dick Nunis (then head of Walt Disney Attractions), and me. Frank said to me, "On the way over, Dick Nunis is going to talk to Carl about WDI becoming part of Walt Disney Attractions. Carl's got to talk Dick into letting Attractions become part of WDI." Frank wanted me to be aware, but I wound up being in the middle of it.

So, just before the flight started, Carl said to me, "Would you consider taking over WDI?

I said, "No, I don't think so. Carl, why do you say that?"

"I'm going to retire. Whoever replaces me will have to put up with Nunis and that BS, and those guys. You get along with Dick [Nunis], and as long as he's going to be around, you could run WDI. You're qualified."

"Carl, I'm a project guy, I like doing operations, and your role is all politics and administration. A guy should do what he does, and stay out of what he doesn't do."

Dick was saying, "I wouldn't want to take over WDI until you clean it up. It's a goddam mess." He started naming names. "That guy should go, that guy should go, that guy should go; you got to control costs, it's out of control, I don't want it."

Carl made the argument that those were all the reasons why Attractions *should* take WDI. "You can clean up the mess. You don't like those people, then you can get rid of them when you can find a better way to operate, because I think we're operating pretty good. I think

Attractions should belong to WDI, because we understand how design and show and operations come together; you don't seem to!"

That flight was long . . . and so was the argument.

Frank came to me at the end of the trip and asked, "So what was resolved?"

I said, "Nothing."

He said, "Well, I'm not surprised."

I bring this up because in many ways, no matter the resolution after that long and contentious argument in the sky, I *did* end up being the administrative leader for both our DLI project teams and the WDI teams in Europe. Jeff Rochlis at WDI, which was responsible for the design, had hired a construction company, Lehrer McGovern Bovis, to manage the construction on the project, but there was no on-site Disney project leadership other than me. Because I was the only Disney guy on the site, and because my "roots" on the project were the deepest, they just gravitated toward me—Imagineering, construction, operational personnel. I just ended up heading up the whole project. When Mickey Steinberg came on board, he was surely the WDI leader, but even Mickey treated me as the client and administrative leader.

When that project was over, Peter Rummell, who was in charge of WDI, said, "Before we start this next project, understand that all the WDI people think they work for you. Let's just make it official. Take the team that's doing the Tokyo second gate, and I'll just step aside—you've got them."

So, we merged the two organizations.

It was just a beautiful arrangement. It worked very well. It was collaborative and communicative. There was no rivalry or interdepartmental ill will. Our shared focus and our shared goal was to create an amazing experience.

In November 1997, the basic construction plan was completed and set down in the "Tokyo DisneySea Project (draft)." With the completion of this plan, we were finally able to announce the specifics of Tokyo DisneySea to the general public on November 26.

Resorts

There was some degree of conflict over how the contracts spelled out the peripheral land-use issues related to the areas directly surrounding the park. There was a long debate as to whether or not Disney should have a right to any claim to it, based on the Disney name, or whether or not OLC could just develop this on its own. Then-OLC president Toshio Kagami didn't want to call it a resort, because he was sure that if we changed the name from Tokyo Disneyland to Tokyo Disney Resort, Disney would ask for a higher royalty. I said no, I promise you, we won't ask that. They were already paying for the "Disney" part, all adding the word "resort" meant was that Guests could stay overnight. We negotiated a certain revenue stream that we felt was fair—and the Japanese felt was fair—so we could just move things along.

OLC insisted that they design peripheral development. We felt that if it was going to be across the street, and appear to be part of the overall resort, that WDI should design it. Again, there was a compromise. They designed it; we supervised what they designed. We either approved or disapproved certain things. Most of what we disapproved, they argued about.

The negotiations with OLC and the prefecture involved a lot of Ringi System wrangling. We negotiated all the expected things, and many that were not. Outside the property infrastructure included not just road improvements but utilities; even seemingly intangible issues such as "additional road wear." But far from being "pork barrel," or viewed as financially based schemes, the Japanese saw all of this attention as a degree of respect for their people, and a level of dignity about their Guests from all over the world that was important to their national pride.

We also built a high-rise parking structure, because the second gate and additional development ate up the surface parking, much as Disney's California Adventure took up the old Disneyland parking lot.

On October 22, 1998, a groundbreaking ceremony was held on-site. After the ceremony, a joint Disney/OLC press conference was held, hosted by Kagami and Michael Eisner. More details on Tokyo DisneySea were made public. At the same time, the name "Tokyo Disney Resort" was first announced for the area in Maihama that encompassed the two parks, the Disney hotels, the Tokyo Disney Resort official hotels (non-OLC properties such as Hilton, Sheraton, Okura, and so on), the monorail system, and Maihama Station.

Shortly afterward, in 1999, I was promoted to chairman of Disneyland International, where my primary focus was to develop and maintain the strategies that ensured the continued growth and success of the Tokyo Disney Resort.

Preventative Medicine

My health went up and down throughout this period. It takes a lot of doing to have as many surgeries and accumulate as many stents as I've earned. There was a fear about whether I'd stay healthy through this project, so the company encouraged me to take my cardiologist with me at the beginning—to monitor my activity and to brief the local clinicians who would be attending me when needed. He shared my records and showed them various video recordings of previous procedures, and made sure that I had the best and most specific care at the ready in case I should need it.

I suffered an annoying and persistent nosebleed at one point (it went on for three days, due to the blood thinners I was on), and went to see my Japanese medics. You'd have thought I was either a head of state or had survived an assassination attempt . . . or both when I checked in with them. I was met at the hospital with grim urgency and swiftly escorted by a team of their best physicians, cardiologists, and nurses. Even the hospital president came to offer his greetings and make sure I had the best of care. I'm not sure if they were disappointed when they realized that they simply had to cauterize my nosebleed and send me away. But it was actually a really impressive showing and quite reassuring, particularly if I were to have a real medical emergency!

A Different Tokyo Disney

Immediately, the differences between my two Japan projects were apparent, and truly rewarding. There were old friends and colleagues embedded there, and infrastructures in place that we had previously had to improvise or build. We had formed an entity called Walt Disney Attractions Japan that Disney employees still operate there as a support unit. This was outside the main TDL agreements—OLC pays for it, and all associated expat costs. I negotiated this at the opening of TDL and the group contained experts from Disney Operations, Food, Merchandise, Marketing, and so on. And naturally, the Japanese had not only gained experience, they'd grown *into* the Disney culture in ways that were satisfying to see, and proof positive that our practices and philosophies were sound and successful. From the very beginning, I felt that Tokyo DisneySea would be a pleasure, and restorative to my old Disney spirit after some trying and disheartening years.

Bill Gair, who had been in France, was the first Disney

executive to be relocated for DisneySea's preparation and opening. He was appointed director of facilities management. I brought him to Tokyo DisneySea, where he later went on to hold the position of vice president of Resort Operations.

Mas Imai, who was in charge of Disney's royalty stream out of Tokyo Disneyland, became our vice president of finance. He was already known and respected there, and was of Japanese-American descent, so a good fit in temperament and identity.

Ray Tanaka was director of administration for Walt Disney Attractions Japan. Ray was the "go-to guy" for just about anything and everything. He was a seasoned and respected liaison between OLC and Disney, and it seemed there was never a hitch or issue that Ray couldn't resolve with efficiency, tact, and intelligence.

Art Kishiyama was the project manager for Tokyo DisneySea. He and I shared some common roots: his childhood was in Los Angeles, where his parents ran a mom-and-pop grocery store. A retired United States Air Force colonel, Art did a great job in coordinating the disciplines, getting people to step in and work together as teams—and then take ownership. A lot of how we got things done with the Japanese counterparts was through Art.

When I first met Jim Thomas, he had been leading the project financial team at WDI for TDL. We worked together on and off when he was a WDI employee the year or so prior to the opening of Tokyo Disneyland. He had relocated to Japan for the last year of the project as director of administration for the WDI team. (In fact, my daughter Michelle babysat Jim's kids from time to time while we both lived near each other in Tokyo.) Jim then went back to Glendale, California, leading project estimating, project scheduling, and project finance; eventually he took over leadership of the entire project management organization.

Jim was very informed about the talent of all the WDI project managers, and advised me in casting the TDS project management talent. We selected John Verity, Doug Leblanc, Bob Pero, Peter McGrath, and Craig Russell (who was already leading the architecture and facilities engineering work on the project); after the project was approved, we added Orlando Ferrante (who had led Imagineering's work on the Disney Cruise Line).

When they made me chairman, I asked for Jim Thomas to take my spot as president of Disneyland International, and he did that through the opening of Tokyo DisneySea. (I asked him to stay in Japan—they were moving DLI responsibilities to Walt Disney Attractions Japan instead of Anaheim—but Jim didn't want to do that; he just didn't want to relocate. So he had to step down and went back to senior vice president in project management at WDI.)

Bob Weis had originally developed the TDS concept and sold the creative. Then he stepped out and a terrific Imagineer named Steve Kirk turned the concept into reality. A Cal State Long Beach grad, Steve had joined WDI in 1976, where he'd been involved with Discovery Bay (a project that never got developed) at Disneyland. Steve did create the characters Dreamfinder and Figment for that project, and then brought them over during his work on the Imagination Pavilion at EPCOT Center.

Steve introduced the TDS project to various levels of management within OLC, unified (and often refereed discussions on) all the design vision of the upcoming park's attractions, and was senior vice president of creative over the whole project. Steve's wife, Kathy Kirk, was director of the creative division at WDI, and his brother, Tim Kirk, is a remarkable concept and creative director who was deeply involved in DisneySea. "The Kirks" were a formidable force at WDI. (It makes me sad that WDI let this remarkable family go during a big layoff in the mid-2000s. So many of those "second-generation" Imagineers have been scattered outside of Disney, and that kind of knowledge, once lost, just can't be recovered.)

Designing DisneySea

With that kind of experience in place, Tokyo Disney-Sea was a dream project—it was a million miles away from Euro Disneyland, and even in many ways better than the Tokyo Disneyland effort had been, because so much of each day was spent dealing with known commodities.

The design team put forward some of the most sophisticated and mature place making designs, from architecture to color styling and water features to landscaping. This was a team of great craftspeople delivering their very best work. The rockwork throughout the park, for instance, is the best I've ever seen, anywhere. It's abundant and all looks like the hand of nature itself. The park really must be experienced to be appreciated—each "port" is a fully unique and transporting realm. Every space is filled with such remarkable detail and immersive environmental design. It is a textbook of Imagineering storytelling.

There were certainly conflicts and disagreements, and I was actually surprised about one of them—"The Battle of the Berm." Walt put a berm, and elevated earthen bank, all around Disneyland, because he didn't want Guests to see the outside world while they were in his park. Imagine being in a rugged Northwest wilderness and seeing a neon motel sign in the piney woods. These "visual intrusions" were going to be a problem at Tokyo DisneySea. What shocked me was that Marty Sklar—the head of Imagineering, the guy who sat at Walt's knee—didn't think it was a big deal to see a resort hotel from inside our maritime fantasy world. So I fought for it, and we got it—and I think it was worth every bit of extra cost and effort.

Marty was a funny guy, though. Over our decades of working together, we recognized a similar sense of humor, and spent a lot of time picking on each other.

He was observant and scrupulous about most things. I did a walk-through of Mediterranean Harbor with him and he eagle-eyed to a roofline two hundred feet away. "There's a cross on top of that building," he noticed. "You know, Jim, we don't have religious symbols inside Disney parks."

"Marty, we're in Porto Paradiso. It's a port city in Italy. It seems like a basilica dome with a cross [that] fits right in with our theme. You want us to put up a Star of David?"

"Sure," he replied with a sly grin.

Opening Day

Mimi and I relocated to Japan temporarily in March of 2001, and stayed until November of that year. The opening day was planned for September 4, 2001, which by no coincidence at all was Masatomo Takahashi's birthday. He had passed away on January 31, 2000. Roy E. Disney had reflected, "Thanks to Masatomo, for years to come, families around the Asia-Pacific region will experience the delights of Disney and its magical theme parks."

After two years of construction and a cost of more than $3 billion (plus another $3 billion for resort peripheral enhancements), Tokyo DisneySea opened its gates at eight o'clock in the morning on September 4, 2001. The Grand Opening Ceremony was held at Mediterranean Harbor, the central area of the park. Like the opening day of Tokyo Disneyland eighteen years before, the skies were gray and overcast, and there was mist and intermittent rain—but when Kagami, Michael Eisner, and Roy E. Disney sailed into the harbor aboard a barge, the rain stopped, and sunlight broke through the clouds.

The dedication for Tokyo DisneySea reads in both English and Japanese:

*Welcome, one and all to a world where
Imagination and Adventure set sail.
Tokyo DisneySea is dedicated to the spirit of
exploration that lives in each of us. Here you chart a
course for Adventure, Romance, Discovery, and Fun
and journey to exotic and fanciful Ports of Call.
May Tokyo DisneySea inspire the hearts and minds
of all of us who share the water planet, Earth.*

*September 4, 2001
Michael D. Eisner
Chairman and Chief Executive Officer
The Walt Disney Company*

September 11, 2001

Just one week later, on September 11, there was a series
of four coordinated terrorist attacks against the United
States. Air travel was immediately halted worldwide. The
entire balance of the world was turned upside down. It was
near midnight in Tokyo when the full impact of what was
happening hit us. We opened the resort the next morning,
and waited for additional information from stateside. We

were soon (and frequently thereafter) briefed by Security and Disney corporate. TDL remained open, but we began looking at admission security procedures, and changed the entire resort entry sequence overnight. As soon as travel restrictions were relaxed, we continued to work together fine-tuning our revisions to policy and procedures.

Since we were only a week beyond opening day, much of my expatriate team was in transit, heading back to the United States. Many of them were grounded in Hawaii. The other significant number were in Alaska. I'll leave it to you to guess who complained, and who didn't.

The outpouring of grief and sympathy for the American citizens in Japan was overwhelming, and extremely moving. Mimi is blonde and fair, and "looks American" to folks in Japan. For some time after 9/11, she was frequently being stopped in the street by people, asking "American? American?" and then expressing their condolences. It was so sincere and touching . . . and so representative of the overall sense of decency that had been a hallmark of our relationship with the Japanese.

Hiromi Imai, wife of Mas Imai, and their daughters, had made these huge, beautiful chains of origami cranes to take to the American Embassy in Tokyo as a gesture of sympathy. An ancient Japanese legend promises that anyone who folds a thousand origami cranes will be granted a wish by the gods. Some stories believe you are granted happiness and eternal good luck, or recovery from illness or injury. There is a famous book in Japan called *Sadako and the Thousand Paper Cranes*. As Mimi and Hiromi arrived at the American Embassy housing compound, they saw that the broad green lawn in front of the complex was completely covered with flowers, thousands upon thousands of paper cranes, and other offerings of shared grief and tribute.

Cultural Decency

I mentioned Ray Tanaka before, but that "sense of decency" in Japan brought to mind another moment in which Ray (a Japanese national) was a key player. After Mimi's mother had passed away, we brought her father over for a visit. Mimi took him over to see Nara, in the Kansai region of Honshu. Nara is a core city in the northern part of Nara Prefecture bordering the Kyoto Prefecture, about three hundred miles from Tokyo. Mimi's dad, a doctor, had been stationed there after World War II ended in 1945.

Mimi and her dad took the bullet train (I was working),

and the two of them saw all the different temples, stopped for meals all over, and stayed down there for a night or two. Mimi noticed that the diamond had fallen out of her engagement ring. She contacted my office and I asked Ray Tanaka to help out—calling all the temples and places that they had visited or taken meals. Ray—and do not ask me how he did it—found that she had lost it while they were at lunch in a remote little village between Nara and Kyoto. The people from this little restaurant brought the diamond all the way back to Kyoto to Mimi's hotel, and refused to take any money, or any reward. They said they were simply honored that they were able to find it, and get it back to Mimi.

I also offered to comp them into the park, but they wouldn't do it. Finally—and this is all due to Ray Tanaka's skills—Ray convinced them that it would make *us* feel better if they took our free admission to the park.

That is Japan. That is the Japanese. I will always be impressed by the journey those remarkable people took me on, from my World War II child's-eye view that the rest of the world was dangerous and untrustworthy—and Japan was an enemy—to the place of utter respect and admiration and deep affection that the nation and its people occupy in my heart and mind today.

Collaboration and Compromise

This mutual respect and collaboration still had its "give-and-take." We continued to add to their Disney fluency, and they continued to mix that into their distinct Japanese view—improving the entire experience in the process.

Sometimes there were simple misunderstandings in cultural optics, such as when we opened Ikspiari, the shopping and dining district located between Maihama Station and the Disney Ambassador Hotel. The flagship Disney Store there was located adjacent to Planet Hollywood—which featured a full-size figure of Arnold Schwarzenegger from the Terminator movie series brandishing a sawed-off ten-gauge Winchester 1887 with a large-lever loop. We expressed some concern about the visual dissonance between Minnie Mouse and that iconic but horrible weapon, and adjustments were made.

That's Entertainment!

Another area where the Disney and Japanese cultures seemed to spark and catch fire was in live entertainment. We started back at Tokyo Disneyland with parades and character appearances, and soon expanded to stage spectaculars and special events and holidays. The Guests ate up every entertainment offering and demanded more, so we spent some time convincing OLC that with more live entertainment they could offer something new more frequently than a new brick-and-mortar attraction. Plus, live shows had a kind of flexibility and ability to repurpose than permanent facilities and systems.

We brought in Larry Billman as creative director of live entertainment. Larry had been a musical performer onstage, and in TV and film, but his writing skills soon led him to Disney live entertainment. Beginning in 1969, he wrote, directed, and/or produced hundreds of live shows at Disneyland, Walt Disney World, and Tokyo Disneyland. Larry also directed six editions of Ringling Bros. and Barnum & Bailey Circus and Disney on Ice.

In Tokyo DisneySea, the variety, style, and subject matter of our entertainment is expansive, and a number of different indoor and outdoor venues offer live shows all day long (and a fireworks spectacular at night, of course).

Tokyo DisneySea also continued a great interactive program that brought improvisational comedy and music directly to Guests, with specific characters roaming the American Waterfront, Port Discovery, Arabian Coast, and the entry areas. These "Atmosphere" players are as popular as classic Disney characters. Guests seek out their favorites and relish the chance to interact—it's a permissible way for the usually-reserved Japanese to let their hair down a little.

A Wish Made in Venice

In the Mediterranean Harbor area of Tokyo Disney-Sea, we have a beautiful, low-key, low-occupancy attraction, a restful ride on a gondola through the romantic Palazzo Canals. Guests board beautiful replicas of ten-passenger Venetian gondolas, and are taken on a tour through the gorgeous architecture of Porto Paradiso. Two gondoliers narrate along the way in Japanese, until they reach our version of the famed Bridge of Sighs, where they begin to serenade their passengers with " 'O Sole Mio" in fluent Italian. (It sounds odd, but it's actually lovely and quite magical.)

Mimi and I had two good friends visiting, Dr. Ray and Colleen Casciari, and when we boarded, I noticed that the gondoliers were not wearing their familiar and iconic hats—light woven straw with colored bands on both the crown and brim. These Cast Members had dispensed with this familiar and important wardrobe detail, and those hats were nowhere to be seen. I thought it was sloppy, and "bad show."

After being serenaded under the bridge, we were told, following Venetian tradition, to make a wish. We left our boat, and made our way to dinner, and as we enjoyed our wine, our dinner guests shared the wishes they'd made— the usual, world peace, understanding, and so on.

"What'd you wish, Jim?"

"I wish the gondoliers would keep their damn hats on."

The Ritual of the Gyoza Sausage Buns

Another example of our collaboration and compromise is a kind of American "churro cart" logic. There's a purely commercial notion that if one kind of a thing, like a churro cart, is successful, then ten must be better. So common fiscal sense says you find a place for eight or ten more churro carts.

They sold a food item when we opened Tokyo DisneySea called a Gyoza sausage bun, which originated in China (and made its way to Japan). It's ground pork and vegetables with garlic, soy sauce, and sesame oil in a heavy dough wrap—a special Chinese-made sausage sandwich, basically.

Guests would line up as soon as the park opened, and it would be a thirty- to fifty-minute wait for what we thought was just a simple snack item. I suggested to them they open up more vending locations for the Gyoza sausage buns. Put a couple on the other side of the park. Our Japanese partners wouldn't do that, because what made the bun so popular was that *this location was the only place you could buy it.*

It wasn't just the sandwich itself; it was the anticipation, and the act of waiting for something special. And they don't wait as individuals. They wait as groups or families; it's a cultural and communal shared experience. It's easy to understand, it's part of the fun of creating those connective moments. In our rush to profit, sometimes we overlook the very aspect of a thing that makes it profitable, meaningful, and memorable—and creates a unique tradition that can endure over decades and generations of Guests.

A Highway in the Sky in Tokyo Disney Resort

As we expanded the offerings at Tokyo Disney Resort, it was clear that the resort property had just gotten too big to walk around. We needed a more efficient and elegant means of getting Guests around what was now several separate destinations.

With Disney, it's never just about moving people from one place to another. It's about moving people through their experience as efficiently as possible—while maintaining the proper atmosphere of theme and show.

So, shortly before the opening of Tokyo DisneySea, the Disney Resort Line opened to passengers in July of 2001. The system is an automated monorail circuit that moves Guests between four station destinations within the Tokyo Disney Resort property, and is operated by the Maihama Resort Line Co., Ltd., a subsidiary of OLC.

It travels in a single direction. A circuit of the entire route takes about thirteen minutes. And even though it never leaves the resort property, it still had to be permitted and approved as public transportation by all the proper government and rail authorities there. It may seem like a simple "ride," but we had to go through a lengthy process, as you can imagine, to get a monorail at Tokyo Disney.

The Japanese saw the monorail as a transportation system, and also as part of the overall show. They are pretty used to trains and practical transportation systems within Japan, so the idea of a monorail itself was not a big deal. Where we brought the Disney difference into the potentially mundane was in making the size of the windows larger, and designing them in the shape of Mickey. Details are more luxurious, from wall coverings to upholstery colors, as well. The cars themselves are wider and more spacious. Even the familiar Mickey silhouette is integrated as a passenger hang strap. These aren't practical necessities—but what they have done is turn a transportation system into an attraction.

In all these instances, the commonality between the Japanese philosophies and behaviors and that of Disney only proved time and again that Japan and Disney were simply a "fit," and a better one than we'd ever expected.

The Best Theme Park in the World

Tokyo DisneySea is, in my opinion, the best park we've ever done.

In the years since its opening, I have heard Tokyo DisneySea referred to over and over again as "the best theme park *in the world.*" Friends, colleagues, Disney fan sites, theme park bloggers, travel journalists, and entertainment critics—as well as tens of millions of Guests every year—have shared this opinion.

I think this sentiment is a reflection on the people

who worked on it and the project. That special alchemy of Disney and Japan; the creative freedom—the ability to dream big—that OLC gave us; a deeply and uniquely experienced group of people on every team and at every level. Tokyo DisneySea was a magic combination of passion, erudition, creativity, collaboration, and a purpose of vision—in creative and craft and business acumen. Nearly everything *worked*, and the things that didn't work were quickly resolved or abandoned.

For me, it represented a culmination of my entire experience and career. It was a crowning achievement. We caught lightning in a bottle.

They say a skilled Cast Member knows how to make a great entrance, but more essentially knows the importance of when to get off the stage.

It was time for me to go.

Part Eleven: Another Homecoming

I T WAS time to retire.

My cardiologist (his name was Ty Cobb—no kidding) told me I had to move on. I told Michael Eisner that. I don't think he ever believed that I had a health problem. But then, I don't think *I* ever believed I had a health problem. Except, now that I've got my seventeenth stent put in—and had bypass surgery two different times—I'm starting to think maybe I *did* have a health problem.

I talked to Michael about it, probably about two years before the opening of Tokyo DisneySea. Dr. Ty Cobb had said, "I always thought you would do well under stress. I think I was wrong—you internalize too much stress. You've had too many heart problems, and you really should retire."

I talked to Paul Pressler about retiring. He was technically my boss, as head of Walt Disney Attractions by then. Michael had always told me, "You work for me. Directly—don't worry about Paul." I actually never had to worry about Paul. He was always very supportive, and he respected my experience and trusted that I did what I had to do.

Michael said, and Paul echoed this too, "We can't really replace you. You have built relationships around the world that go back decades. We probably won't replace your job, because that role was crafted while you were in it, and there's only one you."

After the TDS opening ceremony, Bob Iger asked if I would consider staying on. I told him that I had given several *years* notice that I was retiring—and I wasn't sure my heart could take another project. Bob, being the true gentleman that he is, said, "Please let me know if there is anything I can do for you in the future."

I started delegating more things that I used to do to other people on my staff. I looked for a replacement, and decided on Mas Imai, who had worked on my TDS team as vice president of finance. A Japanese-American, he knew the Japanese well, and they liked him and respected him. But he had to live in Japan. His wife, who was a native of Japan, didn't want to go back there. She liked living in the United States and wanted to stay here. In fact, the last night Mimi and I took them both to dinner, his wife begged me not to "leave her there."

I put together a structure for Disneyland International. But that didn't last too long the way it was established. DLI really became more of an organization of people that interfaced with, supported, and did shipping and receiving for the Oriental Land Company, instead of an international development organization looking at, and looking for, new projects worldwide; the whole group dynamic changed. People left; others were reassigned to other things. Some from the core group are still there, but it's not the same business unit.

Hong Kong Disneyland

I was immersed in the affairs of Tokyo DisneySea, plus planning a succession strategy and retirement, when Michael came to me again. The chief executive of Hong Kong, Tung Chee Hwa, was interested in a Disneyland project for his locale. Much like Tokyo, they were creating a landfill site on the bay to provide a site for the construction. Michael thought it seemed like a natural for me to take on this project. Maybe I could delay retiring by a few years.

I just really did not want to do it; I'd even talked to the Japanese about it before Michael even asked. They were underwriting my salary at that time because of the Disney-Sea project. They had a negative reaction to it. *Really* negative. They didn't want Disney to do a Hong Kong project. They thought it would cannibalize and jeopardize everything they'd done and committed to with TDR.

So my job, then, became convincing them that Hong Kong could be better for them, not worse. I did convince them that Hong Kong was not going to cannibalize the parks they were operating and planning, and I don't think it has.

I did try to convince Disney that maybe a co-op or partnership of some sort with OLC might be a good idea. I thought it could be a good compliment to the Japanese if they had some operating role, or we had them supervise hiring and training for Hong Kong, instead of bringing Americans over to do that. I said, "Believe me, the Japanese know how to run a resort—as well if not better than we do, and they would do a terrific job. And it could go a long way in solidifying our relationship and calming any fears."

Unfortunately, I could never make that fly. And certainly there was no love lost between the two parties.

Shanghai

Bob Iger did ask me to talk to OLC about support and training for the next big park, too, Shanghai Disney in China. Location scouting in Pudong (a district of Shanghai's) had started in 1999, and negotiation for the project began around 2001. Not surprisingly, OLC was totally against it. They were rightfully upset that they hadn't been part of a conversation about going into either of these Asian projects from even before the beginning, but the Chinese would not have accepted that anyway—it was that simple.

I was also called in, pretty early on, to just look over the Shanghai project by Bob Weis, just to offer friendly advice with colleagues in common. I think it was helpful, and both of us, Bob and I, recognized the plan was just too small. That was the biggest part of my advice—I agreed with Bob that over time, unused capacity would fill up, but too much caution would result in a constant and expensive process of catching up to a capacity need.

Bob went to bat for that, and fought for it, and greatly increased the project's capacity from the outset.

Windows on Main Streets

One of the pleasant things about retirement is being recognized for your accomplishments. I won't be falsely humble, it's a really good feeling to be treated like a celebrity, and to see that your hard work has lasting value . . . and that your insights are still useful. Usually, you don't get to hear all of this praise and honor because it's reserved for eulogies.

Ever since Walt's day, a prominent honor for an old Disney guy like me has been "a window on Main Street." The street-level storefront windows display the merchandise on sale in the shops, but if you look at the second-story windows you will see some "testimonials" to make-believe businesses. Initially, the idea was just set dressing, punny names of imaginary enterprises for the observant Guest to get a chuckle, partake in an inside joke.

Walt decided, that in addition to its show value, he could use those windows to honor the many people who helped him make Disneyland a reality. Those he honored ranged from his father, Elias Disney, to Imagineers like

Marc Davis and Ken Anderson. Over the years, Disneyland has kept adding windows to Main Street, U.S.A. with the names of those receiving this honor. And the tradition has continued at the other park sites, including Walt Disney World, Tokyo Disneyland, and Disneyland Paris.

My first window honor actually came long before my retirement, from my WDI colleagues Eddie Sotto and Marty Sklar. I think Michael Eisner was in on it, too. The fictional business of display combines my operations background and my horrible medical crisis. My window at EDL, which was there on the park's Opening Day, is above New Century Notions/Flora's Unique Boutique, and reads: SURGICAL PRACTICE—DR. JIM CORA, "OUR OPERATIONS WILL KEEP YOU IN STITCHES."

A few years later, on April 26, 2002, I was honored with a window on Main Street, U.S.A. at Disneyland. For a former Disneylander, this was a homecoming, and a deeply moving event. How many hundreds of times had I walked that street, and seen and read the names of all those Disney greats. Now I was right there along with them. The window, located above Disney Clothiers, Ltd., reads: GLOBAL EXPORTS AND EXPATS—SPECIALIZING IN LAND AND SEA OPERATIONS—OUR MOTTO: "THE SUN

NEVER SETS ON OUR MAGICAL KINGDOMS"—JIM CORA, MASTER OPERATOR.

Then, on October 30, 2003, a huge three-panel Palladian window was unveiled in World Bazaar in Tokyo Disneyland. The left panel reads: YOU'VE GOT THE VISION—WE'VE GOT THE TEAM. The right panel continues: YOU BRING THE PROJECT—WE'LL BUILD YOUR DREAM. In the center panel is a medallion that features an illustrated graphic of a castle, with a majestic rising sun emerging from the clouds, which states: VISIONARY MANAGEMENT—JIM CORA, PROPRIETOR.

I think that one may be my favorite.

Only three Americans have received windows at World Bazaar—Walt Disney, Frank Wells, and me.

A Disney Legend

We live in a society that flings around superlatives. You hear the word *legend* a lot, but I'm not sure it means that much anymore, because it's been overused and applied to things that don't seem to be worthy of such acclaim. The Disney Legend Award is a little more of an honor in my book. It was started in 1987 by Roy E. Disney. The

Legends are chosen by a selection committee, and since its inception, the program has honored many gifted animators, Imagineers, songwriters, actors, and business leaders as having made a significant impact on the Disney legacy. There are plaques with the honorees names and handprints in a special location at the Studio in Burbank, called Disney Legends Plaza. The plaza features the bronze sculptures of Walt Disney and Roy O. Disney—they're the replicas of the ones seen at Disneyland and Walt Disney World. In addition, there's also a ten-foot-high version of the Disney Legends Award itself.

The Disney Legends Award has three distinct elements that characterize the contributions made by each talented recipient. The **Spiral** stands for imagination, the power of an idea. The **Hand** holds the gifts of skill, discipline, and craftsmanship. The **Wand** and the **Star** represent magic: the spark that is ignited when imagination and skill combine to create a new dream.

I was recognized as a Disney Legend on September 20, 2005. This was Disneyland's fiftieth anniversary, so for this occasion, eighteen Disneyland veterans were saluted at the same time (I was told our years of service to Disneyland and the company totaled 541 years). The event was held in Disneyland's Main Street Opera House, with a luncheon afterward at the Napa Rose restaurant at Disney's Grand Californian Hotel & Spa.

Honored alongside me were Chuck Abbott (one of Disneyland's foremost attractions hosts for thirty-six years), Milt Albright (the first Disneyland employee), Hideo "Indian" Aramaki (master chef), Chuck Boya-jian (custodial powerhouse), Charles Boyer (prolific and beloved artist), Randy Bright (Imagineer and author), Art Linkletter (a close friend of Walt's and a TV star who hosted the big Disneyland TV events in 1955 and 1959— and held the camera and film licenses in Disneyland for some years), Steve Martin (multimedia superstar, though I knew him from his days in the Fantasyland Magic Shop), Tom Nabbe (Disneyland and Walt Disney World Cast Member, who Walt had hired as a kid because he thought he looked like Tom Sawyer), Jack Olsen (master merchandiser), Cicely Rigdon (who initiated the Ambas-sador Program), Disneyland Band maestro Vesey Walker, and Jack Wagner ("The Voice of Disneyland"). I was in some pretty good company.

I was pleased to share this recognition with some people who had been good friends and extraordinary

colleagues in my career: Robert Jani (entertainment inno-
vator), Mary Anne Mang (community relations expert),
Hideo Amemiya (a hotel and resort authority), and William Sullivan ("Sully," my old boss in Fantasyland, who
started on opening day and stayed for his entire career).

It was an exhausting day, plus it rained. There were
so many reunions and recollections, gatherings with old
friends, conversations, and laughter—and an occasional
tear and memories of those not present. It didn't feel so
much like an esteemed honor as much as a beautiful family reunion. Which, to a large degree, it was. Disney is like
that.

Donating Experience and Expertise

My church was a prominent force in molding me, and
I have remained committed to it to this day. Through the
years, my service has varied, but some years back it led me
to a seat on the board of directors of St. Joseph's Hospital. I liked doing that. I had been planning chairman,
chairman of the Leadership Council, vice chairman, and
eventually chairman of the board—and I was held over, in
fact, past my original term limit. Larry Ainsworth, CEO

at St. Joseph's, moved to make me a chairman emeritus, which had never been done at either St. Joseph's Hospital, or any of its other facilities in their hospital system.

When I stepped down as chair, I was asked to join the Quality Committee of the St. Joseph Health Care System, which at the time consisted of twelve hospitals. I felt that this responsibility was right up my alley. My Disney background was especially useful here: "quality" is a Disney value—but in the parks, *safety* was our number one priority, always. I also felt that Michelle's premature death was due to what I still consider a lack of quality care and medical error, and I thought maybe I could do some good here so that wouldn't happen to others.

I really threw myself into that with a passion, and spent a lot of time on it—six years in all on that committee. And I still consult from time to time.

Taylor-Made Health Care

I was also invited to join the board of directors of a firm called Taylor Design. This interested me because it combined two areas where I had gained a lot of expertise: place making and health care. Taylor creates professional medical spaces such as cancer centers, cardiovascular care facilities, and women's and children's health care centers. As ideas about health care evolve, Taylor looks at integrative medicine and a more holistic approach to wellness by creating medical spaces that are humane and patient-focused, as well as offers the latest ergonomically and technologically sophisticated space design. They're kind of like a small WDI to me, because they do concept and creative design, architecture, and construction—but only for health care (and have recently branched out into science and education).

This role is actually a lot of fun, plus it takes advantage of my experience on both sides of the projects—as a creator and as a customer.

Christ Cathedral

The Crystal Cathedral is an iconic edifice in Garden Grove, California. People may remember it as the setting for the TV ministry *The Hour of Power*, hosted by televangelist, pastor, motivational speaker, and author Robert H. Schuller for five decades.

The reflective glass building, which seats 2,248, was designed by the firm of Philip Johnson/John Burgee Architects, and was called "the largest glass building in the world" when it was completed in 1981. (It also has one of the largest musical instruments in the world, the Hazel Wright Memorial Organ.)

Until 2013, the building was the principal place of worship for Crystal Cathedral Ministries (now Shepherd's Grove), a congregation of the Reformed Church in America, founded in 1955 by Schuller. The Crystal Cathedral Ministries filed for bankruptcy in 2010, and subsequently sold the building and its adjacent campus to the Roman Catholic Diocese of Orange. (They had previously purchased land and started planning for construction of a new and larger cathedral in Santa Ana, California, but had outgrown their Holy Family Cathedral in Orange.) The cost of renovating the Crystal Cathedral building for Catholic worship was far less than constructing a new building from scratch, and the other buildings on the campus provided facilities for diocesan administrative offices and ministries with little modification.

During the renovation of this facility, and its operation as the new seat of the Diocese of Orange, my pastor mentioned to Bishop Kevin Vann, the bishop of Orange County, that one of his parishioners was a retired Disney executive. (Bishop Vann is also a huge Disney fan. He even chose July 17—the anniversary of Disneyland's opening—

as the date of the new cathedral dedication in 2019.)

Bishop Vann asked if I would offer my help in adding some "Disney" flair and enhancements to their enterprise. (In addition to its spiritual and televisual function, the Crystal Cathedral had also been a popular tourist attraction.) Now known as Christ Cathedral, the sanctuary (which resides with other historic buildings on a thirty-four-acre property) continues to offer opportunities for visitors that go beyond meditation and prayer. Educational pursuits and enlightenment are promoted and encouraged. There are self-guided and docent-led campus tours provided through the Cathedral Cultural Center that touch upon a range of subjects, such as architecture and art, music, and history.

I advised with docent training and operational improvements, security, costuming, and merchandising recommendations. I worked with Auxiliary Bishop Timothy Freyer, Tony Jennison from the development team, and Kim Binquist, who is now the operations project manager on-site. I also recruited Nancy Valeri to advise them (although she's retired now, Nancy had ended up as director of Marketing Special Events for Disney Resorts Worldwide). She provided tremendous guidance and Disney know-how to the Christ Cathedral Dedication Gala and surrounding events. It was rewarding for me to again combine and cross-pollinate my passions and experiences in a whole new way, and to work with so many dedicated and passionate individuals.

Hope Builders

I joined a group that Mimi primarily supports, called Taller San José—that means *St. Joseph Workshop* in Spanish. It's also referred to as "Hope Builders." They started in Santa Ana, California, in 1995. Sister Eileen McNerney, a member of the Sisters of St. Joseph of Orange, had a goal to develop a program that could move young people from poverty to prosperity, and to also take kids who'd been in trouble with gangs, and try to give them a high school education, teach them a trade—construction, computers, or back-of-the-house medical.

By bringing together sponsors representing local government, churches, corporations, foundations, and individuals, Sister Eileen opened an educational and job-training center in downtown Santa Ana for high-risk youth ages eighteen to twenty-eight.

"Each young person, no matter what his or her history, is precious in God's sight," Sister Eileen said. "And yet many of them are scared, stuck, or broken. It saddens me to walk down the street and see a bird with a broken wing. I can't always fix the bird, but I do believe that with God's help, the young people who walk through Taller San José's door can one day fly."

The mayor of Anaheim, Tom Tait, approached me a few years ago and said, "With your connection to Disneyland, do you think we could start something here in Anaheim like what was done in Santa Ana with Taller San José? We have some similar problems with youth crime."

I contacted Jon Storbeck, then vice president of operations for the hotels at Disneyland and now vice president and general manager of Knott's Berry Farm, and he jumped all over it. Jon gathered all the mayors of Orange County together in one room, including the county's Board of Supervisors, and we talked to them about our goals. They were all in favor of it, and so they put together a program. Jon did a great job corralling those mayors! But Anaheim really stepped up. Hopefully, more companies will support groups like this nonprofit organization that's trying to do something for young people, people who've been in trouble, people, who've never gotten a second chance. So far they've had an 88 percent success rate on getting those in the program placed in jobs. That is remarkable.

But Mimi got more involved than I ever did. She's

done everything from project managing fund-raising and chairing gala events, to wrapping holiday gifts, to teaching art classes. She's an incredible consultant for them; she has strengths and talents and insight in so many areas. Mimi's just really been a loyal and reliable supporter. It's a great charity, and I can't think of any better way to spend the time, effort, and money. The successes are so personal, transformative, and satisfying.

Art and Healing

Florence Nightingale said, "Variety of form and brilliancy of color in the object presented to patients are an actual means of recovery." Mimi discovered this firsthand as an artist when she began teaching art to people with memory impairment at an assisted living facility where her father lived. He had Alzheimer's disease, but his caregivers found that when Mimi was present (of course) his anxieties eased, and that regular activities stabilized their residents' overall well-being.

After Mimi's dad passed, the Sisters of St. Joseph heard about her art education work and asked her to do the same for the aging sisters in the diocese who struggled with memory impairment and loss. Naturalist John Lubbock said, "Art is unquestionably one of the purest and highest elements in human happiness. It trains the mind through the eye, and the eye through the mind. As the sun colors flowers, so does art color life."

Mimi's art has been a source of her joy and inspiration; time and again she has turned that personal experience and satisfaction outward, and in doing so has enriched the lives of so many other people—I'm just one of the grateful hundreds.

VisionMaker

My brother, John, and his partner Dan Martinez started a company called VisionMaker. John had spent thirty-eight years at Disney, including fifteen years as vice president of Disneyland Operations and four years as vice president of Resort Development; he left after Disney's California Adventure opened in 2001. VisionMaker was established to do resort entertainment, either from a theme park consulting standpoint, or actual design, engineering, and construction. John and I were familiar with all those things.

I had retired from Disney, but I then joined Vision-Maker as chairman of the board. We had the talent, and of course access to a lot of additional talent; John's partner started getting some leads on various projects. We worked with an extraordinary firm called the Hettema Group in Pasadena, California. The principal, Phil Hettema, has a long track record in place making and entertainment, from Disney to Universal to DreamWorks, as well as doing some design work for Dubai. We worked with a Saudi prince who was responsible for the project we were doing there, and made several trips to Riyadh, Saudi Arabia's capital, as well as several places in the United Arab Emirates, including Dubai, Bahrain, and Qatar. (Unfortunately, a recession hit, and that project dried up.)

Interesting, certainly, but it really wasn't my cup of tea after Disney. I pulled out after about a year. John is still working in the business; he's got a large project now going on in Spain. My brother and I live within a mile of one another, and get together often. He enjoys his three granddaughters—and has twin grandsons on the way.

Katzenberg's "Brain Trust"

Several years ago, I heard from Jeffrey Katzenberg. Although I was retired, I was at another anniversary at Tokyo Disneyland (I've forgotten what year it was). The

Walt Disney Attractions Japan office there put a call through to me, and it was Jeffrey. By this time, he was long gone from Disney and deep into DreamWorks, which he founded with David Geffen and Steven Spielberg. Dream-Works had made an enormous splash in the animation business with franchises like How to Train Your Dragon, Shrek, and Kung Fu Panda.

"Jim, I'd like you to come to Dubai on a project."

I said, "What kind of project?"

"I can't give you much detail. But since you're in Tokyo it's closer for you to go Tokyo-to-Dubai than LA-to-Dubai. You've been to Dubai before, I understand?"

Jeffrey always did his homework. He assumed that since I was retired, I must be bored, I guess. But hey, I'm always up for some adventure, and since Jeffrey was footing the costs, why not?

"I'll have somebody meet you at the airport. I'll have a helicopter take you around and show you where the site's going to be."

I said, "The site for what?"

Jeffrey was enthused. "I want to do a theme park there. I want [it] to be what Magic Kingdom is to Walt Disney World. I want it to be the central park. Universal's going to be there, Paramount's going to make a pitch. Marvel's going to be making a pitch. Phil Hettema is going to be there, and I want you to be there."

Peter Rummell, Bruce Laval, Judson Green—Jeffrey was bringing a "who's who" of international park and resort experience, people who I knew, and had worked with, and respected.

Mimi and I flew out there. We flew over the site, I looked at a model for almost a full day. (It was a gorgeous model, possibly the best project model I've ever seen.) Then we had an audience with Sheikh Mohammed bin Abdulla Al Thani—people called him Sheik Moe. Everybody who had a "park on the table" did their pitch. Jeffrey had us sit through the whole meeting. At this point, none of Jeffrey's assembled guests really knew what their role was.

All our planes had come in at different times, and we had all been sitting there in the hotel lobby waiting for our rooms to get ready. Everybody was saying, "What are we here for? Anybody know what we're here for?" Nobody at that point really knew why they were there, or what the plan was. But Judson had an inkling.

"I think it's just about faces. Jeffrey wants to prove to the sheik that he can gather the most experienced and talented people together."

As the kids say today, Jeffrey was flexing.

He wanted to show off an unparalleled brain trust.

He showed up two days later, swept into the room, and hugged everybody—and life went on . . . and then the recession hit and they had to cancel the projects, although it's back on now (at least at the time this book goes to press). However, Jeffery's not a part of it.

But I do like Jeffrey, and admire his trailblazing attitude and dynamism. He sees, he wants, he goes for it.

Gone But Not Forgotten?

I think a lot of people decline in their retirement because they think that it's appealing to "do nothing." I am enjoying retirement, and I do like the flexibility and relative lack of stress compared to, say, grappling with a project like Euro Disneyland. But I could never really be still, nor could I be "bored," as Jeffrey Katzenberg seemed to assume. Retirees reading this will understand, if you do it right, retirement is simply a much different style of "busy."

In addition to seemingly endless medical problems, and the aforementioned charity and board work, I'm engaged in—and obligations to home and church—there are abundant ways to fill one's days and feel satisfied.

Sharing the Word

Disney fans always seem to be interested in my works and war stories. I attend every D23 Expo at the Anaheim Convention Center. I sit on panels and have done presentations at The Walt Disney Family Museum, a wonderful legacy to Walt created by his daughter, Diane Disney Miller and her husband, Ron Miller, and their children.

In 2001, the Disneyana Fan Club named me a Disney Legend, and I was the guest of honor at a D23 "Lunch with a Legend" program up at the Studio.

Disney fandom is a very interesting culture in itself, and not unlike a church. There is fellowship, and sharing of the word, and many a lesson to be learned from canon. The hymns are pretty damn good, too. I typically find Disney fans *generous*. It's a culture of sharing. They love Disney, and what makes them happy is the sharing of it. (Some fan cultures are about the hoarding of it, or competitions for specific authority, or expertise.) Disney fans tend to be my kind of people.

Planting and Nurturing

Something I seem never to have retired from is "training and development." It isn't because I'm a genius, it's because of the things I was taught by Walt, and Van France, and Dick Nunis, and a hundred others who shared their valuable insights and eternal truths. The skills and support and dedication of exceptional teams and talented staff contributed to the lessons I learned, and those have become the lessons I teach. The experiences I've had contain not just interesting anecdotes, but valuable knowledge. And as the old saying goes, "If I don't tell you, how will you know?"

Disneyland administration seems to change with alarming frequency, but someone there always seems to have my number or email address. Over the past ten years, I've attended a dozen or more lunches, but I've never really gotten to eat, because I was so busy telling the people who run Disneyland how Disneyland was designed to work, and how we used to organize and implement things at the Happiest Place on Earth. They typically just want validation that what they are doing is in line with what we old-timers believed was Walt's vision. I'm always flattered and happy to accept an invitation to counsel and advise, against the chance that the tiniest shoots can result in a vineyard.

A couple of times I've gotten a call from Brian Alters, Ph.D. in the College of Educational Studies and director of the Evolution Education Research Center at Chapman University, and a dyed-in-the-wool Disney fan. Jack Lindquist was a benefactor at Chapman, and he introduced me to Brian, who has had me come by and present a class lecture. He's become quite renowned himself for his "The Pursuit of Happiness and Knowledge: Walt Disney and Charles Darwin" course.

I haven't a clue what Brian's class is about. I have no idea how my lectures fit into his curriculum. But his students are young, and engaged, and attentive, and largely enthusiastic. So if something I say, or a memory I share, touches off a spark in their spirit, then I've done something. That's *development.*

Training was vital to making our parks and resorts run. But to me, development was the real investment. To put your faith in the raw talent before you, and to guide, enhance, assist, and even sometimes kick it in the ass to reach a potential you could see—and perhaps they did not. I think I spent a lot of my Disney career developing not just "recreation projects," but people as well. That, to me, is as important as any beloved castle or thrilling attraction that is seen and enjoyed by millions. Van France's words still resonate with me. "This isn't about *training*," he'd say. "It's about *developing* people."

It's those people who, in turn, will continue to understand the values and ideals of Disney, to have passion about what we do, and what we represent, and who will continue the lineage and protect the pedigree of Disney long after I'm gone.

Literary Leanings

Doug Lipp was a walk-on interpreter at TDL. He spoke fluent Japanese, and was assigned to the HR division leader in Tokyo. Later, he led the training team within the corporate Disney University up in Burbank. He had mentored under a number of Disney leaders, including Van France. After leaving the company, Doug began consulting with Fortune 100 corporations about training and development philosophies and strategies. Ten years ago (or so) he created a book about the lessons he learned at Disney, to help other organizations create similar successes in understanding and developing their "human resources." I was especially thrilled when Doug asked me to write the Foreword (and participate in a series of interviews used throughout the text) for the book, *Disney U: How Disney University Develops the World's Most Engaged, Loyal, and Customer-Centric Employees.*

It was both flattering and humbling to share the lessons that Walt and Van France had established and shared with me . . . and that I spent a lifetime curating and carrying forward. To know that our ideas were solid, that our instincts were true, and that our efforts had value. To know those lessons will have a large and perpetual "classroom," thanks to Doug's book, makes me proud.

Lawyer, orator, and Congressman Rufus Choate once said, "Books are the only immortality." Working on Doug's book inspired me—and Doug and his wife and partner, Pam, encouraged me, as have several friends and family—to take on the job of writing down my own story.

Epilogue

I WAS born of the American Dream, in the immigrant tradition of innovation and family business. Deeply rooted in ideas and ideals of church and charity, I watched the trauma of a World War replaced by the optimism of the Southern California "car culture" of the 1950s, a world I enthusiastically inhabited. I served in the military, and through sheer coincidence ended up being put onto a career path personally by a master showman, and perhaps one of the greatest innovators of the twentieth century, Walt Disney himself. I was counseled and supported and encouraged and mentored by likeminded colleagues, and followed my instincts and training to teach, carrying those philosophies forward to become a force behind the globalization of the Disney parks for three decades.

In the middle of it all, I was blessed with a family. I'll never brag about my achievements as a husband or a father; I will always feel I could have been better, done better, given more. But I am surrounded by the rewards of fatherhood: my children, and grandchildren, and nieces and nephews and cousins—generations of life—and I cherish that as much or more than anything in my long and satisfying career.

At my side for so long, my heart center, and my best friend—Mimi has been my staunchest support, and my inspiration every day to be better, and to do better.

Along this international journey I lived and laughed, learned and loved—and lost—but I always moved ahead and stayed true to the many beliefs I'd been made a gift of; and ideally I have passed those values on to others, who will in turn plant the shoots, nurture the roots, watch the vines flourish, and taste the ripe and rich fruits of it all.

And at the end of my days, I think maybe a quote from Walt Disney himself sums up my feelings: "When you believe in a thing, believe in it all the way, implicitly and unquestionably."

Now, I live quietly with the benefits of that full life, surrounded by a lifetime of memories. My walls and shelves are adorned with the souvenirs of that wonderful life—photos and art, objects and tributes, awards and accolades of projects and events, family and friends—all my proudest accomplishments remind me every day of *gratitude*, and of Frank Wells's inspiration that "humility is the final achievement."

In my dining room, Mimi and I entertain gatherings of generations of family, and dear friends who have been present for a lifetime. Professional colleagues from every era of my career come to share our memories and relive our adventures, and salute those who have left us, and work on embellishing and exaggerating our legends.

Few of my guests ever notice or comment on the plain rustic vase on the dining room sideboard. But Sitte's yogurt starter pot, a century away from the Old Country, has a place of honor there.

Often our visits and gatherings adjourn outside into the warmth and peace of the Southern California dusk, where we continue to talk and laugh and drink to the life we've all shared together, across the decades, and all over the world. These sublime gatherings are sheltered by a towering grape arbor, nurtured from a tiny shoot, that has been growing and flourishing there for decades.

Acknowledgments

Walt Disney once said, "The whole thing here is the organization. Whatever we've accomplished belongs to our entire group, a tribute to our combined effort."

This book, like all the projects I've been involved with, could not have come together without dozens of dedicated individuals all having a single goal—furthering the rich legacy of Disney. I know in my heart I've been truly blessed to be able to share my story and my Disney adventures because of those who worked alongside me and encouraged me.

I would like to thank, first and foremost, Jeff Kurtti, who worked tirelessly with me in an effort to transform my history and the many stories from the Disney work I've had the privilege of enjoying for over forty-three years. I met Jeff (and hired him to his first Disney job) in 1986. He is a treasure trove of Disney historical knowledge, a wordsmith . . . and his talents know no bounds. It was a privilege to work alongside him.

Many, many thanks to Wendy Lefkon at Disney Editions for her interest and enthusiasm in my life's adventures. She piloted this project these past five years with encouragement and patience. Even in this last difficult year, and despite many personal challenges, she persevered. I will be forever grateful.

I have been challenged for many years to put my Disney stories in writing, but it's the encouragement from the following individuals that has been the motivation I needed to get it done. I have tried to be honest and accurate in my viewpoint; but I have also tried to find humor in the retelling.

I wish to thank my family first for listening endlessly to my many tales, but primarily for sharing with me our vast family history. The stories over the years from my aunts and uncles and many cousins have kept our heritage alive for future generations. I especially appreciate my sister, Marilyn, for her thorough review of the manuscript and her encouragement as it developed, and my daughter-in-law, Bonnie—together they helped provide accurate ancestry background and advice. I'd like to thank my brother, John, who shared not only our heritage but our

Disney legacy as well. And I thank my sister-in-law, Patty Barnett, for her wholehearted enthusiasm and praise for the manuscript.

Our friends Ray and Colleen Casciari are huge Disney fans and have proven to be a great audience for my stories. As my pulmonologist for many years, Ray has kept me alive and laughing throughout my retirement. He's encouraged me every step of the way, plus been a good friend.

Friends and fellow Disney authors Doug Lipp and Marcy Smothers encouraged me to get my stories published. We have all been sounding boards for one another in our documentation of the Disney legacy.

Thank you to my Disney colleagues, from whom I have learned as together we experienced many successful Disney projects throughout the years. My career could never have taken the direction it did without your commitment to our team efforts. I have done my best to recall all those in key positions who made an impact on our many successes, but ask your forgiveness for any who may have been overlooked. There are so many who I had the good fortune to work with throughout my forty-three years at Disney—and I thank you all.

And to those who helped me cull the facts and figures and cast of characters in this book, I thank you for your time, talents, and friendship. To Ron Pogue, Peggie Fariss, Nancy Valeri, Mickey Steinberg, Eddie Sotto, Lee Lanselle, and Wing Chao—your sharing of stories and recollections brought back many great memories of our work together.

And to my friends who made the time and effort to read the many versions of the manuscript—Jon Storbeck, Myron Yeager, Bishop Timothy Freyer, Padre Bill Barman, and Jim Garber—I am forever grateful for your wisdom, advice, and honesty in helping create this book. It's been an "E Ticket."

And finally, to my wife, Mimi, who's shared many of these adventures with me over the past thirty-five years. We've always made a good team, a balance of yin and yang. Thank you for pulling together the many documents, thousands of photos, videos, dates, places, names, and recollections all in support of these stories. Mimi created the first book outline that we shared with Jeff Kurtti, whom she worked with early on at DLI supporting EDL efforts, and helped bring him on board. Mimi's view (as both an eyewitness and a creative artist) was priceless.

We all made a great team to see this project through to fruition, and we certainly hope you enjoyed the ride.

Jim Cora passed away on Sunday, March 21, 2021, after a brief hospitalization at St. Joseph Hospital in Orange, California.

The test of a man is the fight he makes,
The grit that he daily shows;
The way he stands on his feet and takes
Fate's numerous bumps and blows.
A coward can smile when there's naught to fear,
When nothing his progress bars;
But it takes a man to stand up and cheer
While some other fellow stars.

It isn't the victory, after all
But the fight that a brother makes;
The man who, driven against the wall,
Still stands up erect and takes
The blows of fate with his head held high;
Bleeding, and bruised, and pale,
Is the man who'll win in the by and by,
For he isn't afraid to fail.

It's the bumps you get, and the jolts you get,
And the shocks that your courage stands,
The hours of sorrow and vain regret,
The prize that escapes your hands,
That test your mettle and prove your worth;
It isn't the blows you deal,
But the blows you take on the good old earth,
That show if your stuff is real.

—O. Lawrence Hawthorne, 1900